I0816179

A Creek Runs Through This Driftless Land

A Farm Family's Journey Toward a Land Ethic

Richard L. Cates Jr.

LITTLE CREEK PRESS
MINERAL POINT, WISCONSIN

Little Creek Press
5341 Sunny Ridge Road
Mineral Point, WI 53565

ORDERING INFORMATION
Quantity sales. Special discounts are available on quantity purchases by corporations, associations, and others. For details, contact info@littlecreekpress.com

Orders by US trade bookstores and wholesalers.
Please contact Little Creek Press or Ingram for details.

Printed in the United States of America

Cataloging-in-Publication Data
Names: Cates Jr., Richard L., author
Title: A Creek Runs Through This Driftless Land: A Farm Family's Journey Toward a Land Ethic
Description: Mineral Point, WI: Little Creek Press, 2024
Identifiers: LCCN: 2024912201 | ISBN: 978-1-955656-77-1
Subjects: BIOGRAPHY & AUTOBIOGRAPHY / Cultural & Regional
NATURE / Natural Resources
NATURE / Environmental Conservation & Protection

Book design by Little Creek Press
Editing by Don Greenwood and Shannon Booth

All photos unless otherwise credited are by the author, Richard L. Cates Jr.

Cover photo: The Cates Family Farm in the Jones Valley of Lowery Creek, Town of Wyoming, Iowa County, Wisconsin. Drone view looking north by Randy Manning.

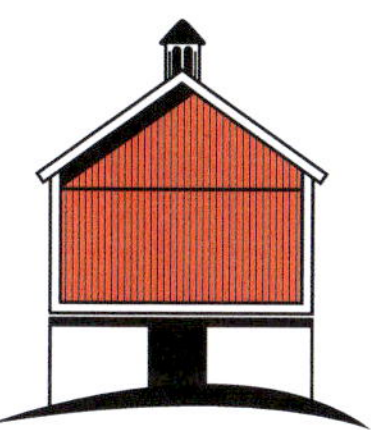

To the love of my life, my best friend and wife, Kim Johnson Cates;
beloved children Shannon, Eric, and Peter (1986–1994); their spouses
Dan and Kiley; and grandchildren Sloane, Peter, Fischer, and Hannah,
who have all enriched my life and have helped make this land a sacred home.
And to my parents Dick Sr. and Marnie (both deceased) who showed
us not only love for family, but love of land and community,
and thus sowed the seeds that inspired our journey.

Additional Praise for *A Creek Runs Through This Driftless Land*

"**The first thing that caught my eye when I visited the Cates Family Farm on a chilly, rainy fall day was this beautiful little creek, running clear and cold down the hillside and under a bridge along the farm lane.** I'm a lover of Wisconsin waters. I was glad to learn that the Cateses had restored their segment of the creek and that, somehow, the brookies had returned. We gathered on the bridge to hear the creek's story, accompanied by the song of its waters. It's a great story. I just wish readers could also hear the song."

—J. Baird Callicott, author of *Thinking Like a Planet: The Land Ethic and the Earth Ethic*

"Immerse yourself in the Cates' meandering journey from extraction to regeneration of the Driftless land—a blueprint for 21st-century agriculture everywhere! **Dick Cates and his family have shown us how to farm in ways that provide for our wants and needs today while building capacity for future generations to do the same.**"

—Randy Jackson, professor of grassland ecology, University of Wisconsin–Madison

"Landowners vary in their care—some may only appreciate a view. Richard and Kim Cates have listened and learned, honing their craft as 'conservation farmers' and stewards. **This book celebrates their ethos, grounded in gratitude, awe, and love of place.** A life-changing experience my family shares through restoring our own rundown farm."

—Steven I. Apfelbaum, author of *Nature's Second Chance: Restoring the Ecology of Stone Prairie Farm*

"What is, **at its core, the story of a family farm in Wisconsin's Driftless region extends, through Dick Cates' poetic language, to portray an ecological and civic community where the past is honored, the present is sustainably grounded, and the future is earned only by the ethical treatment of our natural resources and fellow citizens.** In a time of alienation, with fewer and fewer people connected to the land and to their food, the story of the Cates Family Farm inspires, teaches, and restores hope that our failing farms and communities can be reborn."

—Daniel Smith, retired farmer; agribusiness executive;
author of *Ancestral* and *Poems from the Winter House*

"The generosity and spirit of the Cates family providing a public easement on their farm for public access to Lowery Creek, a Class 1 trout stream, is **one more example of how the family is a role model to the rest of us for so many good causes.**"

—Kathleen Falk, Wisconsin Conservation Hall of Fame 2022 inductee

“This book does not presume to be a template for other landowners. But it does, as you will see, offer key lessons to all farmers and ranchers: stop and listen to your land, employ imagination as well as science, and be a teacher by sharing your own story with whomever will listen. **These lessons may inspire you and are at the very heart of our hopeful future**.”

—Kevin McAleese, president and CEO of the Sand County Foundation

“Wendell Berry once asked, ‘Why do farmers and ranchers do what they do?’ He rhetorically answered, ‘Love.’ **Dick Cates has given us a shining testimony about people, land, and animals—all connected and strengthened by love**. You will feel it pulsing across every page.”

—Rick Knight, professor emeritus of wildlife conservation, Colorado State University; co-editor of *The Essential Aldo Leopold*

“There could not be a more important time to revisit the process of restoring ourselves and each other by learning to understand, care for, and restore land. **This book gives us a beautiful example of this process and reminds us that a land ethic is not simply a concept or philosophy, but a process of humanity, care, and hope**. I am grateful to Dick and the Cates family for sharing their journey in these beautiful writings.”

—Jed Meunier, great-grandson of Aldo Leopold; co-editor of *Aldo Leopold on Forestry and Conservation: Toward a Durable Scale of Values*

“The great American conservationist Aldo Leopold once said, ‘The landscape of any farm is the owner’s portrait of himself.’ In the case of the Cates Family Farm, **the portrait is deeply imbued with love, care, and a land ethic that would have made Leopold proud**. It’s a portrait of a multi-generational family and community, with many lessons learned and ready to share. Get ready to be inspired!”

—Courtney White, author and co-founder of Quivira Coalition

“*A Creek Flows Through This Driftless Land* is a compelling story of a family’s journey on a southwestern Wisconsin farm. **Dick Cates masterfully weaves a tale of love, laughter, and learning, with Aldo Leopold’s land ethic serving as a common thread to tie everything together regarding decision-making on the land**. Following the tradition of other Wisconsin farmers who are also consummate writers about their stewardship duties and their daily observations—such as Ben Logan, Jerry Apps, and Justin Isherwood—Cates shares the struggles, triumphs, and epiphanies that he and his wife, Kim, and the entire family experienced through three generations on the Cates Family Farm with honesty, humor, and wisdom.”

—Mark E. Cupp, executive director of the Lower Wisconsin State Riverway; board chair of the Wisconsin Land and Water Conservation Board

"**Just finished reading the book. What a gem!** On the one hand, we follow the struggles, hard times, low prices, risks, battles with the environment, and all the work of early migrating settlers looking for a better life, which might make you ask, 'Why farm?' On the other hand, we see all that the Cates family has done to create a space using best land use practices while nurturing all that leads to sustainability for future generations—to know the 'why.' What a pleasure to read!"

—Gary Zimmer, farmer and author of *Advancing Biological Farming: Practicing Mineralized, Balanced Agriculture to Improve Soil & Crops*

"The Cates family has brought their hearts, souls, and years of thinking labor to bring their beautiful grazing farm into a high state of alignment with the needs of the Earth while providing them with a healthy income. **This book tells the inspiring story of that transformation in a personal and factual narrative grounded in the natural and cultural history of the Driftless and the peoples and families who have stewarded and farmed it.**"

—Margaret Krome, policy director of the Michael Fields Agricultural Institute

"Dick Cates writes with a generous and curious heart rooted in science and wonder. He gives voice to generations of water and rock, persons and plants that became his beloved farm. **This story is as much about our planet as it is about one extraordinary place in Wisconsin's Driftless region. It was also here where I forged a life in food.** Working with the Cates family taught me that 'local' is a dimension as much as it is a distance. Dick dives deep into the layered complexities of his life in family farming and food and hears a chorus. If you're curious about how smallholder farming holds solutions not only for soil but for society, read this book."

—Odessa Piper, founder of L'Etoile, Madison, Wisconsin's first farm-to-table restaurant; founder of LLC OrganicArts for community-focused cooking

"From the natural forces that shaped it to the First Peoples who cherished it to the Cates family that continues to steward it, *A Creek Flows Through This Driftless Area* is **an intimate story about a farm family and their loving relationship to the land**. I highly recommend reading."

—Patty Loew, citizen of Mashkiiziibii (Bad River Band of Lake Superior Ojibwe); author of *Indian Nations of Wisconsin: Histories of Endurance and Renewal*

"This book is important in the way *A Sand County Almanac* and *The Land Remembers* are important. However, it brings the themes of these influential books together in a new way. Conservation farming, respect for the land, and the experience of life on the farm are told through the story of the land—the central character—and that difference makes this story timeless. This storyteller has the heart and soul of a farmer. This book is not nostalgic. It looks back to learn. More importantly, **the story looks forward with the hope and optimism of every great farmer I know**. This book belongs on the shelf alongside those mentioned above."

—Laura Daniels, farmer; agriculture community organizer; founder of the Dairy Girl Network

“In this, the land of Aldo Leopold, **Dick Cates has shown the next generation of agriculturists, through his actions, how conservation practices can be successfully implemented on the land**. We in Wisconsin agriculture are grateful for his example.”

—Jim Massey, longtime (retired) editor of *The Country Today*

“Our nation needs to learn how to live on our land. We need to experiment and learn how we can live productively in partnership, rather than extractively, with our land. **Dick Cates shows us how his family paid attention to their land and learned**.”

—Martin Doyle, author of *The Source: How Rivers Made America* and *America Remade Its Rivers*

“If we are ever to adopt and implement an ecological worldview, we need examples of what a land ethic looks like in practice. The Cates Family Farm and their story are **examples of how loving care and stewardship redefine productivity, such that the land, the farm, their family, and indeed the world are healthier**. Anyone who cares about or for the land will find insights and inspirations throughout this book.”

—Buddy Huffaker, president and executive director of the Aldo Leopold Foundation

“Aldo Leopold called it ‘the oldest task in human history: to live on a piece of land without spoiling it.’ With great reverence for the land, respect for those who have come before him, and love for those yet to come, this book marks a life's work at this task. **The heartfelt stories and hard-won insights that Cates shares herein are ultimately an invitation: join in the joys of caring for the land and, thereby, for each other.**”

—Keefe Keeley, executive director of the Savanna Institute; co-editor of *The Driftless Reader*

“In an era when factory farms dominate the rural landscape, and their pollution increasingly ravages our waters, **this story of one Wisconsin family of latter-day Leopolds offers a crucial lesson sure to resonate far off their farm—how to make a living off the land without killing it**.”

—Dan Egan, author of *The Devil's Element: Phosphorus and a World Out of Balance*

“It's a pleasure to read about this farm family's journey, especially how they intend to share this land and all they have learned. We learn that a portion of the Cates Family Farm is protected from development—permanently—with a conservation easement that includes a public access easement for a hiking trail (the Driftless Trail). On top of that, they've also agreed to a permanent streambank easement over Lowery Creek, further protecting the creek while opening it to public fishing. **Learning about how this productive farm will allow current and future generations to experience this bucolic setting is an important lesson that I hope more farm families might consider. What an incredible legacy to conservation and community!**”

—Jennifer Filipiak, executive director of the Driftless Area Land Conservancy

Drone view by Randy Manning.

I believe that the manner in which a culture nurtures its agriculture—its practitioners and Earth's gifts required for food and fiber—determines the long-term health, stability, and survival of that civilization. The history of every nation is written in the way in which it cares for its farms, farmers, soil and water, flora and fauna—collectively, the land. So it is my commitment, as a farmer and teacher, to communicate the conviction that the fate of how we care for our land is everybody's future, everyone's vital concern. It is imperative we work together toward the goal of a socially and environmentally just, enduring agriculture across our nation.

—Richard L. Cates Jr.

Papa (Dick) and granddaughter Sloane Helen plant bur oak seedlings, one for each of four grandchildren and a dear friend who had recently passed. They are gifts from the oak savanna and represent beauty, resilience, and hope. Photo by Kiley Cates

Above: On the Cates Family farm we reason, "eyeball to eyeball" with our cattle. Photo by past field representative, Animal Welfare Institute. Right: Hunchy was a Jersey steer that lived a long and peaceful, sociable life on the Cates farm. He wasn't certain if he was a bovid or a hominid ... and neither were we. See the Sidebar on pg 139 to learn more about Hunchy and his antics. Photo by Eric Cates.

The old sentinel bur oak that graces our pastured grassland has been witness to all for nearly two and a half centuries.

Foreword

This is an inspirational story of how the Cates family has developed a strong sense of place and community and honed their personal land ethic over the four generations that they have lived, worked, and learned on their farm in the Jones Valley of the Lowery Creek in Wisconsin's Driftless Region. In the center of their farm stands an ancient bur oak tree that the Cates family fondly calls "our sentinel oak" that has borne witness to the land's history since before European settlers began farming there in the mid-nineteenth century. As Dick Cates reflected on what motivated him to tell readers about the land's remarkable transformation, he mused that the oak "spoke" to him: "You have a story to tell. Your family and neighbors have found a way to grow your food and, at the same time, restore the health of this beautiful valley. It is time to share your story." And what a sweeping story he tells, recounting the land's history from the Pleistocene to the present, from indigenous hunter-gatherers to the farmers who have all lived there, and from land neglect to land health.

Dick's father, who cared deeply about the relationship of people to the land, introduced him at a young age to the writing of conservationist Aldo Leopold—words and actions that influenced and inspired him throughout this story. From Leopold's experiences on his own farm, he described what a great joy and deep satisfaction it is "**...to take a piece of land and by cautious experimentation to prove how it works. What more substantial service to conservation than to practice it on one's own land?"**

Since 1968, the Cates family has gradually come to understand how their land "works" and have overseen a remarkable transformation of their hill-and-valley farm. During the experimentation that led to that transformation, they came to appreciate the wisdom of biomimicry, of finding a way to replicate, within the context of modern farming, the ecological processes that had always sustained their land's health. For the Cates Family Farm, that has meant learning from the land's ecological history as a grass-dominated oak savanna ecosystem that supported native grazing animals moving across the landscape.

But it wasn't always clear how to raise modern livestock in a sustainable and profitable way while maintaining the land's health. The decades-long experimentation includes lots of twists and turns, highs and lows, and many engaging personal stories, both uplifting and sad.

Transitioning from traditional livestock practices that had proven incompatible with land health eventually led to the adoption of a managed grazing system. The farm's pastureland was subdivided into paddocks between which beef cattle were carefully moved on a schedule that kept forage plants productive and maintained continuous ground cover, mimicking the way the natural ecosystem had supported moving herds of grazing animals for millennia. That system reduced inputs and costs and produced high-quality, grass-fed beef for which there was growing demand. In short, it was a true conservation success story, a sustainable system that allowed the Cates family and their animals to thrive on what many might consider a marginal farm.

But the story is about much more than simply finding a sustainable way to make a living producing grass-fed beef. Running through the center of the farm is Lowery Creek, and on the steep hillsides that couldn't be used for grazing, there are oak woodlands. How those ecological components of the farm fit into the Cates family's vision for the land is also an important part of the story. The health of Lowery Creek and its trout population reflects how the surrounding land is being managed. Past farming practices resulted in runoff and other issues that harmed the ecological integrity of the creek, but the managed grazing system reduced those threats and helped a rare, remnant population of native brook trout to recover and flourish. That recovery, as much as any other environmental indicator, proved the success of the Cateses farming practices in restoring overall land health.

Most farms in the Driftless Region have productive agricultural land only in the valleys, while woodlands cover the surrounding hillsides. The Cates Family Farm is typical of the region. Instead of neglecting the farm's uplands or treating their oak woodlands simply as a source of income by producing timber, the family chose to restore and maintain their ecological health through careful prescribed burning. Just as the trout in Lowery Creek provided direct evidence of ecological recovery, so the recovery of uncommon plants and wildlife, like red-headed woodpeckers in the farm's oak woodlands, have repaid the Cateses' effort.

Dick Cates is a great storyteller, and the anecdotes about his family are engaging and revealing of the importance of family in the farm's success. In that respect, his stories include more than just an account of the vision and hard work required to bring a marginal farm back to a model of economic and ecological sustainability. It's also about the underlying human dimensions involving four generations of the Cates family, especially Dick's wife, Kim, and their son Eric and his wife, Kiley. What the family has accomplished on their land is now partnered with similar inspiring work of neighbors through the Lowery Creek Watershed Initiative. This cooperative effort promotes the value of managing the land to maintain the clear, cold waters of the creek that tie these folks together as a community. And in sharing their experiences more widely, the Cateses have welcomed visitors from around the world who come to observe and learn from what they have ventured.

As Aldo Leopold once revealed, "There are two things that interest me: the relation of people to each other, and the relation of people to land." In this book, Dick Cates follows in Leopold's footsteps by revealing that he cares deeply about people and land and by showing us how he and

his family have lived joyfully and sustainably on the land while providing by their example a substantial service to conservation.

Stanley A. Temple
Beers-Bascom Professor Emeritus in Conservation[1]
University of Wisconsin–Madison

Senior Fellow, Aldo Leopold Foundation and Board of Directors,
Sand County Foundation

Past chairman of the Wisconsin Chapter of the Nature Conservancy
and a past president of the Society for Conservation Biology; 2020 Inductee,
Wisconsin Conservation Hall of Fame

From left to right: Shannon, Dick, Kim, and Eric. Photo courtesy of the Cates family.

Lowery Creek, a Class 1 heritage brook trout and bountiful watercress garden.
Lowery Creek runs 3 1/2 miles through our farmland.

Preface

"Our tools are better than we are, and grow better faster than we do. They suffice to crack the atom, to command the tides, but they do not suffice for the oldest task in human history, to live on a piece of land without spoiling it."

—Aldo Leopold, "Engineering and Conservation" in *The River of the Mother of God and Other Essays*

This book is a story of a place through time. I am writing this book to celebrate and offer gratitude for the gifts this Driftless land—never touched by the Pleistocene glaciers—with its soils, water, plants, and animals has offered all who ventured here before us. I am writing this book to celebrate and give thanks for the gifts passed down from all of those who have walked here before me and cared for this place gently and passionately. From the First Peoples who called this place home for millennia to the European immigrants of the middle 1800s who "stuck" and farmed the land with stewardship—to all who raised families and built communities here together. And to my family—my mother and father and four siblings, my spouse and our three children, and now our grandchildren—who followed the first immigrants a century later.

I am writing this book to tell the story of my family's journey here. Much of this journey involves my foibles and my impetuous nature as I was driven by long-held myths of the meaning of success. I believed that by working harder—even at the wrong things—I would somehow earn grace.

Eventually, this becomes a story of listening to and learning from the land and embracing a "land ethic." Essentially, this means honoring nature's wisdom and taking personal responsibility for doing the right thing once we recognize what it is. In equal part, it is a story of listening to my best friend, my wife, Kim, who saved the farm and saved me from myself.

I listened, and I survived. I found peace and gratitude and hope again ... and the joy of farming.

Globally, we see alarming trends: population increasing through the middle of this century, overuse of marginal farmland causing desertification, water scarcity across many bioregions, and the increasing intensity and frequency of severe and destructive global weather events.

Wisconsin farmland—and our blessed water—will become increasingly significant, essential to our overall well-being, economic future, and food production in America and beyond.

The challenges we face in the realm of soil and water conservation across America and the world are real and significant. We continue to despoil our water—the most precious resource upon which all life depends. *Our* water does not imply that it belongs to *us*, but rather, it is a gift to all life on Earth. It is a gift that needs to be cherished and nurtured by us, *Homo sapiens*, because we have the capacity, unique among all species, to destroy this gift. Access to clean water will always be a matter of war and peace, of life or death.

In Wisconsin we have no oil and few precious minerals. But we are in the center of the largest fertile region on the planet because we have rich soil, and it rains more often than not when our crops need it. All my adult life I have been aware of and proud of the culture of agriculture in Wisconsin, a culture that should be cherished and nurtured. We stand on the shoulders of giants of the generations before us, and we are the beneficiaries.

Yet, in Wisconsin we are paving over or otherwise converting farmland at an alarming rate. In 2020 alone, Wisconsin lost one hundred thousand acres of land in farms,[1] which is equal to losing one average-sized Wisconsin farm every day.[2]

We continue eroding our soils where agriculture is practiced without cover crops, without thoughtful, strategic tillage or no tillage, or maintaining a perennial cover (grass or tree crops). New research indicates we are eroding our soils across Midwestern America at ten to one thousand times the rate they are forming.[3] Yes, read that sentence again. This lost topsoil ends up in the Gulf of Mexico and creates the largest hypoxic or "dead zone" on the planet (an area that some years measures eight thousand square miles), a zone where algal growth and decay depletes dissolved oxygen to the extent that fish and other aquatic life can no longer live.[4]

I am going to plant a flag: The greatest existential crisis human civilization faces is the destruction of the natural conditions necessary for our survival. We've got but one shot at checking human-induced climate change and species extinction. We must do it within this generation, or the game is over.

But we must not act out of fear. We need to act out of the joy that the love of our place has to offer. By listening to the land and learning from it, learning to treat the land with reciprocity, with justice, we will restore what we love and, in so doing, save ourselves, as well.

Albert Schweitzer lamented regarding Western culture: "The great fault of all ethics hitherto has been that they believed themselves to have to deal only with the relation of man to man."

Enter Aldo Leopold—ecologist, conservationist, lover of land—and his now classic treatise *A Sand County Almanac* (1949), where he championed an ethical relationship between people and the land they own and manage, a land ethic, which he called "an evolutionary possibility and an ecological necessity." Leopold observed:

> All ethics so far evolved rest upon a single premise: that the individual is a member of a community of interdependent parts. The land ethic simply enlarges the boundaries of

> the community to include soils, waters, plants, and animals, or collectively: the land. In short, a land ethic changes the role of *Homo sapiens* from conqueror of the land-community to plain member and citizen of it. It implies respect for his fellow-members and also respect for the community as such ... A land ethic, then, reflects the existence of an ecological conscience and this in turn reflects a conviction of individual responsibility for the health of the land. Health is the capacity of the land for self-renewal. Conservation is our effort to understand and preserve this capacity.

Leopold's words have challenged and nurtured me throughout my life.

A pristine, cold-water trout stream, named Lowery Creek for the past half century, birthed in the distant Pleistocene epoch, runs through the Driftless Area farmland my family and I are blessed to live on and care for. Our community of diligent land stewards along Lowery Creek has chosen to care for this natural gem and, over the decades, has learned how to do so.

In Wisconsin, we are who we are precisely because of our connection to our land, *our place*. The land has enriched our families, our community of friends—all of us. I believe that a land ethic can and will emerge out of a respect for land as a living organism and our mutual obligation to the great biota we call our Earth.

I write with the hope and faith that by cultivating not just crops and animals but embracing and living a land ethic, these gifts will continue to be offered to our children's families and their communities and to many generations beyond.

Leopold reminds us: "Nothing so important as an ethic is ever written ... it evolves in the minds of a thinking community." We need to imagine the future we desire and then get to work, collaboratively and collectively, to create it.

So, I am writing to celebrate and give thanks to the growing number of folks who recognize and support the imperative of an agricultural future guided by a land ethic, one that we continue to imagine and build.

I invite you all into this vision, especially all of the next generations who dream of a life of purpose on the land, on planet Earth, *our home*.

Every place through time has a story. Every farm is a story. We need to tell these stories and make the time to listen and learn from the land. We need to imagine a future of gratitude and hope for our grandchildren and beyond. We need to learn to cherish Earth's gifts.

And in the Lowery Creek watershed, the native brook trout are back after a century-long hiatus.

Introduction

We Ask Our Sentinel Oak for Acorns of Wisdom

"The landscape of any farm is the owner's portrait of himself."
—Aldo Leopold, *The Farmer as a Conservationist*

"The land is the real teacher. All we need as students is mindfulness."
—Robin Wall Kimmerer, *Braiding Sweetgrass: Indigenous Wisdom, Scientific Knowledge and the Teachings of Plants*

Every farm is a story of the land and of a family or community working on the land and with the land. So every farm is a story of relationships between people and between people and the land.

Our family, as well as every other farm family I know, spends a long time working toward being "extant," that is, still existing, surviving. Being here not just yesterday but also tomorrow. It doesn't always work out. There is a lot of hard work involved. Luck is always part of the equation, but there is also that piece that is hardest to quantify—imagination.

Albert Einstein told us, "Imagination is more important than knowledge." What does that mean, and how could it be related to a farm? First, seek knowledge, of course. But to build a successful farm business, one must *imagine* how to use this knowledge.

Over the decades, our family has done a whole lot of imagining—we just plain had to figure it out.

Today our farm runs on sunshine and rain, healthy soil, and good relationships. Period. It took us a long time to understand and accept all of this.

In the years since my father purchased our farm from the Stapleton family in 1967, our family is the only one in the rugged terrain of the Town of Wyoming, in Iowa County, Wisconsin, that has started and maintained a farm business over the past fifty years. Three livestock farms and a couple of crop farmers started and operated for a decade or so. Now, a few crop farmers rent some of this land. A small-scale vegetable farm and a livestock farm that started later are still operating, with no apparent heirs. Many dairy farms were already in place in our town through those years, and all but three small herds are gone, only one with an apparent heir. Our farm livelihood has transferred to the third generation in this time.

This book is our story and the story of folks before us who have lived along our beautiful trout stream through the millennia. It's also the story of the stream's renaissance, a result of discovery and living a land ethic, a community of care, and collective love for our place.

Today, as I write, a magnificent, majestic sentinel bur oak, an old *Quercus macrocarpa* tree, stands alone almost in the middle of our family's grazing land. This deep-rooted oak has watched over all who have called this valley home for the past two and a half centuries—at least ten generations of *Homo sapiens*—since the time of the birth of the United States of America.[1] Yet this old tree is but a newcomer.

Towering over the pasture and serpentine Lowery Creek, our sentinel is the landmark that lets us know we are home. I know I'm never alone when I look upon this tree, though my company changes with the seasons, with the weather, with the sun and moon. The tree gives me a feeling of grounding but also a heightened sense of things. Under the shade of its foliage, under its protection from the rain, under the falling of its brown leaves, under its snow-covered branches, I, too, find myself rooted here.

Tonight, on this full "worm" moon, I am comforted by the thought that spring is arriving once again, with all its promises of new life. A million earthworms find the frost retreating and their home in the soil coming alive. The first colorful flowers are blooming, Dutchman's breeches and soon the pasqueflowers. Canada geese in V formations, racing to return to the northern marsh, are honking overhead. Ruffed grouse will soon be drumming, and a solitary great blue heron, who each year rules the Lowery Creek, will be returning. With snow and heavy rainfall, this March has indeed come in like a lion.

Most Wisconsin farmers call this "mud season." I certainly do. For years I stressed over the arrival of early spring—cold, wet, gray, inconvenient. But after years of care, our grasslands have become more productive, more dense, and more protective of our precious soil. So, what little spring mud that may still churn up is but a minor incident in the annual cycle of life here on this farm.

We recall and connect the proverbial dots each year. Mud means water, and water is life. Water means grass, and grass means more life. My journey on this farm would have been less arduous if I had observed the lessons of nature from the beginning, but like most farmers, I had to unlearn before I could learn. Water is what gives this place its genesis, its fecundity for all of the sentient beings that have been fortunate to call this home over the ages.

It is the land, all the life that depends upon it, and Lowery Creek that runs through it that we have stewarded here in this valley. I hope that our sentinel oak has been proud as it has watched us learn to work with this land and not against it.

This is a book of stories of the land and the people, stories of my family, and my own story. They are true, and they are full of joy, pain, and reverence for this land, as well as love.

I have always been a student, and I have spent a good deal of my life as a teacher. I have arrived at a time in my life when I want to share, more than anything else, matters of the heart.

Our sentinel oak represents perhaps the fortieth generation of the line of *Quercus macrocarpas* that have graced the creek that runs through our pastures since the savanna replaced the boreal forest some eight millennia ago. Close your eyes and stand quiet and still under its enormous embracing arms and try to imagine all that this tree and its forebears have borne witness to.

Beneath its spreading boughs, I think of how it has seen this same annual drama unfold year after year. The oak stands erect, stalwart, and patient, and it shows me that this is the only way to live and love this landscape. Perhaps an old tree can at least whisper. I am listening. My hope is that you will also.

These stories of this land, the people, and my life are braided together into a cord that can never be undone. They have evolved together and could never just stand on their own. They are eternally bound.

Our grassland harvests sunlight and weaves it into grass, fancy straw. Our cattle harvest the grass, and the bugs in their belly turn it into sugars and protein—so much like turning straw into gold. This, in turn, feeds and grows our children and grandchildren and those of so many other families. All this is a miracle and one of so many of Earth's gifts.

Before we begin our family's personal journey, I will introduce you to our land—the geologic history of how it came to be the unique Driftless landscape that it is. Then I want to introduce you to the people, the long lineage of *Homo sapiens* who name this place their ancestral home, or who came much later for the "takings," and those who arrived later still, stayed, and came to call it their adopted home. The land shaped these peoples, and in turn, they altered and shaped the land. This is the first part of our journey together.

If the Earth Were Only a Few Feet in Diameter

If the Earth were only a few feet in diameter, floating a few feet above a field somewhere, people would come from everywhere to marvel at it. People would walk around it, marveling at its big pools of water, its little pools and the water flowing between the pools. People would marvel at the bumps on it, and the holes in it, and they would marvel at the very thin layer of gas. The people would marvel at all the creatures walking around the surface of the ball, and at the creatures in the water. The people would declare it precious because it was the only one, and they would protect it so that it would not be hurt. The ball would be the greatest wonder known, and people would come to behold it, to be healed, to gain knowledge, to know beauty, and to wonder how it could be. People would love it, defend it with their lives, because they would somehow know that their lives, their own roundness, could be nothing without it. If the Earth were only a few feet in diameter.

—Don Jones, a pioneer in the profession of art therapy and one of the founding members of the American Art Therapy Association

The people would declare it precious because it was the only one, and they would protect it so that it would not be hurt.

Photo by Terry McNeill.

PART I

The History of the Driftless Land Along Lowery Creek and the Peoples Who Have Called it Home ... or Stopped by for the Takings

Photo by Randy Manning.

Our Driftless Home Shaped by Water— A Creek Runs Through It

"Let creeks and rivers deepen crevices in rock, and gullies form and soften under wind. Let oaks take root, and shagbark hickory, and elderberry, yarrow, bee balm, clover, big and little bluestem, rattlesnake master, downy gentian, boneset, dogbane, ragweed, and thickets of sumac, blackberry, blackcap, rose. Let black soil deepen over limestone seabed."
—Patricia Monaghan, from *Getting to Black Earth* (2013), the eastern edge and start of the hills and valleys of our Driftless Area

Nį̄na wakąc̨ąkšaną—Water is Life in Hooc̨ąk, the language of the Ho-Chunk, First Peoples of this region.[1]

The cold, clear spring-fed waters of Lowery Creek emerge to greet the light of day from cracks in the limestone and sandstone bedrock laid down by an ancient ocean half a billion years ago when the North American tectonic plate was part of an enormous landmass known as Laurentia. At that time, the Driftless Area was located in the vast ocean near the Earth's equator, just beginning its long, slow slide to the north.

Today, I am walking down our farm lane across our grassland to Lowery Creek, hand in hand with my young granddaughter, Sloane Helen Cates. When we arrive at the bank and look down into the waters, I don't just see our reflection. I imagine all the creatures that have moved through this valley over the eons, this cold, clear water quenching their thirst, and the surrounding bountiful landscape providing sustenance and shelter.

Sloane points down and asks me what is moving in the water. Could be fly nymphs. I tell her, "Trout dessert," and she giggles at my playful word choice as she so often does. The alluring and iconic brook trout, a native of the Driftless Area for the past several million years, had been gone from much of Lowery Creek for the past century, an unintended consequence of generally poor European farming practices.[2] But within the last decade, biologists discovered their unexpected, astonishing revival.

I look more closely and allow my mind to wander beyond my reflection. What I see are the first humans to encounter the Driftless Area, so many millennia before me, trekking down from the edges of the great ice sheet to the north, hunting woolly mammoth and mastodon, then later deer, elk, and bison to feed their families. I see the first farmers raising a few hills of beans, corn, and squash to supplement the bounty of the hunt.

I see the early Europeans making their way to the lead mining district in the 1820s and '30s and bringing the lead to Daniel Whitney's shot tower just to the north along the Wisconsin River in Old Helena. I see the Lloyd Jones clan from Wales arrive in 1844. Frank Lloyd Wright, their most famous son, came here in 1879 from Richland Center at the age of twelve to work on his uncle James Lloyd Jones's farm (now the Taliesin estate). And from Ireland, the Thomas Stapleton family made its way across nascent Midwestern America in 1855 to put down roots on this very land that eventually became the Cates Family Farm.

I hear the water of Lowery Creek swirling past where Sloane and I are standing. I know this is the sound that has connected all of us through all these millennia. This water is the lifeblood of this valley. It is, indeed, along with the flesh and blood of my granddaughter, one of Earth's innumerable gifts.

Since I was a boy, I have often been soothed by the sound of the water in the stream moving, always moving, from the high ground in the south to the north through this narrow-grassed valley toward the Wisconsin River. In its six-mile course as the crow flies—just over nine miles on the meandering course a trout would have to maneuver—the main channel of Lowery Creek drops over five hundred feet from its spring-fed origins in the hills to the merging of its waters with the Wisconsin River. From there, its waters flow for another sixty-five miles, dropping just sixty-five feet before emptying into the mighty Mississippi and continuing another thousand miles to the Gulf of Mexico.

Unlike much of the Midwestern landscape shaped by the advance and retreat of glaciers during the geologically recent Pleistocene Ice Age—the past two and a half million years—the Driftless Area is not a new landscape. Our topography is ancient. The waters that formed Lowery Creek have been coming from our hills and ridges and carving these fertile valleys since the early Paleozoic, five hundred million years ago, so long ago that it seems like forever.[3] All the land surrounding the Driftless Area was ground flat by the glaciers, but the dynamic force that shaped the landscape of our farm was simply the steady, unrelenting action of water moving from high places to low places, carving its way through the rock on its journey back to the sea. (See Sidebar: The Driftless Area Has an Epic Story to Tell)

In the eight thousand five hundred square miles that are the true Driftless Area,[4] almost exclusively in Wisconsin, there are roughly thirteen thousand miles of free-flowing spring-fed cold-water streams.[5] Lowery Creek represents just over fifteen miles following the three primary channel meanders. Two channels traverse the Cates farm, the main course and one of the two tributaries, which are about three and a half miles of stream channel.

Lowery Creek was eons in the making. I know our family is here for just this present moment, a split second in the long history of this wondrous landscape shaped by the power of water. As the current stewards, life on this land is at once guided by a deep reverence for its well-being while we are here and grounded in the joy of knowing we will be passing it on and on and on. My family and our neighbors share the responsibility of caring for our land together. There is power in that responsibility, often unspoken between neighbors, as we share both what can be seen and what lies beneath our feet. It must be this way because

Aerial view of a portion of our Town of Wyoming. The rugged driftless terrain is evident, with ridges about 300 feet above the valley floor. Lowery Creek meanders across the upper right of the photo, and under our farm lane, on its journey north to the Wisconsin River three miles away. Photo by WI DNR.

The Driftless Area Has an Epic Story to Tell

From its equatorial beginnings in the Cambrian Period to avoiding the Pleistocene ice sheets, the Driftless Area has an epic story to tell. The geologic strata of Lowery Creek and the Driftless Area is a warped layer cake of sedimentary rock layers laid down through the slow accumulation of mud and sand and the calcified remains of early forms of sea life at the bottom of shallow tropical seas. The process began more than five hundred million years ago when the Cambrian Period was yielding to the Ordovician.

Understanding our place in time and space requires us to attempt to grasp this grand timescale. At the outset, the Driftless Area, a mere flyspeck on the huge Laurentian land mass straddling the equator, was submerged under a vast sea for more than two hundred million years. In time, a portion of the Earth's crust floated on the molten rock deep below and slowly began to drift. By the middle of the Cretaceous Period, some one hundred million years before the present day, our place on the North American tectonic plate had made its way to somewhere near 43.1410 N, 90.0705 W. These coordinates are the latitude and longitude where Lowery Creek empties into the pond at Frank Lloyd Wright's home, Taliesin, before it spills into the Wisconsin River. This is the location of our home today.

For eons before that and for all the time since, there has been a colossal march of global change—continents colliding and drifting apart, massive-scale volcanic eruptions, meteor impacts, and mountain ranges forming from the buckling and heaving of the thin crustal surface of our planet.

More recently, through only the past two million years, the Pleistocene epoch that we refer to as the Ice Age emerged. During the Pleistocene, glacial ice sheets, sometimes more than a mile thick, bulldozed much of the Northern Hemisphere, rearranging entire landscapes, taking down anything and everything in their paths. Time after time, the advances and retreats of the Pleistocene glaciers avoided the Driftless Area, leaving its unique landscape and biome untouched.

Since Cambrian times, our Driftless landscape has essentially been shaped by water. This time it is the erosive action of water moving from higher places to lower places. Some of the precipitation that fell as rain or snow on the hills moved overland and began to cut channels and then hollows between the hills. Over millions of years, much of the water settled through the soil to the rocks, finding its way into small cracks and fissures. Over time, the fissures became caves as water moved through the rocks and dissolved calcium carbonate sediments. Eventually, this groundwater would always find its way to the surface and daylight, emerging as cold-water springs that fed cold-water streams that braided and sinewed down and down, cutting and widening valleys before joining to form our region's rivers.

Why is the Driftless Area here? What anomaly of geology, or fate, allowed this place—our home—to remain unglaciated through the numerous glacial advances and retreats of the Pleistocene?

Professor James Knox "wrote the book" on the geology of the Driftless Area. According to Dr. Knox, there are three principal reasons why the Driftless Area escaped glaciation.[1] First, there is a deep down-warping (technically a syncline) of the bedrock at Lake Superior that acted like a siphon for the glacial ice that was coming off the Laurentide ice mass in Canada. This syncline channeled ice south and west into Minnesota. Second, on the eastern side of Wisconsin is an old pre-glacial lowland composed of relatively weak rocks, primarily shale. This rock was easily scoured by the glaciers and served as a sluiceway to channel an ice lobe south and east.

"So you've got two siphons, basically, pulling the ice away from what became the Driftless Area," Knox explained. The third factor, according to Knox, is that Wisconsin structurally is an arch with the bedrock bowed up. The high spot in the igneous bedrock begins in the central part of the state and widens to an arched shield to the north. The hard crystalline rocks of this bedrock arch resisted the ice flowing south.

So there you have it ...

At the outset, the Driftless Area, a mere flyspeck on the huge Laurentian land mass straddling the equator, was submerged under a vast sea for more than two hundred million years.

the water has no natural boundaries on this landscape. Like the creatures who inhabit this place, our stewardship maintains the circle of life that has always been here. Developing a land ethic in this present moment is essential for the future.

As I look up from my stream reflection, I direct my gaze just to the east of where Sloane and I are standing on the bank of Lowery Creek and take in our sentinel oak and her young progeny. Sloane knows these oaks as part of our family, through the stories I've shared with her about how they came to be here. Like many stories about our farm, the story of our oaks is centered on the power of conservation, and as Wendell Berry states: "It all turns on affection." Sloane and her brother and cousins will be the future stewards this land deserves, so guiding them with love of the place, the water, and its creatures is the bigger piece of how a farm family lives.

Telling these stories is shaped by understanding our place in time and space in relation to the grand timescale. The Pleistocene epoch is often referred to as the Ice Age for good reason. During the Pleistocene, glacial ice sheets, sometimes more than a mile thick, bulldozed much of the Northern Hemisphere, rearranging entire landscapes and taking down anything and everything in their paths. During the glacial advances, spruce-dominated boreal forests existed to the south of us and across the Driftless Area. During the long interglacial periods, the boreal forests moved northward, and prairie ultimately developed. Time after time, the advances and retreats of the Pleistocene glaciers avoided the Driftless Area, leaving its unique landscape undisturbed. Once the cold Pleistocene epoch relented, our place eventually developed as oak savanna—oak trees interspersed in tallgrass prairie grassland—one of the rarest biomes on Earth.

From where we have stopped on our walk, I look across our pastures and imagine the progression of the woolly mammoth, the mastodon, the retreat of the boreal forest, followed by the coming of deer, elk, bison, and oak savanna.

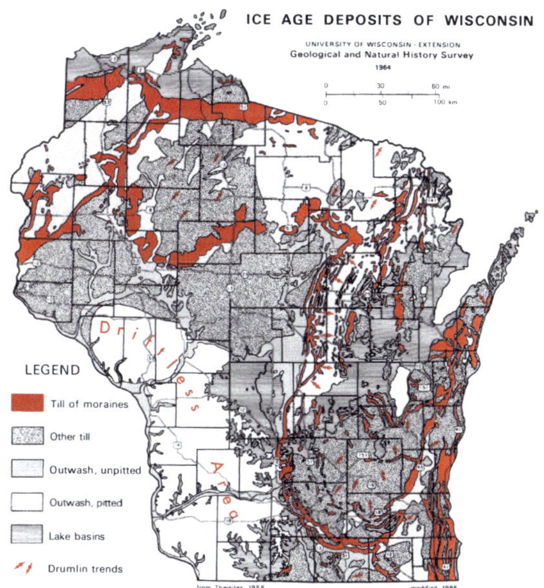

Source: Ice Age Deposits of Wisconsin

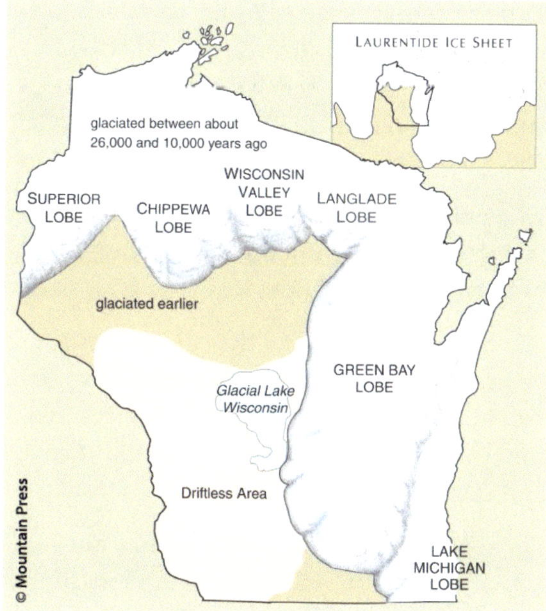

Source: Wisconsin Wetlands Association.

The Laurentide ice sheet—the most recent of the Wisconsin glacial stage—began to retreat fourteen thousand years ago and was largely gone from the Upper Midwest three to four thousand years later. As the new epoch, now termed the Holocene, progressed, the boreal forests were replaced for the first time by deciduous forests. The climate continued to get warmer and drier, and about eight thousand years ago, grasslands began to replace forests.[6]

The Driftless Area was at its hottest and driest for several thousand years. Eventually, a shift to wetter and cooler conditions began approximately four thousand years ago, ushering in a climate more like what we have today with predominantly westerly winds and interactions of Gulf moist air creating precipitation and the region's pre-European settlement vegetative pattern.

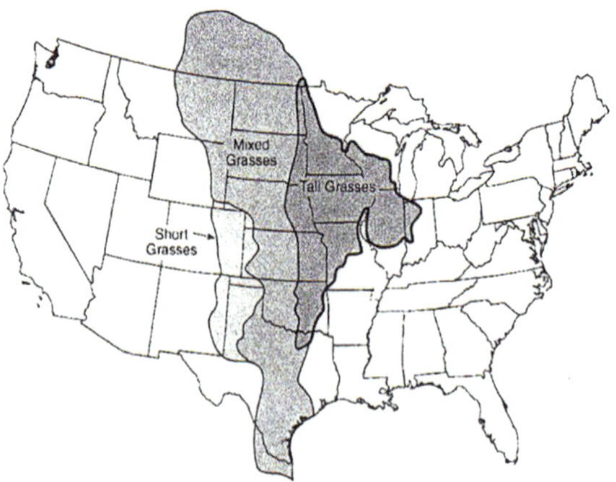

The tall grass prairie and other major prairie areas in the United States prior to European settlment. Source: Risser, P. G., E. C. Birney, H. D. Blocker, S. W. May, W. J. Parton, and J. A. Wiens. 1981. *The True Prairie Ecosystem*. Hutchinson Ross, Stroudsburg, Penn.

As noted, some of the tallgrass prairie developed as oak savanna, and Lowery Creek is in the heart of this historical savanna. Oak savanna, also known as "oak openings," is dominated on the uplands by dispersed bur oak, *Quercus macrocarpa*, some white oak (*Q. alba*), occasional black oak (*Q. velutina*), mesic prairie grass and forbs species, and on the lowlands by swamp white oak (*Q. bicolor*) and wet prairie.

On our farm, we can see firsthand an oak tree that reached maturity in open savanna grassland. Rather than growing tall and narrow in a race to the top of the forest to scavenge what little sunlight can be reached, their branches are spread out wide, as if in celebratory jubilation. As Sloane and I stand under the massive canopy of our sentinel oak, we also celebrate a long life, a quarter of a millennia, and a graceful reminder of time and place. As any kid knows, these trees make the best climbing trees, and we are fortunate to have many of them on our farm.

This unique oak savanna is now even more so one of the rarest biomes on Earth. It is estimated that prior to European settlement, most of this biome, 5.5 million acres, existed in the Driftless Area of Wisconsin.[7] Now, less than a tenth of a percent of those acres remain.[8]

The tallgrass prairie and the oak savanna are fire-induced biomes. This means they were created by fire that came about during regular stretches of dry weather over thousands of years. Weather records over the past century show the region has experienced severe to extreme droughts in some years. The incidence of drought is much lower in the forested regions to the north, south, and east.

The tallgrass prairie and oak savanna are also located in one of three prime areas of thunderstorm activity in the United States. Thunderstorm-induced lightning frequently occurs in autumn and early spring when the abundant grass created during the growing season is dried out and most flammable. The topography of the tallgrass prairie, with its absence of major water bodies or barrier mountain ranges, also enables a fire, once started, to run its course.

In addition to lightning-caused fires, indigenous peoples set fires to keep the savanna open as part of their hunting strategy. The most significant effects on the Driftless landscape vegetation were caused by the elimination of fire when the Europeans came to the area. They put out the fires, and the forest grew on the steep slopes and over any ground that wasn't plowed.

Englishman George W. Featherstonhaugh was hired in 1834 by the U.S. government as its first geologist. In 1837, he described the land as he traveled from Madison to Blue Mounds, Wisconsin, an eastern gateway to the Driftless, giving a very clear picture of the dominant prairie and oak savanna in the region and the scattered nature of oak forest:[9]

> We got into one of the most exquisitely beautiful regions I have ever seen in any part of the world. The prairie that had hitherto been distinguished by a regular rolling surface, here changed its character and took the form of ridges somewhat elevated, which frequently resolved themselves into masses of gracefully rounded hills, separated by gentle depressions, that occasionally became deepened valleys. In whatever direction our eyes were turned, the most pleasing irregularities of the surface presented themselves. But that which crowned the perfection of the view, and imparted an indescribable charm to the whole scene, from the knoll where we stood, to the most distant point, was the inimitable grace with which the picturesque clumps of trees, that sometimes enlarges themselves into woods, embellished this rural landscape from the hand of Nature … America will justly boast of this unrivaled spectacle when it becomes known, for certainly it is formed of elements that no magic could enable all Europe to bring together upon so great a scale.

Today, we live in a relatively quiet time in the shifting geology on our dynamic planet. Since the retreat of the last continental ice sheet that spared the Driftless Area from its grinding ice bulldozers, Earth's major upheavals and volcanic eruptions have mostly left humans alone to evolve to where we are today.

During this "interglacial period," humans have learned innumerable ways to work together, grow food, and harness energy. Today, we must use the opportunity as a global community to address the reality of climate change and the power of imagination to find solutions.

Scattered throughout our planet are special places of overwhelming beauty and welcoming abundance, like the maternal hills and fertile valleys of the Driftless Area, home to Lowery Creek—our home, our place.

A view south looking over what is now the Jones Valley and the Cates farm toward the headwaters of Lowery Creek. Drone view by Jack Whaley.

Millennia of First Peoples Along Lowery Creek—Resilience and Reciprocity of Earth's Gifts

"The Honorable Harvest asks us to give back, in reciprocity, for what we have been given ... It was through actions of reciprocity, the give and take with the land, that the original immigrant became indigenous."

—Robin Wall Kimmerer, *Braiding Sweetgrass: Indigenous Wisdom, Scientific Knowledge and the Teachings of Plants*[1]

There is a crumbled stone cairn on the high ground at the headwaters of Lowery Creek. Getting to the cairn on foot involves a six-mile walk with more than a five hundred-foot vertical climb from the mouth of Lowery Creek at the Wisconsin River. The walk takes you across the wetlands below farmland owned by the Lloyd Jones family and what is now Frank Lloyd Wright's Taliesin and Midway Barn. You continue up and across farmland once lived on and worked by a dozen or so Irish families and the British Yankee Goodwin Lowery, and now my family. All of us arrived only after the First Peoples had been here since time immemorial.

The family that presently owns and has farmed the high ground since the early 1900s informed me that the European immigrants from whom their great-grandfather purchased this land told him there was an Indian burial mound. They requested the new owners to "Please respect it. Don't let the children play up there, and please leave it intact." The family has done so for more than one hundred years since that piece of land last exchanged hands.

This site was, and is, sacred to someone. I am grateful to the family for guarding and protecting something they, or I, will never fully comprehend. There is more to this site than its mere physicality. They have respected the sanctity and the mystery of another culture and its manner of honoring their dead, long after this human ancestor was placed in their final resting ground.

This location of the cairn is high on the landscape. If all the brush were gone as it was when the First Peoples managed the landscape with fire, one would be able to view a full 360-degree panorama. The crumbled pattern of stone shows evidence of being oriented toward the rising sun at dawn. A spring at the headwaters of the main tributary of Lowery Creek is a few hundred feet downslope, and a south-facing cliff is just a short distance to the west.

On a recent visit to this sacred spot, I gazed out from the high ground, breathing in the moist air all around me, so saturated with life. I heard only resident bird song, the wind in the trees and the grass, and my own heart beating. In my bones I felt the sanctity and mystery, and I was overwhelmed with how long human souls have stood right here, perhaps just like me, absorbing the beauty and gift that is this place.

I contemplate how long ago someone was laid to rest here and wonder why their loved ones chose this place. The mystery of all that I will never know allows my imagination to run free. The only thing I do know for certain is I am thankful that so many before me cared so deeply for this place and that the chain of care has remained unbroken through the ages.

For years, archaeologists have taught that the first humans likely arrived to the American continents twelve thousand years ago, having wandered across Beringia, the land bridge that existed between Siberia and North America about the time the most recent continental glacial ice was receding. However, evidence of human occupation along the western coast of South America, as far back as thirty thousand years ago,[2] lends support to a coastal migration theory that people first arrived to this continent by boat.

Contemporary tribal historians push back at such efforts to date human occupation. According to the origin stories of most Indian nations in Wisconsin, the tribes have been here from "the beginning of time."[3]

The first cultures were comprised of nomadic hunters who followed the indigenous megafauna, the large mammalian herbivores such as mastodon, woolly mammoth, giant beavers, ground sloths, and ancient bison species as they foraged and grazed their way across the continent.

Isolated megafauna fossils have been found throughout the Driftless Area. The best documented early kill site in our region is near Boaz in Richland County, just thirty-five miles to the northwest of our farm—a mastodon with an adjacent Clovis fluted spear point, the kill dated approximately twelve thousand years ago. Additional sites similar to Boaz likely exist in our region, but the deep covering of sediment that blankets most valleys complicates their discovery.[4]

At the headwaters of Lowery Creek, there is a site near year-round clear-water springs and overhanging rock outcroppings that could have served as shelters or windbreaks for fires, cooking, and sleeping for small bands of hunters and their families.

Much of this high ground has been under the plow since European farmers first broke the oak savanna grassland in the mid-1800s. A measurable amount of the original topsoil has since eroded and been lost downslope. Due to this soil loss, along with the annual freeze-thaw cycle that moves stones and other hard objects to the surface, items once buried by time or discarded in encampment middens often become observable at or near the surface.

In the mid-twentieth century, the young son of one of the European immigrants farming near the headwaters of Lowery Creek used to follow his father's horse-drawn plow just to see what turned up. Fortunately for us, he sometimes saved what he found. Other pieces were identified during a barn site excavation there when the soil was disturbed to greater depth. The result is a collection of stone spear points and arrowheads (projectile points, or biface tools), as well as other cultural items of varying age, all unearthed at the headwaters of our small watershed after having been carefully crafted and then likely passed down through generations.

Early spear points (possibly as late as 8,000 years ago in some locations in WI). I would like to thank Joe Stapleton, Spring Green, WI, for sharing his collection of cultural items from the Stapleton-Wyoming Campsite. The site has been registered with the WI Office of the State Archaeologist and Smithsonian Institute, Washington, D.C. Photos by Adeline Amble, Spring Green, WI.

The Thebes notched and St. Charles notched points are representative of the nomadic hunters who traversed this landscape nearly ten thousand years ago.[5]

At the head of our valley, my friend unearthed stone tools that were elegantly crafted ten millennia ago, hundreds and hundreds of generations ago. Ten *thousand* years ago, men and women, their hopes and dreams not so different from yours and mine—potentially in some trepidation over an oncoming storm, certainly in anticipation of the joy of a next meal, all while doting on their children in tow—trekked along the waterway we now call Lowery Creek from the Wisconsin River to their camp in the high ground, or back again, right through what are now our farm's pastures. I could have waved at them from where I write today or joined them in a few quick steps. I hold this in my mind's eye, and the wonder and awe of it gives me chills.

It deeply stirs my imagination to know that the First Peoples were in our neighborhood and community so many years ago, hearing the same sounds of the swirling creek water and the wind

All spear points and the Madison Triangular-Adams County arrowhead were identified at the Stapleton-Wyoming campsite.[7] Collection by Joe Stapleton and photos by Adeline Amble.

in the grass as I do today. I like to think they weren't so different from us, united by a love of this place for its gifts of life and its overwhelming fecund beauty. As we do now, they cherished their hopes and dreams and lived with a will to thrive, not just survive. Of this I feel certain.

The people living during this period experienced a rapidly changing environment. The Pleistocene megafauna likely became extinct in part from the shift to a warmer and drier climate as the glaciers retreated north.[6]

This era is marked by the first divergence from a nomadic way of life to one of "seasonal rounds" or an annual subsistence round. People began to move across the landscape in search of particular plant, fish, or animal foods that were abundant at different times of the year. (Western archaeologists tend to divide cultures of Native peoples in the Driftless Area into four main periods based on perceived changes in technology, subsistence practices, and lifeways: Paleo-Indian prior to 9,000 years ago; Archaic 9,000 to 3,000 years ago; Woodland 3,000 to 1,200 years ago; and the Mississippian-Oneota 1,200 years to European contact. These periods likely do not fully reflect the complex history and reality of the First Peoples and their cultures in the past, as they are based on the limited data of observable changes in cultural items and sites that are visible to archaeologists.)

Peoples likely passed through the Lowery Creek corridor during the autumn months, "when the deer paw the earth," and again in the spring, "raccoon breeding" month. This corridor would have been a travel route of relative ease for families or clans on foot passing through this otherwise rugged country as they made their way between winter shelters in the uplands near the headwaters of the creek and their summer home, likely along the Wisconsin River. The Kirk Corner notched point uncovered on the farm at our upland site is representative of the early part of this period, and the Raddatz side-notched point later.

None of these tools and weapons traveled with their hunters from some great distance to arrive at these uplands. Nor are they here as a result of trade with exotic groups living in far-off places. They were all crafted from locally sourced Galena chert. Extensive chert beds exist along the Military Ridge, the local area's highest landscape just a few miles south of where these items were found.[8]

The landscape was in transition, shifting from forest to oak savanna and tallgrass prairie, similar to what the first Europeans encountered so many millennia later. Climate change pushed the shift from conifers to deciduous oak-type forests. Eventually, as a result of fire, from both lightning strikes and human intent, the landscape shifted again to predominantly oak savanna and tallgrass prairie.

The native herbivores preferred to feed on the newly emerging shoots of grass that appeared after fires burned off the overlying dead matter. First Peoples, having observed this, regularly set fires to establish hunting grounds.[9] "Rather than domesticating animals for meat, Indians retooled whole ecosystems to grow bumper crops of elk, deer, and bison," writes Charles C. Mann in his 2005 book *1491: New Revelations of the Americas Before Columbus*.[10]

In the summer months, people congregated in large groups along the Wisconsin River, *Nįoxetexųnųnįk* (in *Hoocąk*, the Ho-Chunk language), and other tributaries where water resources, including fish (*hoo*), turtle (*keecąk*), mollusks, lamb's quarters (*raxgemąkejahağep*), arrowroot, and wild fruits and berries, and *haas* were abundant. Cattail shoots (*wiici*), other edible greens, (*wažącosake*), and wildflowers were abundant in the spring and summer. In the fall, hickory nuts (*pąąjagu*), walnuts, (*cage*), acorns (*huuc*), wild rice (*sii*), sunflower seeds (*xąąwįhoxerexete suu*), among other wild seeds, were gathered. Domesticated corn (*wicąwąs*) and beans (*huunįk*) joined squash (*wicąwą cozu*), a food of choice for five thousand years, as part of the diet about one thousand years ago. With abundant food and water (*nįįI*), these riverine locations were able to support large groups of people.

In the winter, people dispersed in small family or clan groups, traveled into the interior of the Driftless Area, and sheltered from the cold in caves beneath overhanging rock outcroppings or in wigwam structures (*ciiporokes*), covered with cattail mats or hides. These small groups relied heavily on hunting for food and hides and supplemented their diet with dried fruits and nuts. White-tailed deer (*caa*) and American elk (*hųųwą*) were the main species hunted, and to a lesser extent, buffalo or bison (*ceexįį*). Archaeological analysis of unearthed bones shows that modern bison were present in the Driftless Area at least three thousand four hundred years ago.[11]

Patty Loew, Lowery Creek, and the Driftless Area is Ho-Chunk Ancestral Homeland[1]

Excerpt from *Indian Nations of Wisconsin: Histories of Endurance and Renewal,* by Patty Loew

"A thousand years ago, after carefully preparing red, black, and blue-gray paints, an artist sanded the walls of a rock shelter hidden in a stand of mixed hardwoods in present-day Iowa County. Satisfied that the "canvas" was properly prepared, the artist—a historian really—began to record a remarkable story. The walls filled with painted turtles, thunderbirds, and a mythic hero who wore human heads as earrings. Supernatural athletic contests and "giant" slayings unfolded in pictographic detail.

"Members of the modern Ho-Chunk Nation recognize this composition as the story of Red Horn, an ancient Ho-Chunk hero. This origin epic, told by generations of tribal members and preserved in a cave known today as Gottschall, testifies to the enduring power of the spoken word and persistence of Native American oral tradition. Gottschall also provides other clues to the pre-Columbian Ho-Chunk past. Along with the Red Horn paintings, the cave contains pottery shards of the Effigy Mound Builders, whose earthen works first appeared about 3,000 years ago, and unusual soils associated with sacred rituals of the Mississippians, whose agriculture-based economy and impressive trade networks emerged about 1,000 years ago. The connection between Ho-Chunk oral history and the physical evidence at Gottschall suggests that rather than being separate peoples, later cultures evolved from and intersected with earlier ones.

It is clear how resourceful and imaginative these First Peoples were as they made their way along the "seasonal rounds" to provide abundant sustenance, utilizing perennialized oak savanna encouraged with fire for animal hunting, harvesting nuts and fruits from the forests, foraging wetlands for perennial grains and greens and waterways for the native brook trout, and more.

About three thousand years ago marked the introduction of stone grinding and more complex burial rites. Burial patterns from that time indicate distinct regional populations as well as an egalitarian social structure.[12] The Kramer point is representative of this era. Stone was also ground into more diverse cultural items such as grooved axes, gorgets, and plummets, which could be used as net weights or bolas.

And people here had become more in touch with others across the continent. They began to utilize exotic materials secured through trade networks: marine shells, copper from the Lake Superior region, Knife River flint from the western plains, and obsidian from what was to become the Yellowstone Park area. Red ocher, an iron oxide sourced from ground hematite or other iron-enriched minerals, began to be used as a powder or paint with human burials.

Mound building and the first appearance of clay vessels characterized the next shift in social and material culture. The Waubesa contracting stemmed point and the Steuben expanded stemmed point identified at the Lowery Creek headwaters site are representative of the first half of this era beginning about two thousand five hundred years ago. Also uncovered was a Madison triangular (Adams County) arrowhead—likely one of the first for the new bow and arrow hunting tool that was introduced here just over one thousand two hundred years ago. This type of arrowhead was fashioned until about the time of European contact.

The Ho-Chunk—Hochungra, "People of the Big Voice"—were concentrated at the Red Banks near present-day Green Bay at the time of first European contact by Jean Nicolet in 1634, but also had settlements in the southern Driftless Area. Much of the Driftless Area, including Lowery Creek, is Ho-Chunk ancestral homeland. (See Sidebar: Patty Loew, Lowery Creek, and the Driftless Area is Ho-Chunk Ancestral Homeland)[13]

When the first Europeans arrived here, it is estimated there were between fifteen thousand to twenty thousand mounds or earthworks in present-day Wisconsin, more than in any other area of North America. Mounds were especially abundant in the southern Driftless Area.[14] Most of those mounds have disappeared because of plowing, road construction, development, and, of course, curiosity seekers and their shovels.

Thankfully, many mounds are still extant, and now, with modern tools like LIDAR (light detection and ranging), previously undetected mounds continue to be identified.

Although mounds can be round, conical and oval, linear, enclosures, or flat-topped bases for "temples," effigy mounds are most mysterious and truly unique to our area. The effigy mound builders sculpted the earth into more than one thousand groups of animals and supernatural beings on what was likely their ceremonial landscapes. Typically used as burial places, such emblematic mounds are "not found elsewhere in the world in such concentrations and certainly constitute an archaeological world wonder," wrote Robert A. Birmingham and Amy Rosebrough in their 2017 work, *Indian Mounds of Wisconsin*.[15]

"The Gottschall site, a place of obvious cultural and religious significance, is just one of more than one hundred rock art sites identified in Wisconsin, most of them in the Driftless Area of the southwestern part of the state. From simple grooves and incised geometric designs to elaborate painted birds, animals, and human forms, these cave drawings may have been created for spiritual or sacred reasons inspired by dreams, fasts, or rituals. Perhaps Native artists carved or painted these motifs to educate the young or commemorate the dead. It is likely that the ancestors of today's modern Indian nations used pictographs as mnemonic devices to help tribal members remember important events or complex ceremonies ...

The walls filled with painted turtles, thunderbirds, and a mythic hero who wore human heads as earrings. Supernatural athletic contests and "giant" slayings unfolded in pictographic detail.

"Along with other intriguing fragments of the past rock art, picture writing, and wampum are useful in reconstructing the experiences of Native cultures before they encountered Europeans. It is a history that encompasses a vast expanse of time ..."

Some mound groups correspond to Ho-Chunk clan divisions and cosmology; for example, there are eagles and thunderbirds of the Sky World, bears of the Earth World, and water panthers symbolic of the Underworld. Patty Loew, a member of the Bad River Band of Lake Ojibwe, notes that some mound groups may be maps, calendars, or astronomical devices.[16]

The Driftless Area effigy mound-building ancestors of the modern Ho-Chunk people eventually became the first sedentary farmers in the upper Mississippi Valley. This transition was based on increased reliance on corn-based agriculture. Interior landscapes like Lowery Creek were (to some extent) abandoned in favor of concentrated agricultural settlements along the Mississippi River and east and south of the Driftless Area. People were tied to localities where crops were grown during the growing season, and surplus crops stored for the winter months provided another impetus for more permanent settlements.[17]

Let's return to the crumbled stone cairn on the high ground at the headwaters of Lowery Creek and the still unanswered questions: If, in fact, this is a burial mound, how long ago was someone laid here to rest, and why?[18]

The cultures that constructed conical mounds, or cairns, built some of them out of stone. Cairns are generally defined as a mound of stones built as a memorial, monument, or landmark, typically on a hilltop or ridgeline.

A conical stone cairn has been recorded across the Wisconsin River a few miles farther north. It was excavated in the 1920s and was found to contain the remains of a young male with a raven headdress. It was, indeed, a burial mound.

The cairn at the top of Lowery Creek is built on top of rock with only a thin layer of soil. Could it have been merely a landmark for travelers, ancient or not so ancient? It certainly would have been visible for miles in any direction. There is likely more to its purpose.

The cairn was constructed of several types of red, black, and white rock. The rock the cairn is built on is St. Peter Formation sandstone, a type of bedrock widespread across the region. The majority of the rocks in the cairn have a reddish tint. The color comes from oxidized or "rusted" iron embedded in the rock. A significant number of somewhat smaller, black-faced rocks are also St. Peter Formation sandstone, "faced" with hematite (another form of iron oxide) or goethite (an iron oxide hydroxide) precipitate layer. There are no outcrops of black-faced St. Peter sandstone nearby, so this rock was carried for some distance. The white or light-gray colored rock of the Platteville Formation is dolomite, the rock layer immediately over the St. Peter Formation and frequently visible as the "capstone" layer of sedimentary geological formations in this region, according to geologist William Batten, who visited the site.

So why would a burial site be placed on bedrock and under a rock cairn instead of in or under the earth? One possible explanation is the family lost a loved one during the winter hunting season

Cultural pieces (not datable) from the Stapleton-Wyoming Campsite.
Collection by Joe Stapleton and photos by Adeline Amble.

when the ground was frozen. Placing the body in a cairn constructed of stones of three sacred colors would have honored the loved one and protected the body from the ravages of scavengers.

The following spring, it is possible that when the family returned to the clan's larger gathering site along the Wisconsin River, the loved one's skeletal remains, at least the long bones, may have been bundled and carried along on the trip and then enshrined in an earthen mound. We don't know what spring that would have been in the past, but it is likely that the family traveled across the grassland along Lowery Creek, where our cattle graze today.

On top of a hill overlooking this grassland, the ash remains of *our* family's loved ones are here in the soil, on this land. Headstones mark their resting spots, as is our custom, but also arranged stones—cairns in their own right. These stones vary by color and type. Some are white or light gray local limestone with pieces of chert, pink and black-flecked granite from a special place about two hundred fifty miles away in northern Wisconsin, and multi-colored riverine stones from the nearby Wisconsin River. These stones are of great meaning to those who rest here as well as those of us who placed them. Not so different, really, from the special manner our neighbors from so long ago sought to memorialize their own loved ones.

In a solemn yet soulful way, I feel a kinship with this Native family—a bond of grief for our losses yet love and gratitude for all that the ones we have lost taught and shared with us.

First Peoples have, through their oral traditions, passed on for millennia their spiritual connection of respect and gratitude for their homelands. Robin Wall Kimmerer writes in *Braiding Sweetgrass* (2013): "Being naturalized to place means to live as if this is the land that feeds you, as if these are the streams from which you drink, that build your body and fill your spirit. To become naturalized is to know that your ancestors lie in this ground. Here you will give your gifts and meet your responsibilities. To become naturalized is to live as if your children's future matters, to take care of the land as if our lives and the lives of all our relatives depend on it. Because they do."[19]

In Aldo Leopold's turn of a phrase: the millennia of First Peoples here lived, and do to this day, in accordance with a land ethic.[20]

On our farm website, my daughter-in-law, Kiley Prusso Cates wrote, "We celebrate and honor the people who first called this land home. We remember the struggles and tragedies they've endured and continue to endure. We recognize and honor their place and shared story of America."

I have gratitude for the millennia of First Peoples who have lived here for so long caring for this place. By doing so, they set the stage and provided the opportunity for the Stapleton and Cates families to follow and live well. We can only hope to repay them with a pledge of reciprocity.

Our family's eternal resting spot on the hill above our home.

European Immigration—Earth's Gifts of Beaver, Lead, and Soil, Free for the Taking: A Diaspora Without a Land Ethic

"Welcome to Wisconsin, the watery navel of a big-bellied country—no oceans but a couple of seas on two sides, Old Man River on another—some few hundred thousand spit-drop ponds and drooling creeks swimming with fish and warm cuddly things, mink and muskrat, and of course the reason we're all here in the first place, beaver, King beaver, who gave rich hats to fine gentlemen for gold and whose souls stack up like cordwood in the marshes and hollows and repined forests ... This is a body-warm mother of a prairie, where we live, where the mongrel Yankees, and Slavs and Bohunks and Vikings and Welsh and famine-ravished Irishmen and war-ravished Prussians came in search of a God, a kiss-inspired dream, a sack of potatoes or at least a good beer."

—David Allan Cates

"Be fruitful and multiply, and fill the earth, and subdue it; and rule over the fish of the sea and over the birds of the sky and over every living thing that moves on earth."

—Genesis 1:28

"We abuse land because we regard it as a commodity belonging to us. When we see land as a community to which we belong, we may begin to use it with love and respect."

—Aldo Leopold, *A Sand County Almanac*

During September and October 1832, John Mullet, deputy surveyor, surveyed the exterior and township lines of T 7N R 4-5-6 East. At the intersection of Sections 5, 6, 7, and 8 he identified "corner trees" as was the practice of the day. A yellow oak (now more commonly called a black oak) of sixteen inches in diameter was identified in Section 8 (to the SE), and bur oaks of six to seven inches in diameter were identified in Sections 5 (NE), 6 (NW), and 7 (SW).

Only the bur oak identified in Section 6 remains today. This sentinel oak of our valley would have been about a half-century old at the time, a similar age and breadth—a mere ten inches at breast height—as her progeny close by is today, still in its youth. The next generations are growing up on the grasslands as they have for the past eight millennia.

Our sentinel oak was in place well before the first farmers arrived along Lowery Creek. If she and her cohort sent messages with the wind across the Driftless, they would have been laden with shock and awe about something entirely new under the sun. "Who are these new kind of *Homo sapiens* bent on taking from the Earth, ignoring the honorable harvest and acts of reciprocity?"

However, prior to filling in the story of the parade of immigrant "takings" across nearly four centuries, I want to introduce you to the Stapleton family and their Irish brethren who arrived to Lowery Creek in the 1850s, escaping the ravages of the devastating Irish Potato Famine. Unlike the plethora of immigrants who came to skin, dig, or exhaust precious resources—anything mostly free—and move on when the "going got tough," Thomas and his wife, Mary (Hogan) Stapleton, and soon their children, were some of the first to settle and build a farm along Lowery Creek. They farmed to their own drummer, and they farmed to last. With their first land purchase in 1855, they began to put together the parcels that only much later became the Cates Family Farm, and we are the most fortunate beneficiaries of their farming legacy.[1]

Soon after Thomas and Mary Stapleton's arrival, the banks and highlands along Lowery Creek and across all of what became the Town of Wyoming were filling up fast with fortunate survivors of the Great Hunger, one of the most salient examples of the failure of monoculture agriculture in human history. Making their way across the Atlantic in tall wooden sailing ships and crossing a thousand miles of continent with hope and the will to build lives of dignity and three square meals a day, Irish families arrived in our Driftless Area of Wisconsin in great numbers. They had seen and lived through what *doesn't* work on the land. Willing to take a second chance, I can only assume they had allowed themselves to grow wiser.

Andrew Sullivan and his wife-to-be, Mary Lewis, emigrated in 1852 and settled on a parcel northwest of what would become the Stapleton farm. Edmund Lawton, Ellen Sullivan, and later, James Rowan found their way up the hill to the west, with John Carmody and Margaret O'Brien just to their northeast. Within a few years, John Laughnan and Margaret O'Grady settled to the east of the Stapletons. Sullivan's son James and Laughnan's daughter Mary married. John Ryan purchased land contiguous to the southeast of the nascent Stapleton farm in 1857. The Hogans,

Thomas's wife Mary's family, were to the south and east of the Ryans. Within a couple of decades, there were several Thomas and Mary Stapletons, three John and Mary Ryans, and ... well, you get the picture.

By the time of the 1860 U.S. Census, Thomas and Mary had two (eventually six) children, and Thomas is listed as a farmer with a net worth of $700 in real estate and $100 in personal property.

Enter the lone Yankee, Goodwin Lowery, in 1863, onto the farm contiguous to the north along the creek that was to become his namesake. Goodwin was descended from early English New England families. He and his wife, a native of New Orleans, bore no children but farmed here until Goodwin's death in 1889. Every Irish community requires at least one stone wall, and the Stapleton-Sullivan-Lawton-Rowan-Carmody-Laughnan-Ryan-Hogan community had theirs, about a half mile's worth of carefully assembled stone boxing off the Lowery farm ... but to what end? Perhaps in this neighborhood, the majority believed that a good stone wall could make a good "certain" neighbor. (See Sidebar: The Stone Wall)

Richard and Mary Thomas Lloyd Jones arrived here from Wales in 1865—the only other non-Irish immigrants to our part of Lowery Creek—to farm a short distance down the valley where Lowery meets the Wisconsin River. Our valley then became known as the Jones Valley, adjacent to the larger Wyoming Valley. The Lloyd-Jones family established their farms and school at what became known as Hillside, and in 1911, the Taliesin estate was created there by their famous architect grandson, Frank Lloyd Wright.[2]

The Stapleton farmhouse from the 1890s with porch and half second floor addition. The original portion of the Stapleton, now Cates, farmhouse was built in the 1860s with four rooms and a basement root cellar. Thomas and Mary died in their farmhouse in 1869 and 1924, respectively. Photo courtesy of the Stapleton family.

It was an abundance of beaver that lured the first European fortune hunters here. During a time when the hats made of beaver felt were the height of fashion in Europe, French explorers were the first to encounter this furry mother lode-in-waiting in the north woods of the New World.

There is some evidence that Étienne Brûlé may have explored the upper Great Lakes in the 1620s,[3] but the first European generally credited to have reached what is now Wisconsin was Jean Nicolet. In 1634, Nicolet was sent from Quebec by the governor of New France to contact the Ho-Chunk people and expand the fur trade and possibly find a water route to Asia. With Huron guides, Nicolet traveled by canoe through Lake Huron and Lake Superior, then into and down Lake Michigan. Nicolet probably came ashore near the Red Banks along Green Bay, the ancestral home of the Ho-Chunk people. Nicolet remained with the Ho-Chunk through the winter before he returned to Quebec.[4] Subsequent French-led fur trading forays headed into the Lake Superior region.

The first European expedition into the southern Driftless Area of what is now Wisconsin occurred in the spring of 1673. Father Jacques Marquette, a Jesuit missionary, and Louis Jolliet, a French trader and explorer, departed from Green Bay and traveled by canoe to the headwaters of the Fox River near present-day Portage.[5] A mile and a half portage brought the expedition to the Wisconsin River. From there they paddled downriver, eventually passing the mouth of the tributary stream we now call Lowery Creek on the south bank in the area that would later become the Town of Wyoming.

British fur trading interests gradually moved into Wisconsin during and following the French and Indian War (1754–1763) and

The Stone Wall

Good fences make good neighbors, as the famous poem "The Mending Wall" by Robert Frost contends. Here in the Driftless Area of the North American continent, there generally are not enough stones lying around for wall building. That's because there is no glacial drift. So, there are no stone walls in the Driftless Area. At least that's what I used to think. There happens to be a stone wall on what was the Thomas Stapleton farm, and now it is the Cates farm. I stumbled upon it several decades ago. I was stunned by my discovery. I thought, *This is not possible. I'm seeing things—a stone wall that climbs the steepest hill on the farm and drops down the other side!*

I investigated the matter, but no one I talked with had any idea of its origin. There is no oral history related to the wall and virtually no written record except that it shows up in an official survey record dated April 19, 1881. I enlisted veteran Iowa county surveyor John Halverson to pursue the matter.

Several decades ago, John needed to check the section corner at which the wall makes a T. In doing so, he needed to set a steel corner at the wall's zenith on top of the hill. John told me, "Whoever built that wall, those old boys were spot on." The stone wall makes its T at the exact point, within a couple of inches, of the section corner John established with modern-day satellite assistance.

It turns out that the property boundaries along which the wall was constructed led to a section corner with only three different landowners in 1881, not four as could be imagined: two Irish immigrant farmers, Andrew Sullivan to the NW and Thomas Stapleton to the SE; and a Yankee gentleman of English heritage, Goodwin Lowery, to the NE and to the SW. Mr. Lowery owned two parcels contiguous only by their corners. All of those landowners had been in place since 1863, when Goodwin Lowery was the last to purchase. And, as lore has it, they all ran sheep on the hills at that time.

Everyone likes a good mystery. Well, I do anyway. In time, I took photographs of the wall in its much disheveled, moss-covered state, measured its length, and estimated—based on the cross-section of the piles of stone from the crumbled wall—its original height and width. It was about a half mile long, three-plus feet high, and up to two feet wide. That's about 15,840 cubic yards of limestone, or at 165 pounds per cubic foot, about 1,307 tons. If an oxen-drawn wagon could haul approximately four tons per load—twice the weight of two one-ton beasts—that's 327 loads! But where did it come from, who dun it, and why?

With the assistance of a professional geologist, we determined that the stone from the wall and an abandoned quarry about two miles away across the high country were a match. It seemed an oxen or horse wagon loaded with stone across undulating terrain, but more or less on the contour, seemed doable.

So, it seems to me that this wall was built by at least two Irish families sometime between 1863 and 1881.

Though our sleuthing had led us to who built the wall and when and where the rock likely originated, the yawning question remains: Why?

With tongues planted firmly in cheek, my neighbor Joe Stapleton and I have postulated, "Well, it was a great way for all the Irish families in the neighborhood to get together and do what they all had done back home for centuries, build a good old stone wall to keep the sheep in. And in this case, an Englishman out."

I don't think we'll ever really know for sure. Good fences can make good neighbors ... but stone walls in the Driftless Area?

became dominant for the next hundred years. The influx of Europeans brought not only war but Old-World diseases. Native peoples had no previous exposure to these diseases, so they lacked (biological) immunity. Thus began the tragic decimation of a once flourishing indigenous population.[6]

The fur trade steadily declined over time, as well, reaching a low in 1850 as a result of habitat destruction and the unregulated killing of tens of millions of beavers.[7] Silk hats replaced beaver hats in fashion, and in a few years the beaver pelt trade was over.

The next major European incursion to the Driftless Area came with the lead rush of the early nineteenth century. American industrial expansion and military ventures had created a strong and ever-growing demand for lead. Lead mining became the new get-rich-quick scheme and was perceived to be much more promising to potential settlers than either the fur trade or farming. The Ho-Chunk and Meskwaki (Sac and Fox) peoples of the southern Driftless Area had been mining lead deposits at and near the land surface for thousands of years for trade, ornamentation, implement construction, and grave offerings long before the Europeans arrived.[8]

European settlement of what was quickly becoming known as the "lead region" remained slow until a series of "treaties" between 1804 and 1832 ceded all Indian lands south of the Wisconsin River to the United States.[9] The treaties use the term "cede," but the treaties actually amounted to the forcible removal of the region's First Peoples from their traditional homelands. In the case of the Ho-Chunk, the removals were repeated again and again, but some members of the tribal nation, thankfully for us today, always found their way back to their home here.

The lure of quick reward eventually brought a steady stream of settlers into what would become Iowa County (originally delineated in 1829 when it was a part of the Michigan Territory, Iowa County later became part of the Wisconsin Territory created in 1838).

Some of the first miners in the region came up the Mississippi from Missouri, where a similar lead boom had occurred a few years earlier. By the 1830s, experienced miners also began arriving from Cornwall in southwestern England and, to a lesser extent, from Ireland.[10]

According to the 1881 *History of Iowa County*, the first known miners to find their way to the hills and valleys of what became our Town of Wyoming arrived in the early 1840s. A man named Snead located lead at the headwaters of what later became his namesake, Snead (now Sneed) Creek, located just a few miles west of Lowery Creek.

Oxen and large draft horses hauled wagon loads of lead ore from the mines, passing by what later became the Stapleton and Lowery farms—now the Cates Family Farm—on their way to Daniel Whitney's shot tower on the cliff above the Wisconsin River at Old Helena. Lead was melted on-site and then dropped in the molten phase from the tower into a cooling well down below. After polishing and grading, the resultant "shot" was transported down the Wisconsin River to the Mississippi River and downriver to growing communities like St. Louis. The shot tower operated until 1861.

Lead mining in Wisconsin peaked and then declined rapidly. By the mid-1840s, miners were departing for copper and iron mines and the new logging industry to the north and west. The discovery of gold in California in 1849 led to a mass exodus of remaining miners to the West. A few stayed here mining for zinc found in deeper rock layers. There was a time in the late nineteenth century when Mineral Point, twenty miles southwest of the Cates farm, boasted the largest zinc smelting facility in the world.[11]

In 1849 the jurisdiction of our Town of Wyoming was established. Previously known as Percussion Precinct, named for the local landmark Percussion Rock, the new town took the name of the principal valley and the Wyoming Church located there.[12] The name Wyoming may have first come from an Iroquois word for a green valley in northeastern Pennsylvania, or later from an Algonquin name meaning "large prairie place."[13] The first school in our town was in place by 1845, and the first post office was established soon after that in 1848, both before folks settled on what to name their town. They had their priorities for sure.[14]

With mining diminished in importance, the stage was set for a boom in agriculture. By 1860, the former lead mining region of southwestern Wisconsin had become one of the most desirable agricultural areas in the state, and the monoculture of wheat growing became the next "taking." With railroad companies offering free or cheap land and the passage of President Lincoln's Homestead Act (1862), even the poorest immigrants gained rapidly in land ownership. Some even rose to local political leadership.

Free land on the frontier, taken from the First Peoples, created opportunity and democracy for the European born. After 1884, Native Americans were allowed to homestead, but only if they renounced their tribal affiliations. Of course, few were willing to enter this lopsided bargain.

Wheat farming had made its way to Wisconsin with the Yankee farmers as they moved west. In Wisconsin, the uprooted Yankees found fresh land that had been covered with native prairie and oak savanna for millennia. The fertility of the soils they encountered was a result of the immense, dense web of grass roots that provided organic carbon matter—nutrients and sugars for microbial life, which, in turn, feed the plants. Wisconsin's wet, dry, and mesic prairies include four to five hundred plant species. These prairies are among the most diverse polycultures on Earth. In a square meter or two, one can find twenty-five to thirty-five species in intact high-quality prairie remnants.[15]

Immigrant farmers turned this sod over with their plows and replaced the polyculture with fields of single crops, monocultures of grain, primarily corn or wheat. In the winter, the land would be left bare except for the dried grain crop residue, open for the wind and rain to erode the soil and scour gullies into the landscape.

Native prairie grasses and forbs, six or more feet high and with undisturbed root systems just as deep, were extremely challenging to turn over, or as the term became known, "to break the land." With a heavy wooden beam and long moldboard, the "breaking plow" required as many as ten oxen to pull.

Witnesses to the historic "prairie breaking" from Ohio, west across the North American plains, liken the sound of the snapping of millions of grass roots to an endless cacophony of rifle fire.

Wheat yield and resultant income declined in part because soils became depleted of nitrogen as the soil's native fertility was consumed or eroded, but also because of the emergence of the fungal leaf disease, wheat rust (*Puccinia triticina*), and insects, which always, given enough time, find the Achilles heel of any monocrop culture. In wheat's case, it was the chinch bug that decimated the crop. Chemical fertilizers to replace soil fertility were not yet available, and wheat farmers had neglected the age-old wisdom of raising sufficient farm animals for natural fertilization.[16]

In pursuit of higher yields, many Wisconsin farmers moved again, as the railroads offered "unbroken" grasslands farther west. These lands to the west provided new fertile grounds for the doomed-to-fail-again lure of wheat monoculture.

Wisconsin farmers who stayed put shifted to a different method of agriculture, one more diversified and more fitting for the land. Rather than depending on a single crop, thoughtful farmers had learned to invest in multiple opportunities for income. Other crops, including corn, rye, barley, oats, and hay, began to take the place of wheat, and livestock numbers of sheep, poultry, hogs, and cows also grew significantly. In time, it was the dairy cow that was to reign supreme.[17] By the end of the nineteenth century, Wisconsin agriculture had shifted away from wheat to a multitude of small dairy farms. Cheese-making plants spread across the rural landscape.

But in the 1930s, the Dust Bowl of the North American plains played out in Wisconsin as the "gully bowl" where torrential rains washed, or eroded, bare soil from high ground to low ground ... again.

Monoculture agriculture has always been precarious and has failed repeatedly throughout history, but farming without a commitment to, or even recognition of, the imperative of conservation fails as well. Unfortunately, plowing on the contour simply wasn't a part of the farming practice of most immigrants. They had not done this back in the Old Country. When a heavy rain landed on fields of intensively worked crop rows running straight up and down the slopes in Wisconsin's Driftless Area, the water would surge with an unstoppable force down the landscape and carry prodigious amounts of soil with it.

This Driftless landscape, often too wet or too steep to plow, was best suited for "re-grassing" or planting in grass and clover cover. In essence, it was a replacement of the native prairie and oak savanna that had been "broken" by the first immigrants.

The peoples of our earliest agricultural cultures understood regenerative methods and polyculture. These methods are far from new. They were used by the Romans and long before by the Chinese. The Roman poet Virgil offered practical guidance to farmers:[18]

"A harvest of flax exhausts the ground, oats exhaust it, and poppies exhaust it ... but by rotation, the labour prospers: don't be ashamed to saturate the arid soil with rich dung and scatter charred ashes over the weary fields."

The Romans and Chinese also interplanted fields of herbaceous crops or grazed pasture with olive groves, mulberry trees, and vineyards (practices not yet termed *agroforestry* and *silvopasture*). As noted previously, the First Peoples kept the land covered and used fire to keep the land open for grazing herds (a perennialized landscape). They employed the triad of corn, beans, and squash planted with minimum soil disturbance for a thousand years (no-till and crop diversity).

Of Coon Valley in the 1930s, a watershed in the Driftless Area, Aldo Leopold wrote that it became "one of the thousand farm communities which, through the abuse of its originally rich soil, has not only filled the national dinner pail, but has created the Mississippi flood problem, the navigation problem, the overproduction problem, and the problem of its own future continuity."[19] In a matter of a few decades, Lowery Creek, like Coon Creek, once a deep, cold-water trout stream, became a shallow, muddy water course prone to flooding.

Gullies developed where torrents made confluence. Many of the photographs of the day clearly show the resulting "canyons" that made farming nearly impossible and, at the same time, polluted some of the best trout streams in the region.

Fortunately, this tragic loss resulted in a paradigm shift for the better in some of the worst-impacted areas. Many farmers, other landowners, as well as professional conservationists began to realize that simply "adjusting" present agricultural production practices wasn't enough to solve the devastating destruction caused by the loss of precious topsoil.

The Coon Creek Watershed Project, which encompassed Coon Valley, was initiated in 1933, and it became the best-known early effort to recognize and reverse the ravages of soil erosion in the

Coon Valley area in the Driftless Area of Wisconsin, mid 1930s. Photo by USDA Soil Conservation Service.

Driftless Area. It was the first collaborative conservation effort on private farmland—working land—of its kind in the nation. Aldo Leopold was one of the principal architects and farmer-trainers on this project until his passing in 1948.

Soils & Men: Yearbook of Agriculture 1938, written by the United States Department of Agriculture, a great practical treatise, offered detailed and experimentally proven methods employed at Coon Valley for restoring improperly farmed soil: crop rotation, plowing across hillside slopes, and manure application to recycle fertility.[20] In essence, many of these practices are a nod to imitating—biomimicking—the polyculture of the native prairie, which thrives as a result of plant diversity and nutrient recycling, processes that built the fertile soil. Farmers and society could see the benefits of these wise practices, and many of the original farm families and their heirs have continued with these conservation practices to this day.

The first soil map of Wisconsin was published in 1882. Soil survey work began in earnest in the early 1900s. From the 1960s to the 1980s, county soil mapping was updated and mostly completed. On May 16, 2006, Wisconsin became the tenth state in the U.S. to have soil survey information for the entire state on the Web Soil Survey. From this historical work, we know that many acres of agricultural lands have lost a significant fraction of topsoil and some, all their topsoil.[21] In some locations in the Driftless Area, more than six feet of soil has been lost.[22]

The families who made up the European diaspora to farm in our ridge and valley landscape in the mid-nineteenth century are the folks who came after the First Peoples were pushed off the land. These Europeans had nothing where they came from, and they arrived here to build families, communities, and lives from their own labor—an elemental calling.

As the immigrants came, they brought with them a different way of seeing the world. Many of them were just trying to make ends meet, to tend plants and animals for sufficient food and barter to raise a family. Some of them were greedy opportunists. Some of them did the right thing by the land, but many beyond Jones Valley did not.

People came with the wind and blew away with the wind. Fur traders, miners, loggers in the north, and then the wheat farmers, many with the same mentality. In the history of this place, this land had never been asked to "make money." It had, for time immemorial, been asked to grow and provide food for its nonhuman and human inhabitants. The relationships that endured were, by necessity, reciprocal. The rights and opportunities to live on the land were in balance with the responsibility of care for the land. This was the First Peoples' wisdom, and it is nature's wisdom. But, from the time the first immigrants arrived, the land had been asked to do something new under the sun: provide an income in cash. Species were lost. Soil was lost. Water was polluted.

This routine abuse of the land and failure of stewardship did not extend to the Stapleton family, however. I note, with reverence, that the Stapleton family valued keeping that soil in place. They

Margaret Ellen (Peg) (1919–1997) and Michael Edward (Ned) (1921–2005) Stapleton—Farming Here in the Early Twentieth Century

I recorded this conversation with them in 1989

Peg: Mom was a Carmody [Mary C.] from the farm up the hill next door. She was thirty-three when she got married, but Dad [Thomas H.] was forty-five. He was an old man when we were born. And he was only two years old when his dad [Thomas] died. His mother [Mary] was a very domineering woman. She came from Ireland. She didn't let Dad get married for a long time. He had to grow up.

Grandpa and Grandma died in this home ... fifty-five years apart! Dad and his five siblings were all born in this house, and Dad died here. Mom passed in 1979 after a number of years in an elder care facility. I was born here as well as my six siblings. There weren't any hospitals around then. Each town had a doctor, but that was about it.

Ned: My best fields were where I could haul the manure in the spring. In the winter, I tied the beef cows up in the barn. We didn't leave them loose in the barn. I used to have to clean the barn out about every other day. That was all hand work.

We always had sheep, hogs, and chickens in addition to the beef cows. We milked for about fifteen years in the '30s and '40s, but no one milked in the winter. My dad used to have over one hundred sheep on this farm at one time, but the wolves got so bad he had to sell the sheep.

We plowed only about twenty-five acres out of almost 290 acres on the farm, some oats and corn grain for the hogs and beef cows. The balance was woods and grass-clover pasture or hay. We never did grow wheat. Wheat wore out the soil.

But you see, the thing of it is, now there's no-till planting. That's a pretty good thing. I've seen a lot of good corn that comes up with no tillage. You just direct plant and spray it, and that's it.

We had two big grass pastures, the front and the back part of the farm. You have the better idea. Just move them around all the time. That way you got pastures three to four weeks old sometimes. I never thought of doing that. No one did.

When the cattle weren't on the grass pastures, they'd go in the woods all the time. The neighbors all pastured. Everybody pastured, but that all kind of went out of the picture after the war [WWII]. Everyone else went to stored feed [feeding livestock in a confined area]. Not on this farm, however.

My dad used to have over one hundred sheep on this farm at one time, but the wolves got so bad he had to sell the sheep.

We hauled our water from the pasture; there's a spring in the low spot there. It used to drain out into the creek. It was all dug out, and it'd put out a good stream of water.

Peg: And the bottom is quicksand. Anytime one of us was missing, Mom would run to the spring.

cultivated a limited acreage of corn and oats in rotation with clover and alfalfa for their small sheep and cattle herds but did so only on the flat bottom or ridge-top fields. Primarily, they operated a pastured "grass" farm for cattle and sheep for 112 years. They never cultivated wheat for sale off the farm, a practice that for so many early farmers resulted in exporting their soil nutrients to the marketplace, or worse, down Lowery Creek. Joseph Patrick Stapleton told me his uncle Michael Edward (Ned), who farmed here his whole life, taught him to understand that "wheat wears out the soil." This wisdom had been passed down for four generations of Stapletons on their farm. (See Sidebar: Margaret Ellen (Peg) and Michael Edward (Ned) Stapleton—Farming Here in the Early Twentieth Century)

What did they know or feel that others didn't? Why did they keep this farm mostly in grass, the crop it had produced for thousands of years? The Potato Famine, which overtook their homeland and the lives of many loved ones, must certainly have played a significant part. We don't know. We do know that we have been the beneficiaries of their wise choices. For this, the Cates family owes the Stapletons a deep debt of gratitude.

In 1967 my family was fortunate to become the next caretakers of this farm along the mid-section of Lowery Creek. The Stapleton family retained enough land for Joe and Theresa, the next generation of Stapletons who wanted to farm. They are our friends and contiguous neighbors.

The truth is the Stapleton and Cates families have, in fact, been the beneficiaries of topsoil that originated from farms in the farther upper reaches of the watershed.

The soils on most of the pastured area of our home farm along Lowery Creek were (of the Soil Taxonomy order) Mollisols, that is, soils originally formed beneath oak savanna. They were classic grassland soils—biologically active, naturally fertile, rich in organic (carbon) matter, and therefore dark colored. These soils developed in the deep glacial loess that blew into the Driftless Area during times of glacial retreat throughout the Pleistocene epoch, and most significantly during the early Holocene as the Wisconsin glacier began its final retreat fourteen thousand years ago and continued until all of the ice was gone several thousand years later.

In the area of the valley where flooding happened too frequently, the soils were and still are, as a result, less developed. They are of the order Entisol, but they had the stamp of the classic dark surface soil of a Mollisol.[23]

In the photos of the soil profile along Lowery Creek as it flows through our farm grassland, the original soil surface, pre-European settlement, is clearly visible as the upper edge of the darkest layer at about twenty-four inches deep.

There it is, in black and tan, the story of the history of the first European immigrants' relationship with this land. They came and plowed up and down the hills, year in and year out, turning the grass wrong side up. Free to roam and now lighter in color due to loss (oxidation) of the once rich organic carbon, the soils just settled in here, carried with the rain and creek water from higher ground. Most of it was likely from fields of farmers in pursuit of the ephemeral returns of "king wheat" in the hopes of a cash prize, as promised, in exchange for the basis of life—good grassland soil washed away.

The pre-European settlement oak savanna soil surface—dark in color from higher organic carbon levels—is visible at about 24 inches. Above this level is soil—lighter color, less organic carbon—that eroded here from higher ground, a result of past poor farming practices.[24] Photo at left by Eric Cates.

I am sometimes embarrassed, always humbled, whenever I think again about how the Stapleton and Cates families have, for so long, been the custodians of someone else's loss. But there it is, in black and tan.

"We are eroding our soils across Midwestern America 10 to 1,000 times the rate they are forming," as the new research cited in my Preface to this book indicates.

The Food Security Act of 1985 established conservation programs such as the Conservation and Wetland Reserve Programs that set highly erodible soils and wetlands aside from planting. Conservation compliance was another feature of the bill. A farmer was not eligible for commodity programs unless they had an approved conservation plan in place. The legislation also introduced programs that limited the plowing of grasslands or wetlands. Together, these programs had a dramatic, immediate impact on reducing soil erosion and loss of nutrients (of primary concern are nitrogen and phosphorus which in concentration are pollutants) from farms in Wisconsin and across America.

Sadly, the progress made then has now largely been reversed. Many thousands of acres of livestock forage crops, land set aside for conservation (USDA Conservation Reserve Program and others), and native prairie and oak savanna—all perennial cover on the landscape—have been replaced with row cropping of annual grains, principally corn and soybeans.[25] When and where conservation practices, such as minimum (mulch or strip) or no-tillage at planting and seeding of cover crops at grain harvest, are employed, they should be lauded. However, most of these acres are plowed some years or left unseeded following autumn harvests.[26]

Climate change has also increased the frequency and intensity of extreme weather events in our region. Beginning in 1990, the upper Midwest, including the Driftless Area, experienced an unusually high occurrence of extreme rainfalls and floods.[27] Where land conservation practices have been put in place, extreme weather events are sometimes enough to overwhelm their efficacy, particularly when and where improvements have been incremental.[28]

However, there is another path, but it took me some time to find it.

In the fall of 1967, Thomas H. and Mary C. Stapleton's daughter, Joe's aunt Peg, informed Richard Lyman Sr. and Margaret Cates that her home farm might be coming up for sale, and it did.

We now turn our story to learn the journey of my family and our pursuit of an enduring farm livelihood, a land ethic, gratitude, and joy.

Aerial from the 1930s. The Stapleton and Carmody farms occupy much of the eastern half of the photo. Forested areas are much more dominant in the 2020s, a result of nearly a century more of fire suppression. However, prescribed fire, commonly practiced by First Peoples here, is now experiencing a revitalization. Photo publicly available.

PART II

Our Journey—Making a Life on the Grasslands Along Lowery Creek

The Cates family (1971) "making hay." From left to right: Father Richard (Dick) Sr., dog Dutchess, mother Margaret (Marnie), brothers John (with puppy, Racoon MacDoodle MaGoo), David, Bob, Dick (the author), and sister Christine riding Lass. Photo courtesy of the Cates family.

Dick discing a corn field early 1970s on an International Harvester Farmall 400. Photo courtesy of the Cates family.

My Family's Arrival—Making Hay

"Farming, you can work for yourself, determine your own destiny. The highest office in a free country is a free human being ... Aldo Leopold writes about farming that makes sense not only from the human side but from the environmental side. We've got a hell of a lot of land to protect, and we need the farm families to take care of it."

—Richard L. Cates Sr.

One spring day our sentinel oak observed a light blue Rambler station wagon pull up to the Stapleton home. Likely before the car had come to a complete stop, out jumped five towheads—four apparent brothers and their lone sister—followed by their hesitant mother and exuberant father. Our sentinel likely mused, "Well, this is going to be an adventure."

My family with a farming history were Yankees before coming to Wisconsin. My father's family, Anglo-Saxon Cate (later Cates) arrived at the area known as Down East in Maine a few years after sailing from England and landing in Virginia in 1663. This old Yankee line was primarily made up of farmers, fishers, and lumbermen.[1]

It was primarily because of my father that I became motivated, some might say obsessed, to follow the path of farming. So I will describe some of his background and how it led to the Cates Family Farm.

Richard Lyman Cates Sr. was born in New York City in the Bronx in 1925. During the Great Depression his parents became unable to support themselves, as well as their only young child, so they placed Dad in an orphanage there that sheltered and fed other children of similar circumstances. From ages six to ten, he lived in the orphanage. His mother would visit him religiously once a month, his father not as often. While living at the orphanage, he attended Public School 73.

Sports were his means of developing a sense of self-worth, particularly stickball, a crude form of baseball, played on the streets of the Bronx by "street urchins" as Dad would recall later in life. In time, he became an outstanding young baseball player, and through this talent he earned a scholarship to attend high school at New Hampton, a private boarding school in New Hampton, New Hampshire. Now old enough, he chose to spend those summers doing the hard physical work on the family farm, then owned by one of his uncles, near Dixmont, Maine, on the south end of Penobscot County.

After America entered World War II, my father enlisted in the Marine Corps as soon as he was able, prior to the requisite eighteen years of age (he misrepresented his age by several months). Following basic training he was selected for two years of officer training conducted at the University of Rochester, Rochester, New York.

By the summer of 1945, Dad was a Marine platoon leader heading to Camp Pendleton, California, where he was to ship out to Japan for combat duty. However, the war ended abruptly that August with the dropping of the devastating atomic bombs, and our father remained stateside and eventually received an honorable discharge.

After the war ended, Dad returned to college and finished his undergraduate degree at Dartmouth College in 1947. During this period he returned, seasonally, to the farm in Maine. It was through those farm experiences as a boy and later as a mature young man, that he developed a love of farming and promised himself he would make working the land a part of his future family life.

Dad's experience as a marine had a profound impact on him. He had been asked to give his life for something bigger than himself. During training at the Marine Corps Base Quantico, he was impacted in a way that would shape his life by an older marine, a captain, recently returned from savage combat overseas where he'd lost most of his company. The man told Dad, "This war is worth dying in. Our nation believes in freedom and dignity for individuals. The enemies we have been fighting care nothing for human beings." Those words had a profound impact on my father, and in his own words, he was "branded for life" to pursue, unwaveringly, a commitment to the ideals of freedom and dignity for all. He came to embrace the notion that in a free and democratic republic it was the rule of law—where the laws and procedures apply equally to all citizens—that was the "vehicle to man's freedom."

The rule of law thoughtfully and reasonably applied, he maintained, was the only peaceable means to protect and safeguard the inalienable rights of individuals. Continuous vigilance against the great forces of wealth and power—forces that could crush the individual—was essential. He believed in his bones that "freedom isn't free," and he committed his life to this notion.

Following graduation, he applied to several well-known law schools on the East Coast, and to the University of Wisconsin–Madison. He was accepted at all of them but decided to make his life in the Midwest and chose to enroll at Wisconsin.

Another keystone belief our father held dear was the ideal of an agrarian democracy, where individual farmers made "the most valuable citizens" with the truest commitment to civic duty.

Liberty and the inalienable rights of the individual are central values, and the sovereignty of the people is held as the source of all authority in law.

Dad had seen pictures of farmland in Wisconsin and the many small productive farms. To him the farms seemed light years ahead of those he grew up around in Maine. He thought of Wisconsin as the land of milk and honey—rich fertile farmland and a society where folks, with hard work, could follow their dreams and become who they wanted to be in life. He arrived in Wisconsin early in the summer of 1948, many months before the start of law school, and needed work and a place to live, so he went down to what was called the "unemployment" office in those days.

A Norwegian immigrant farmer named Hans Breiby, whose home and farm were just outside of Madison, arrived at the office shortly after Dad did, looking for a farmhand. On the spot, Dad took the job. The terms: room and board, no pay. So by the next day he was milking cows, pitching hay, and cleaning barns in Wisconsin ... and in heaven.

Mother and father through the years. Photos courtesy of the Cates family.

He ate like a king, and he told us that Hans and Mrs. Breiby, long after they'd finished their meals, would sit and watch him eat, spellbound. As the weeks wore on, Hans would shake his head and say, "Cates, I should have hired you for wages. It would have been a lot cheaper!" Dad continued working for the Breibys, milking cows before classes every day until winter set in, and the roads became so unreliable he had to move to town.

My mother and father met each other in the summer of 1950. Dad was waiting tables at my mother's sorority house on campus to help pay his way through law school, and Mom was enrolled in summer school to further her education having just graduated from the University of Pennsylvania. Mom's mother had attended the University of Wisconsin for her undergraduate studies, and I believe she wanted to explore the campus her mother spoke so highly of. In February 1951 they married. Dad finished law school in June, and the newlyweds packed and moved to Camp Lejeune, North Carolina, a Marine Corps Base. Dad had been called to serve for one year during the Korean War. I was born during this tour of duty on February 18, 1952, in Wilmington, North Carolina, the nearest town to the base.

That spring of 1952 our small family returned to Madison, where Dad soon established a law practice. In 1958 he and labor attorney John Lawton founded Lawton and Cates S.C. They remained partners for thirty-two years until John's passing in 1990. Dad served a term in the Wisconsin State Assembly in 1959 and 1960, but he really just wanted to be a litigation attorney trying cases, something he did almost until his passing in 2011.

My parents had five children, of which I am the oldest. I came of age in a time of much civil unrest in America, and especially in Madison, with frequent anti-war protests, and a burgeoning counterculture. Both my parents were vehemently opposed to the Vietnam War on ethical and fiscal grounds and supported the protesters across America. At the same time, they also witnessed a growing youth culture they felt was somewhat devoid of purpose and lacking in meaningful work. Dad especially felt this way and often stated he didn't want his kids "growing up lazy in town." But if the honest truth were to be known, Dad had been dreaming, ever since he left his uncle's farm in Maine and the Breiby family here, of getting back to the farm—any farm.

Every business day he took his mid-day meal at the lunch counter at Rennebohm Drug Store on the Capitol Square. There he got to know Peg Stapleton, who worked the counter. One day she told him her family was selling a farm in northern Iowa County near Spring Green. It was a hill-and-valley farm where the Stapleton family had raised beef cows, sheep, hogs, and chickens, and occasionally milked cows since 1855. Dad took Mom out to see the land in the fall of 1967, the first time she had ever set foot on a farm. Mom, who professed to hate anything that had to do with "country," said she would go along with the purchase, as it was "a pretty farm." Dad likely used his best courtroom-honed powers of persuasion to make the case for buying the farm.

So, just a few months later a ten-year land contract with 20 percent down and the balance at 6 percent interest was drawn up between the two eldest surviving Stapleton siblings, Edward (Ned) and Margaret (Peg) Stapleton, and my parents, Richard (Dick) and Margaret (Marnie)

Cates. The price was $50,200 for the 287.44 acres with a modest farmhouse, barn, and several small outbuildings, amounting to (including these buildings) $174.65 per acre.

Most of the acreage was hills covered with oak forest. The balance of the land was pasture at the foot of the hills or in the valley bottom, some of it wetland, with a few small cropped fields, but all traversed by Lowery Creek and one of its two main tributaries. Almost all the land was too steep or too wet to plow. There was also a modest-sized ridge field three-quarters of a mile from the farmstead up a rough narrow-track ridge road.

Later I learned that agricultural land is categorized according to its agronomic "capability," its sufficiency for growing crops. Capability Class 1 is the kind of land every farmer wants. On our farm there were a few acres of Capability 2 land, while the balance was steep and/or wet Capability 3 and 4, and steep and stoney Capability 6 and 7. The capability system only goes "down" to Class 8.[2] It seemed the only landforms the farm didn't have were actual mountains, or sand dunes (as I was to verify not much later in life).

Little did I understand at the time, precisely because most of the open land had never been plowed and couldn't be plowed. It had remained as oak savanna and grassland with interspersed trees. The deep soil underneath much of this grass pasture was rich, black, and alive, having been originally deposited as wind-blown loess with the retreat of the Pleistocene glacier just twenty miles to the east, supplemented since European farming began by topsoil on the move from higher in the watershed carried in with rain wash and flood waters. It was a literal carbon vein of biological, ecological wealth. Over time, I came to understand, and be thankful, that this farmland had the potential to grow lots more grass.

At the time of our arrival, most of the farms in that valley were being sold to non-farmers, as the farms were too small, too steep, or too wet to be productive units for the kind of modern thirty- to fifty-cow dairy operation that was the success model of the day. In fact, at the time, a person with 20-20 vision for the future—and enough cash—could have purchased much of the land in the Jones Valley all at once.

I'll never forget working alongside my dad that first spring when John Kraemer, the owner of the farm contiguous to the north, walked the quarter mile across the field separating us, up and over the small knoll in the middle—right past the great sentinel bur oak—to pay us a visit. He addressed my father and asked if he would purchase his farm of 104 acres at a similar per-acre price. The Kraemer farm was mostly good valley soil, so this would have been quite a bargain, but Dad declined. Mr. Kraemer ended up selling his family's farm soon thereafter.

It wasn't until 2016, forty-eight years and three owners later, that Kim and I and our children, Shannon and Dan Bloom, were finally able to purchase the Kraemer farm. This was the sixth opportunity to purchase this land since 1968 and, of course, the price of land *always* goes up. A want-to-be-clever friend of mine inquired at the time of our purchase, "What's wrong, Dick? Wasn't the land expensive enough the first five times?" (See Sidebar: The Old Lowery Farm Soon Became the Kraemer Farm, John Kraemer—Reminiscence of the Good Old Days)

When I was three years old, Dad strapped some tiny skis on my feet and let me slide down the little hill on the golf course near our home in Madison. Once we reached the bottom, he simply tossed me over his shoulder and carried me back up. Three decades and thousands of downhill runs later, I was doing the same for my three kids. So skiing was the first love I learned from my father, and it has remained a life-long passion for my family and me.

I tell you this because by the time I was a teenager, skiing meant long, long snowy trips in the car, first with all of the family, and then mostly just Dad and me. It was on those odysseys that our life-long conversation about farming began to take root. But through those years, and well into my early twenties, my primary passion was as an alpine (downhill) skiing athlete. I was determined to take that dream as far as I was physically and mentally able. I loved the challenge, and to me, it was the marrow of living.

Dad rode his three-speed bicycle to work from the Madison suburbs to the downtown Capitol Square for over a quarter century, a bit over six miles to and from work every day. His usual route took him through the University of Wisconsin Arboretum of which Aldo Leopold was the principal motivator and architect.[3] During all these bicycle commutes, he had time to think about what it was he wanted out of life to share with his children.

Christmas 1971, my father introduced me to Aldo Leopold and his thinking. I was nineteen years old, and he gave me a paperback copy of Leopold's 1949 book *A Sand County Almanac* as a present. He told me how significant he felt Leopold's writing was in defining man's relationship with land, and he suggested that

The Old Lowery Farm Soon Became the Kraemer farm, John Kraemer (1932–2022)—Reminiscence of the Good Old Days

I recorded this conversation with John, autumn 2016

NOTE: John and his family sold this farm in 1968–69. After that, there were three sequential owners prior to the Cates family purchasing this 104-acre farm in 2016.

My family purchased this farm in 1911 from James Van Blaricom. Van Blaricom bought it from Goodwin Lowery [after whom the creek through our valley got its name]. Our barn was built in 1921 and 1922 by my dad's brother, Edward Kraemer, from Plain. That's how Ed got started building barns and houses. Then he went into the road and bridge business. [Now, Kraemer North America does major bridge, rail, and marine projects across the continent.]

Years ago there were lots of different ways to make a living. My wife took care of the garden, cooked, and took care of the kids. Every farm had some sheep and hogs and chickens. In the fall of the year, people would sell their lambs, and in the spring they'd shear sheep and sell the wool. Mother gathered and sold eggs, and this would bring in cash to buy the groceries. The milk cows and hogs took care of the payments and other expenses. I mean they always had some money coming in.

We grew corn, oats, hay, and alfalfa. We tried wheat once in a while, but it would only get this tall [stunted on the wetter bottomland that characterizes this farm]. My dad put in drain tile so our bottomlands could drain. Our whole farm used to be in tile, and it used to grow real good crops. Then the next landowners busted them out to make wetlands, and what do you do with it then?

I used to love to work that field of Frank Lloyd Wright's. Well heck, that's the nicest piece of land there is. We used to take a [International Harvester] Farmall M and a three-bottom plow, and come in behind with a disc pulled by a Farmall H. Then with a little Ford tractor pulling a two-row corn planter, we'd plant corn and (soy) beans. We never worked that ground until about after the fifteenth of May. We had an old-fashioned Allis Chalmers combine, and it would lose about as many beans as it would save, but the field would yield forty-five to fifty bushels an acre. They don't get any better than that now with their expensive seed and all that spray.

And the woods, years ago in the middle of April, they'd all be on fire, set on fire by the farmers. That'd clean out all the dead wood. The bugs would be burned up, and the fire would kill the waste trees that would come up. The woods had sheep or cattle in them in the summer, and they were like parks to go hunting. Didn't hurt the oaks because it wasn't a big fire; it went real quick. We didn't have any mosquitoes either.

When we were growing up, we helped each other with everything. We had more than fifty kids about my age out here. There were four Irish immigrant families in a row: Ryan, Stapleton, Sullivan, and Carmody. We were German, Richardsons were Norwegian, and the Davidsons were Swedes. It didn't make any difference. We all worked together. Religion was never brought up. We said the Pledge of Allegiance to the flag. But that was as far as religion went. Yeah, we all played together, and we all respected each other whatever they believed.

I used to love to work that field of Frank Lloyd Wright's. Well heck, that's the nicest piece of land there is. We used to take a [International Harvester] Farmall M and a three-bottom plow, and come in behind with a disc pulled by a Farmall H.

I take a look. Well, I had a few weeks before my college sophomore classes resumed for winter semester, and I read the entire book, not comprehending much, or any, of it.

However, I did understand that the ideas expressed in Leopold's book were important to my dad. In retrospect, I now know this gift launched a life-long conversation between my father and me focused on the farmer's responsibility as steward of his or her land, and all that entails. The gift of a book, and those conversations, changed my life and set me on a course from which I have never looked back.

Everything I feel about the land, land conservation and stewardship, was because of those conversations I had with my father about land, farms, and farming. Those conversations also inspired Kim and I and led us to the farming practices we experimented with and eventually put in place. With good fortune, years later, I also got to teach and pass what I had gleaned from Dad to the next generations as an instructor at the College of Agricultural and Life Sciences at the University of Wisconsin–Madison.

I don't honestly recall what my impression was when my father took me to visit the land for the first time. I do recall that within the first couple of visits I realized that this place, as far as my dad was concerned, was a place of WORK! I didn't know the plan, nor did I have the slightest idea what constituted productive work, but it didn't take me or any of my four siblings, or my mother, very long to realize that it was mostly all hard work that made the muscles sore first and then strong. We also quickly learned that it was easiest just to "do what Dad said to do." He also "lent" our labor to a local dairy farmer. It was a good deal for the dairy farmer as long as he told us what to do. We could work hard. We just didn't know anything.

Dad bought an old-fashioned cattle truck, the kind with a box-like enclosed cattle structure behind the cab. During the early years, we rode to the farm from our home in Madison, about an hour's drive, in the cattle enclosure, sitting on tires along with all the tools and supplies needed for the day. We all worked on the farm together, and we loved it—the sweat and the camaraderie—as we tackled the tasks at hand. We loved the freedom of farm work. We were our own bosses, at least when Dad wasn't around.

Most significantly, the farm presented an opportunity for the five siblings to get to know each other as true friends. We came to depend on each other through every difficult task the farm tossed our way. Everyone pitched in even though there was often no clear goal. Each one of my brothers and sister wanted to do their part and to be with and learn from each other. Working together we built a respect for each other that has lasted a lifetime, a priceless gift. (See Sidebar: My Siblings and I Learned to Work Together and Care for Each Other)

It was much later that I realized what a saint my mom was. Although the farm was not her dream, she thrived seeing how much it allowed her family to bond in a real and meaningful way. She learned to drive the tractor and hay baler when she was in her forties! She was good at it too, never in a hurry, and I don't remember her ever wearing out a clutch or tipping over a load of hay bales. She also saw to it that hay bales placed on the conveyor to the mow were properly positioned so they'd make it all the way to the top. Her other big job, and she was in charge of this one, was raising calves who lost their mother, something she did in the basement of our suburban home.

I think I have always loved farming. I don't recall at what point I was actually able to verbalize this, but something about being on the land for me is as essential and intimate as breathing. I always enjoyed the work no matter how hard it might be. Like the ongoing training to become a proficient skiing athlete, I loved setting goals that could be measured and accomplished. On the farm they became the numbers of hay bales mowed, fence posts driven, healthy cattle raised to market, and more.

We loved the physical and mental challenge of hard work. Sweltering hot summer days in the hay fields were a form of torture to endure, and we took pride in being able to thrive no matter what was thrown our way. All of us five siblings liked or loved farming. I'm the one who stuck with it. I know now that I had farming in my heart, the heart of a farmer. It was not really a choice, but more a fact that took time to bubble to the surface and come to life.

That being said, I came to dislike *this* farm in the worst way. Building a fence in the woods on the side of a Driftless Area mountainside, I thought of it as so "#$%@&* hilly!" (These days there's an annual bicycle tour named "The Horrible Hilly" that goes right by our farm.)

Then there was that darned creek that went right down the middle of the pastureland. The cows always seemed to be on the wrong side of the creek whenever Dad told us to gather them for vet work or weaning. It seemed like they knew precisely where to be in order not to be

My Siblings and I Learned to Work Together and Care for Each Other

John: Dad loved farm work—he had since he was a boy, but he started farming here, in part because he wanted his kids to learn how to be together. This was a gift he gave to us, to have the opportunities to spend time together, learn to work hard, learn to improvise, learn to care about each other.

Chris: Mom and Dad liked the way that I took care of the horses. They gave me that privilege. None of us at those early ages knew what we were doing, but I was given that opportunity. I was really in my element with those horses. I loved them.

Dave: Yeah, it's like a friend of mine's story. He also came from a family of five kids and with cousins nearby. The backyard was always a mess. They had a donkey back there and all sorts of other pets, a menagerie. And the neighbors in that suburban neighborhood complained and essentially said to his dad, "It's a mess back there. Your yard is full of crap! What the hell are you doing?"

To which my friend's dad replied, "I'm not growin' a lawn; I'm growin' children." So in the same way, really, our dad wasn't growing a farm; he was growing children into young adults.

Bob: My friends at college would ask, "How are you so close to your family?" My answer was always because we worked together on the farm, and we learned so much about each other. That was the right answer. You know, we just had these incredible relationships with one another because we had these opportunities to work together.

Chris: We did everything together. We took vacations together. We sat around the dinner table, not for ten minutes, but two hours sometimes. That's what our family is used to, and that's what Mom and Dad instilled. "You're going to sit here—Bob, you can be underneath the table if you want to—and all your friends can come and join, but we are all going to sit here." That's what our family did. And we traveled together, skied together. It seems we did everything together. Do other families do this?

John: I've never felt self-conscious in my house. I never felt like somebody was judging me. I never felt like one of my brothers thought I was weird. I mean, it's just so meaningful.

How does that not happen? And I look at my kids now, and I look at their cousins—my brothers' and sister's kids—and I'm just in awe. I am in awe of how they all really care about each other. They all promote one another. And it's such a beautiful thing. My kids have had a tribe to watch.

You know they're not just getting signals from me. They're getting signals from all of my brothers and sister about life. And it's a lot easier to raise kids in a tribe. Dad and Mom get the credit.

Dave: Well, I think the farm distinguished us from other suburban families. It really made us different. And we all thought of ourselves as different. The farm stamped us. It made us feel the way I felt when I drove into the Memorial High School parking lot in the farm truck when I was seventeen years old. I felt different. I felt like I knew something about the world that my peers didn't have the experience to know.

Chris: And I remember how many friends wanted to join in and be a part of that, all our friends that pitched in to work on the farm voluntarily.

Bob: In a most significant way, this time together shaped who I became for the rest of my life. I am thankful.

John is the second sibling. He is much taller than I am, standing at six feet four inches. He earned his J.D. degree and worked as a trial lawyer. He lives in Madison and is married with five children, eight grandchildren and counting.

Dave is the third sibling. He is more than six feet four inches tall. He earned an MFA and is a novelist and poet and humanitarian working for weeks each year in Honduras. He lives in Missoula, Montana, and is married with three children, three grandchildren and counting.

Christine (Chris) is the fourth sibling. She was a saint to put up with all that four brothers could dish out. She has worked in the service industry throughout her life. She lives in Louisville, Kentucky, and is married with four children, ten grandchildren (and counting?).

Robert (Bob) is the fifth sibling. He grew the largest and stands about six feet six inches tall. We claim he grew the largest as he got to hoard all of the food once we had flown the coop. Bob earned his MD and is a family physician. He lives in Monroe, Wisconsin, and is married with three children, five grandchildren and counting.

From left to right: Marnie, John, Dick Sr., Chris, Dick, Bob, David, Dutchess. Photo courtesy of the Cates family.

where we needed or wanted them. (There were no improved rock-bottomed stream crossings in place on this farm until I made the first one in the late 1980s.) The cows did not act as if they had any recollection of how to get back across the creek. One thing they always remembered though was how best to avoid us. Over the years, if we didn't see the cows on a dewy morning in early autumn, we knew darn well they had found the neighbor's cornfield over the hill. The only two questions were, over which hill and to which neighbor?

I just wanted a nice flat, black piece of farm ground. I wanted something on the level, something I could turn over, and it would be pretty and black and go on forever. I dreamed of land like I had seen out in Iowa and central Illinois. Those boys, I imagined, had their cake and could eat it too. Not so on the Cates farm.

We had a horribly hilly and wet farm, and cropping wasn't in the cards. We had a few beef cattle and no experience. I decided I would seek out a job on a real cattle operation. After a long letter-writing campaign, I landed a summer job between my junior and senior years of high school as a member of a hay and fencing crew on a working ranch in western Montana. I loved the hard work and the learning that accompanied working on someone else's farm or ranch, and I returned the following summer. Dad had three other sons and a daughter and only a few cows, so I had convinced myself he didn't need me.

I graduated from James Madison Memorial High School in Madison in the spring of 1970 and began college at Dartmouth College in Hanover, New Hampshire, the next fall. I had success as a downhill ski racer in high school, competing at the national level, and Dartmouth had one of the top collegiate ski teams in the nation. I skied successfully for Dartmouth, and after graduating, I spent a year competing across the U.S. I had hopes of landing a spot on the national team and a berth on the U.S. Olympic team to compete in the Winter Games in Innsbruck, Austria, in 1976. It was a dream I feel fortunate to have had the opportunity to pursue, but like most athletes, the pinnacle of the sport eluded me.

Dartmouth didn't offer courses in agriculture, but it did offer courses in cultural anthropology, where I could learn how cultures across the globe had taken care of their most basic needs. One of those needs, of course, was procuring an adequate food supply. From nomadic hunters to seasonal sedentary hunter-gatherers to the first farmers ten thousand years ago, I was taught how society and civilizations were structured around food and water resources. The geography department offered courses on food and the stark reality of hunger in the world. In those years we were also taught how the Green Revolution had "saved" millions of people in India and other parts of Asia and Latin America from starvation.

I continued to work on the Cates farm when home on college breaks or between ski races, and I cherished the physical challenge, which I just thought of as more dry-land training for ski racing. But as my dreams of athletic glory headed "downhill," my love of farming and ranching continued to grow. (See Sidebar: Brother Dave on Dick's Passion to Farm ... a Humorous Story of Trial by Fire)

Brother Dave on Dick's Passion to Farm ... a Humorous Story of Trial by Fire

Dick and I were working together in the fall of 1974, right after he graduated from college and I from Memorial High School. I was going to go to the University of Montana, but classes didn't start until later in September, so we stayed in the trailer on the farm together. I remember him reading Ken Kesey's book, *One Flew Over the Cuckoo's Nest*, which he loved.

One of Dick's recurrent themes I discovered in those few weeks when we were working together was how little he thought he knew about anything. He had graduated from college and yet didn't feel he knew anything very well and was really irritated by this. So, for example, together we started learning the names of all the species of trees on the farm.

And I know a lot of trees because of what we did together then. But besides learning things like the kinds of trees, Dick wanted to learn how to do this and do that, how to fix and maintain things and build stuff. These were the kinds of things we really didn't learn from Dad, who didn't like machines and wasn't particularly handy with tools. Anyway, near the end of September, I left the farm to go back to college. Later that fall, Dick was working with Dad. Dad told me the following story:

He was in the barn working on the cattle squeeze chute, lying down on the barn floor, trying to get a bolt in place or something, and he was straining. He says while he's doing that, Dick comes in from working on the truck out in the driveway and says with some enthusiasm, "Dad, Dad, guess what I learned today!" This is something, according to Dad, that Dick had

We always used to say that if there was a simple way to get a job done on the farm, it eluded our father. One of Dad's long-time law partners, Bruce Davey, recalls the autumn he was recruited with other greenhorns from the Lawton and Cates law firm to sort cattle. Dad carefully instructed his recruits, "Our job is to sort the big ones from the little ones." The goal was to end up with only the "little ones" in the barn and then run them through the head catch, give them their shots, and castrate the males. By "big ones," Dad meant the mother cows—well over a thousand pounds each—and by "little ones," he meant the calves that were now almost a year old and many of which weighed well over five hundred pounds.

Bruce recalls that after a long hard chase around the farm to finally get most of the herd in the barn—this was a wild bunch of beef cattle that wasn't used to humans giving orders—Dad barked instructions as to the function each man was to perform and precisely where they should stand and be ready. Bruce, being one of the younger still-athletic partners, was assigned to guard the only barn exit. He recalls taking his post, standing in foot-deep cattle manure, clad in full hockey protective gear and wielding a sturdy, heavy oak gate panel. (Cattle not used to being handled would kick you as soon as they looked at you.) He was to hold the panel in front of him, blocking the barn exit when a small one approached, and move the panel aside to allow the big ones outside to freedom on the pasture.

Things got underway with Dad hollering orders. It seemed like everyone was learning their role, and the plan was working. It wasn't a well-oiled plan, but a plan nonetheless. About this time, Dad hollered once again, "Bruce, it's a little one! Bruce did as he had been doing all afternoon and hauled the heavy gate in front of himself and the barn opening. The little one hit the gate head-on at full speed, knocking Bruce over into the crap, and ran right on up over the gate panel and Bruce's front side.

As Bruce slowly recovered and pulled himself up out of the trenches, ego bruised and covered with manure head to toe, Dad looked over at him sheepishly and muttered, "Bruce, I forgot to tell you we have a blind one."

We all lamented our father's mistrust of the internal combustion engine, having been brought up farming with horses and a pitchfork. Dad bought a tractor with a front-end loader so that it would be easier to clean the barn when it was full of manure. But instead of going in and using the bucket to scoop the manure, he'd drive the tractor into the barn, drop the bucket down, turn the tractor off, and then proceed to use a hand shovel to fill the bucket. After a long stint of shoveling, and the bucket finally full, he'd start the tractor, back it out of the barn, and dump the bucketload into the manure spreader.

The only thing that made this job a little bit easier and simpler than not having a tractor with a loader bucket was not having to walk each shovel full of manure to the end of the barn or corral where the manure spreader was parked. We'd say, "Dad, this is just stupid."

He'd reply, "Well, we don't want to wreck anything."

In addition to making all the hay on our own farm every summer, one year, Dad hired us four boys out for custom hay baling. I can't imagine what he was thinking. Our hay equipment was so old and rickety that we could hardly keep it running to make the hay on our farm. But Dad was the boss. We put up about twenty

been saying every day. Like a little kid. And so Dick knew that Dad was probably getting tired of hearing it.

Anyway, Dad hears Dick say the same thing on this day, and despite lying on the barn floor and struggling with what he was struggling with, Dad says, "What did you learn today, son?" and rolls over and looks up.

Dick is standing there with his head and face completely black, dripping with what appeared to be motor oil. "I learned that when changing the oil on the truck, don't put your head under the oil pan when you pull the drain plug." Dad loved that story and told it over and over again. He loved how Dick made fun of himself ... with a smile.

Dick wanted to learn how to do this and do that, how to fix and maintain things and build stuff.

thousand small square bales, all hand-loaded and stacked. That's a lot of hay, considering our barn at home could only store about five thousand bales. As the oldest, when things broke, it was my responsibility to fix them. I hated it when our old equipment broke and had to be repaired in the broiling hot sun, all while the hay sat and rain was in the forecast. (See Sidebar: Barns)

Because of these breakdowns, we'd get behind schedule. We were hard drivers, though, and I recall we unloaded hay for one of our clients at his horse barn somewhere near midnight.

Years later, Dad was talking to a guy he met in a handball tournament at the local YMCA, and in conversation, Dad said he was in the farming business. The guy said his wife had a couple of horses and they ate a lot of hay. The guy then said, "One year, I ordered hay from some boys who showed up to unload near midnight!" Dad didn't have the heart to tell him that those were *his* boys.

From an environmental standpoint, some of our practices would have had Leopold rolling over in his grave. Our handling of manure and chemical pesticides would not have met Rachel Carson's approval either. Brother David and I, who operated the farm in our young adult years, both feel ashamed of our ignorance and carelessness at the time.

We'd spread manure heavily on the fields, all of which were at the bottom near the creek, as soon as everything started melting in the spring. Some of the manure surely ran right into the creek. Most farmers were doing this at that time (but most have since learned and changed their ways), so we didn't think much about it. An old farmer once told me, "We used to put the cattle in the creek, and that would make the fish grow big. The manure, the fertility, the food; that's what the fish would eat."

Thinking back on it, the ignorance of our actions and the consequences made us cringe.

We used creosote as a cheap wood preservative for retaining wall timbers, fence posts, and corral boards—anything and everything Dad had us build around the farm. Creosote was then suspected, and now is known, to contain carcinogens. We did all the creosote application, all the herbicide and corn rootworm insecticide handling and spraying without protective masks, wearing only shorts, no shirt or gloves. (Some farmers still used stockpiled DDT and chemically similar pesticides, including organochlorines, well into the 1970s.)

Those were the kinds of jobs we really enjoyed. We would say, "We're going to spray weeds," or "We've got to creosote all these boards." We felt we were doing something that had a start and a finish and a clear purpose. My brothers (while I was away on the ranches in Montana) put in more fence posts and nailed up more boards in those early years than they could count. Dad would say he wanted a board fence across the middle of a field, and it was as good as done.

I have a very clear and not-so-fond memory of tipping over our old, rickety herbicide sprayer on a hurried trip out to the pasture to spray thistles. I was young and trigger-happy, and I just wanted to get the darn job done. Well, I was traveling too fast and tipped over the sprayer on a bump in the pasture road, just feet away from the creek and on the pasture where the cattle were to be for another month or so.

I was angry as hell because I had to repair the old contraption. I never even considered blocking and containing the spill before it ran into the creek or even whether the cattle might lick it up and suffer somehow. At that time, we simply believed that chemicals were "good things," and that there was no downside to their use.

Our pasture grazing management was ... well, there was no grazing management. As I noted earlier, it was not a managed farm. The cattle would be in the back part of the farm for the first half of the summer and in the front part for the second half. The thistles grew taller than we stood. While there are always "new" invasive species—by this, I mean non-native plants out of place in Wisconsin—the one persistent, always dependable, obnoxious, and noxious weed is the thistle. In the Driftless Area, these are primarily the plumeless (*Carduus acanthoides*), a biennial often nicknamed Russian thistle, and the Canadian thistle (*Cirsium arvense*), a perennial.

It's not that I was born hating thistles. I'm an equal-opportunity farmer. It's just that if one grazes livestock of any kind, they need to have something to eat. Grass and clover are preferred. In an unmanaged pasture in Wisconsin, thistles eventually dominate as they grow tall quickly to dominate sunlight, sending down roots quickly to hog the water. Additionally, they grow prickles or thorns on all their leaves, so nothing wants to bite and chew them. The result is that unless otherwise controlled, both these types of thistles crowd out the short-stemmed, Kentucky bluegrass-dominated pasture (*Poa pratensis*, a shallow-rooted perennial also known as "June grass" as it stops growing when the ground dries up

Barns

Beyond nostalgia for our rural heritage, beyond the fascinating and ingenious examples of folk architecture, Wisconsin barns stand as a lasting testament to our unique struggles and triumphs as agrarians from distant lands who came together in this welcoming wilderness and made a life, a culture, and a society. Europe may have its cathedrals, but Wisconsin's story is warmly told through its glorious barns.

These structures speak volumes about a time when most of us grew our own food, were intimate with the land we lived on, and shared our days with the animals we depended on for labor, transportation, clothing, and sustenance. Each barn instructs us about self-sufficiency, inventiveness, problem-solving, thrift, integrity, and other values we hold dear.

Perhaps the most poignant fact about these edifices is that we don't build them anymore. Our lives, our technology, and our culture have moved on. And most of the magnificent barns of Wisconsin's past centuries are no longer standing. People who own an old barn know they have something special, something that won't come our way again.

The cornerstone of the old barn on the Cates Family Farm in Iowa County displays 1893 as its completion date on what was then the Thomas Stapleton farm. Its two-foot-thick foundation of native quarried sandstone and limestone is built into a hillside, a bank barn. Stapleton family lore tells us that the mason earned a dollar a day for the thirty days it took him to lay up the foundation.

Zuber Hanson, a Norwegian craftsman, and his helpers constructed the 32-by-56-foot and 40-foot-high-at-the-cupola post-and-beam, wooden-pegged frame using white pine logs that had been floated down the Wisconsin River, then milled in Spring Green at the

King Lumber Company. Timbers, boards, and labor came to $1,500. The Irish community along Lowery Creek raised this barn, and the barns of the valley, together.

Though my family continues to farm here, we have long ceased using our old barn for its original purposes. To this day, whenever I am near the barn, I have vivid images of my parents and sister packing the haymow elevator with small square bales of hay and my three brothers and I in the mow stacking thousands of bales a summer—sweat-glistened, dusty boys striving to be men.

Out of kindness, or perhaps in celebration of an exalted symbol, my family and I chose to renew our barn. Its restoration stretched over decades, rebuilding portions of the stone foundation, the mow floor, and walls. Block and tackles were fastened to trees on the hillside, and, little by little, the structure was pulled back up straight and re-braced, negating the leaning aspect from its century-long battle against the prevailing southwest wind. Three layers of shingles came off, and new shingles went on, and our barn was ready for its centennial party in 1993, with many more parties to follow.

For me, the old barns are a source of wonder and awe and are important to preserve. These barns, built by practical folks of modest means with hand tools, were not built simply to be functional. They were constructed with such care to last for generations as a testament to hope and love of place. Their builders valued commitment and community, and they shared an optimism that the fruits of the good earth, well-tended, would serve their children, and their children's children, and generations beyond. In a culture where everything else seems to change so quickly, these barns are evidence of the enduring faith of our forebears.

As I have also grown older, the barns have taken on a deeper meaning. I now see them as a symbolic tie that binds the next generations to all those who came before, tending the land and livestock.

Even in these changing times, the old barns of Wisconsin are part of our legacy. As such, they should be cherished and preserved as a constant reminder of the values of the peoples and culture that passed them to us.

Left: A barn dance in our refurbished barn, originally constructed in 1893.

in midsummer), and they win the competition for water and soil nutrients. Of course, no grass means no livestock.

What management we did apply in the early years mostly consisted of hauling out a herbicide sprayer when we weren't busy with our other assigned chores. By then, the thistles had already gone to seed, which meant the herbicide was useless anyway.

I met the love of my life, Kim Denise Johnson, in the autumn of 1974, and my life immediately began to grow richer in every way. Kim plays an essential part in the bigger story of this book, and I will bring her back later and pay homage to her wisdom. For now, she figures in a memorable thistle story.

The summer after Kim and I met, one of her sisters visited. Kim was excited to show off the land her potential husband's family owned and on which she enjoyed riding horses. She was especially fond of the spring-fed ponds on the "back" part of the farm. Originally installed by the Stapleton family in the early 1960s with USDA cost share funds, the ponds were a common conservation practice employed on farms in the Driftless Area to capture water and soil runoff from tilled fields and steep woods where livestock grazed. The larger of the two, the overflow pond, was just barely warm enough to swim in, and largemouth bass and panfish could easily be caught with a hook and worm (in a heartbeat).

The two sisters, decked in shorts, swimsuits, and tennis shoes, set off on the half-mile walk across the pasture. However, Kim had not been back to the ponds in a while, and she forgot what to expect in July. What we called the "back pasture" was closer to a tangled jungle of uncontrolled, pink-flowered thistle plants than lush grass-feeding grounds.

Kim and Kaye made it halfway back to where the two-track pasture lane petered out. After a heroic attempt to forge on with scratched forearms and legs and eventual frustration, they abandoned the quest for the pond and turned back for the comfort of the shade on the porch back home in Spring Green.

Later that day, when Kim and Kaye shared with me their misadventures in the back pasture wilderness, I vowed a lifelong battle with the thistles, one that my family and I gladly took on, and eventually prevailed (with plumeless thistle, but continue the battle with Canadian thistle ... darn).

Over time, we all began to realize that Dad really didn't want to be in charge of this family farming adventure. He just wanted to be what he called "the hunkie," the name his fellow workers called him when he worked one year as a young man shoveling pig iron in a steel mill in Sparrows Point, Maryland. He wanted to do simple, hard work with his body as a relief from his stressful life as a litigation attorney.

When Dad was in Washington, D.C., in 1974, engaged in the Watergate hearings as a General Counsel to the House Judiciary Committee, he took time off to return home to his family and his farm—to nurture his body and soul by making hay with the family.

I remember I was home from college that autumn and spending part of the day on the farm doing whatever Dad asked me to do. Two of my friends had just arrived from their homes in New England.[4] We were preparing to head west for ski training on the early snow before the winter racing season started. On this day, I was excited to tell Dad about all that we had accomplished together on the farm.

Plumeless thistles in flower (purple and white) and junk discarded on the pasture.

I went through a litany of things: how we repaired this and cleaned that up, where the cattle were and how they seemed to be faring, on and on. Eventually, I could see that Dad wasn't that interested in all of the details I was offering, so I paused. Dad looked over to me and said, "Son, I just want to know if the cattle are still the same color." My friends never let me forget that story.

All Dad really wanted was a place to work physically like a bull and, at the same time, to see that this place provided the setting for his children to learn the skills he didn't have, to learn to work together and get along in life, and to kindle a grander view of why farming and caring for land was significant work. And it turned out well for me. I had a growing passion for farming and doing so with a land ethic. I just didn't know how to get started.

In 1976 Dad purchased a chisel plow, a conservation tillage tool that doesn't turn the ground over like a conventional moldboard plow. It was the moldboard plow that allowed the European settlers to turn the prairie and oak savanna into black arable fields for row crop agriculture by severing the extensive labyrinth of living grass roots and turning the sod over. Rather than turning the sod over, the chisel plow lifts and loosens the soil and keeps the previous year's crop residue—which farmers in those days called "trash"—on the surface to help hold soil, water, and nutrients in place where the new crop can utilize them.

We were one of the first farms in the area to own and use a chisel plow. The first time I hooked the strange-looking new unit to the three-point hitch on our International Harvester Farmall 706, it was April, and the cornstalks from the previous fall's corn harvest lay thick on the soil surface. I ripped through the field at full torque. When I looked behind at the furrows, I thought to myself, *I really don't like the look of that. It just looks trashy.*

So I ended up pulling the chisel plow through again, then again, and then again crosswise to no great effect. It still looked trashy to me. Then I hooked up the disc harrow and disked and disked and disked. So much for the fuel savings that were supposed to be a bonus of reduced tillage. My neighbor, Brandoch Peters (son of famed Frank Lloyd Wright colleague, William Wes Peters, and wife, Svetlana Stalin—yes, Joseph Stalin's daughter) had been watching all of this. After Brandoch couldn't take it any longer, he stopped over. He had some sheep but wasn't so much a farmer as an artist and philosopher. Nevertheless, as I look back on it so many years ago, he was right on point. He said, "Dick, it's supposed to look like this. Just park the tractor and enjoy life."

It took me a while to get used to conservation tillage. It was the right move, away from moldboard plowing. It was the way to go at the time, but in reality, our land wasn't appropriate for tillage agriculture. Most of our land is either too steep or, in the floodplain of the creek, too wet. There's also the inconvenient truth that a creek runs right through the middle of it all.

Studying how cultures secured food and how agriculture began and armed with Leopold's notion of a land ethic—and now a conservation tillage tool—I began formulating and asking basic questions about the "whys" of agriculture. How much soil does a chisel plow save by reducing erosion? What is the difference between a good soil and a poor one, and why? How does fertilizer work? What is the difference between an annual grain and a perennial forage for holding soil in place? What is the potential of our farm in the rugged Driftless Area of Wisconsin? What is going to be my personal Green Revolution?

My curiosity about these matters was growing, and I wasn't able to immediately secure sufficient answers to satisfy it. I knew that there had to be people somewhere who had at least some of the answers, but where would I find them?

I knew the University of Wisconsin had several campuses with colleges of agriculture, as did many other land-grant universities across the nation. Still, I didn't have a clue of the size of the immense collective repository of world-class knowledge found behind thousands of

Unlike a conventional moldboard plow, a chisel plow's straight shanks (above) can pull straight through the soil without turning it over. Photo from public access publication.

laboratory doors on campuses scattered across America until I made a stop at the campus of Montana State University, Bozeman, Montana, in March 1976.

I had traveled with my parents to visit my siblings, David and Christine, who were attending college at the University of Montana in Missoula. One of my friends from Dartmouth had been attending graduate school in geology at Montana State, and I thought it would be fun to visit him. Besides, I knew the university had a top-notch ski team, and I wanted to check out the famed powder snow off the chutes at the top of their ski area, Bridger Bowl.

During my short visit, I also scheduled a couple of interviews at the College of Agriculture, and that visit changed the course of my life. I hadn't been there for an hour, visiting with down-to-earth yet vastly intelligent professors of plant and soil science, when *I knew* that this was where I belonged.

I proposed to Kim that spring, and we were married on September 4, 1976. We packed everything we owned into an old Subaru station wagon (one of the first in the U.S. we continue to claim) and headed to Montana the next week. We honeymooned in a tent in Yellowstone National Park and started our lives together in Bozeman. During our three years on campus in Bozeman, Kim was a soil science major and earned her undergraduate degree in land resources, and I completed a Master of Science degree in soil science.

We were both strongly encouraged by mentors, for whom we had a great deal of respect, to continue our academic training. I was deeply driven to understand and respect our soil resource, which, along with clean water, is the source of all life on Earth. Early in 1979, I recorded my "Reasons for Graduate Study" to submit to the University of Wisconsin–Madison College of Agricultural and Life Sciences:

> I have chosen to study at the PhD level because I see it as a means of pursuing professional, as well as personal freedom. I am referring, primarily, to the freedom of thought. This freedom is of great value to me, and to its end I will strive.
>
> I am interested in soil as an entity in and of itself, and as an essential part of the ecosystem. But most significantly I am interested in soil as a valuable yet exhaustible natural resource. To the extent that man respects soil is the extent he shall thrive.
>
> Specifically, I am interested in questions such as: What is the effect of man's various activities on soil? To what extent does, or can man make use of the soil, without using it up?

Kim and I returned to Wisconsin later that year, where both sets of parents still lived, and in early 1980, I began a PhD program, and Kim began her master's, both in the Department of Soil Science at the University of Wisconsin–Madison.

For a while, Dad had rented the farmhouse to a family who took care of daily chores as the five siblings were all away from home for their schooling or other work and only available seasonally. Mom and Dad, who couldn't and didn't want to care for the farm alone, were considering selling!

But in the spring of 1981, my brother David and his wife, Rosalie, returned after living and working in Costa Rica. David, a talented developing novelist, and Rosalie, a community organizer, also both landed work as editors at our local newspaper. Dad asked if they would come live on the farm and take care of things for him. This greatly appealed to David and Rosalie. They moved into the farmhouse and managed Dad's herd and the farm, and within a few years started their young family here. As it turned out, the commitment David and Rosalie made to the farm allowed Kim and I to come back to a farm that was still in the family.

The close proximity of the university, within an hour by car, to the farm allowed me to make frequent trips back and forth to assist David and my father. The diversion of helping on the farm from the intense demands of my doctoral research and writing work was a blessing and greatly cherished.

My research topic involved an investigation of nitrous oxide (N_2O) production, already a greenhouse gas of concern, from soils. I explored under what environmental conditions and by what biological mechanisms oxides of nitrogen are generated and released from soils. Soil, as it turns out, is the major planetary source of N_2O, a greenhouse gas approximately three hundred times more potent than CO_2. It also causes destruction of the ozone layer.

The research was conducted in the laboratory, as well as field-farm based. The field research was conducted on the Leopold family's Shack Prairie, my family's farm, and other locations. Throughout this research, I served one of the first Leopold fellowships and spent much time with Nina Leopold, Aldo's eldest daughter, and her husband, Charles Bradley. These two exceptionally brilliant, talented, and caring people became dear elder friends and mentors who, in addition to my father, shaped the beginnings of a life-long journey to discover my own land ethic.[5]

During this time home again, my love for farm life flared from a flicker to a burning flame. Although I *knew* I wanted to farm, I was clearly hoping this academic effort would provide opportunities for Kim and me sometime in our future. I didn't have to wait long.

TOYOTA

A Sojourn in the Desert—Rediscovering Our Place

"The care of the Earth is our most ancient and most worthy, and after all our most pleasing responsibility. To cherish what remains of it and to foster its renewal is our only hope."
—Wendell Berry, *The Art of the Commonplace: The Agrarian Essays*

"Farming is a high calling. You have an opportunity to be a steward of our nation's most valuable resources, our soil and water."
—Richard L. Cates Sr.

In the early spring of 1988, our sentinel bur oak again witnessed something new under the sun. The farmer was setting up cross fencing and then moving his herd of cattle from one plot of grass to another every few days. "But wait," she recalled, "this is not all new. In my youth, before the cows came to the valley, the native grazers moved across the land, and the grass grew thick and tall."

Kim and I had a strong desire to work overseas before settling down here to raise our family. We firmly believed, and still do today, that there is no more powerful and productive experience than working in a culture very different from ours. In this way, one has the opportunity to view from a different lens just what it means in the world to be an American, what is unique and of lasting value about our culture and, quite frankly, what is not.

One evening in the winter of 1982–83, when Kim was completing her master's degree and I was working to complete my dissertation, we got a call. It was a friend working in Saudi Arabia offering me a job as soon as I could get there. The Kingdom of Saudi Arabia?!

Kim and I learned from him that he had worked for several years in Libya before migrating to Saudi Arabia in 1983 to help start what was to become the world's largest dairy farm.[1] His job had been to start a crop production operation to raise the crops on irrigated sand in the central

Arabian desert to feed what was, at first, a small dairy herd. Within three years the herd had grown to six thousand milking cows, many of which came from farms in Wisconsin and were flown overseas in retrofitted C-47 cargo planes. He was calling me because he was leaving this job for private work in "The Kingdom" (of Saudi Arabia) and wanted to know if I was interested.

My research in Montana was focused on the reclamation of saline (salt in general) and sodic (salt dominated by sodium) soils. When the sand of the Arabian Desert is irrigated with ancient salty water from deep aquifers, saline and sodic "soils" are the result. So the major impediment to raising crops in the Arabian Desert was not water quantity, provided one could obtain the necessary permits from the Saud family to drill deep enough. The big problem was that the salty irrigation water could significantly reduce crop yield and even cause soil sterility, especially when huge amounts of fertilizer (also salts) were added. In our situation, we were dependent upon inert sand as the growing medium for year-round crop production.

Kim and I had one child at that time, Shannon, who was just six months old, and we were planning to expand our family over the next few years. We were both going to be finishing our graduate work by spring. We considered the offer seriously for about a week—both sets of parents told us we were crazy to consider traveling to, much less living and working in, Saudi Arabia—and then we called our friend back and said, "Yes. We'll give it a go!" Why not help build the largest dairy farm in the world in the Arabian Desert?

By April, I had completed my PhD dissertation. In May, I traveled alone to what was to become our new home, a dairy farm in the middle of the Saudi Arabian Desert, on the edge of the Rub' al-Khali, "The Empty Quarter," where temperatures soar to more than 120°F in the summer, and in some years there is no rainfall at all.

In my early morning farm rounds I would often find camels belonging to Bedouin herders. Camels were ridden or led secretly over the farm perimeter earthen berm at night to graze irrigated alfalfa in preference to sparse desert shrubs.

After a protracted five-month visa process for Kim and Shannon, which involved many tea-drinking sessions with my Saudi bosses, my two loved ones were finally able to embark on the journey to join me. I reunited with them in Madrid for a few long-awaited days so I could escort them for their first time arriving in Saudi Arabia. Our arrival to Jeddah coincided with the Muslim pilgrimage, the hajj—the annual migration of two to three million Muslims to Mecca—one of the largest human migration gatherings on Earth.[2] Jeddah was a point of arrival and departure for many of those millions. Kim and Shannon, blonde and red-headed females without head coverings, quickly drew much attention as we struggled through the airport, stepping over a multitude of pilgrims from across the Muslim world who were camped on the floors as they waited, sometimes for days, for a seat on a flight to Mecca or back home. Welcome to the Kingdom.

For the next three years, my job was to oversee growing forage crops, including alfalfa, oats, sorghum, and some corn on five thousand acres of irrigated sand under fifty center irrigation pivots. All this to feed six thousand and eventually ten thousand milk cows and a total of twenty thousand head of cattle, including heifers, calves, and bulls. This was and continues to be the largest integrated dairy farm in the world, with all livestock, milking, and milk processing facilities at one location.

An international company with a subsidiary in the U.S. originally hired me. In time, the Saud family "nationalized" the farm company and kicked the other business partners out of the country. So after a year and a half, I was employed directly by the Saudi company. (After about six months of employment, I received a stack of business cards, Arabic on one side and English on the other. I don't know what the Arabic said, officially, but I became known as Abu Shannon, father of Shannon, which was good enough for me. The English side had me as Dr. Richard *Cales*, which was also good enough for me.)

During my three years, I also built and managed our crops and soils laboratory to test and monitor soil and plant salinity and experiment with methods to mitigate this problem. I oversaw a crew of forty-five men from northern Europe, East Africa, the Middle East, and the Philippines, and I was responsible for a $4 million annual budget (more than $11 million at today's value).

At the same time, Kim, who did most of the work in the home, and I were raising a growing family. Eric, our second child, was born a U.S. citizen in an Austrian hospital in Riyadh, Saudi Arabia, in May 1982.

Kim was employed in the crops and soils laboratory for part of our first year until the Saudi management decided to enforce the rule that women couldn't work with men, and her employment ended. However, she thrived on the camaraderie of the other spouses from around the world, helped initiate an on-farm preschool for all the young children, and enjoyed visits with friends to Riyadh and neighboring farms.

My equipment inventory would have made my farmer friends back home drool with envy: We had four of the largest eight-wheel drive articulated Steiger tractors made in the world at the time, many John Deere four-wheel drive tractors, Hesston big square hay balers, hay racks towed by semi-trucks, D9 Caterpillar equivalent dozers, huge front-end loaders, land levelers, thirty-six-foot harrows, and meter-deep soil rippers to break up sand compaction. My friends may have been envious, at least until I told them I couldn't keep it all running because obtaining spare parts from overseas on a timely basis was next to impossible. If we could keep two or three of four of anything running, we celebrated. Although diesel fuel for all the field equipment was pumped from big storage tanks, gasoline to supply the five hundred farm employees' pickup trucks and personal vehicles came in truckloads of twenty-liter (approximately five gallons) plastic Jerry cans. The gas was tube siphoned, always mouth initiated, to the gas tanks because there were no gas pumps.

Water is precious, and water truly is life in the desert. In town, gasoline could be purchased at a pump for the equivalent of $0.22 per gallon, while a gallon of potable drinking water went for $2.70.

Top: Bedouin herders brought sheep in at night as well. I even got to wave at this herder. Bottom: Dick dancing with Bedouin in a desert tent home; Dick on skis on top of sand dunes preparing for a run in the Rub' a Khali, the "Empty Quarter." Bottom two photos by Kim Cates.

The growing season was 365 days a year. With LOTS of irrigation water—ten feet to meet the crop needs and another twenty-four inches to flush, or leach, the water's salinity past the plant root zone—we could harvest ten to twelve cuttings of alfalfa and ten to twelve tons of dry matter per acre. For comparison, in Wisconsin, we depend on about thirty-five inches of rain each year, get three or four cuttings per growing season, and a yield of five to six tons from a really good stand of alfalfa.

When I first arrived, irrigation water was being pumped from an aquifer about four hundred feet below the surface, but that water source was running dry. Because my job was to raise the crops to feed the cows in a desert without rain, this was a big deal. I continually tried to convince my Saudi superiors that this was a significant problem that needed attention. Finally, the well closest to the sheik's on-farm palace went dry, and the green crop turned brown. Then the center pivot, empty of water to hold it in place, blew over in a sandstorm. I was convinced these incidents would get the sheik's attention. They did, but the sheik simply began construction on a new palace on a different part of the farm.

Eventually, we began to drill wells to about two thousand feet, but that was into an aquifer barely flowing enough to grow a crop. Toward the end of my tenure, I oversaw the first wells drilled to the Minjur aquifer over five thousand feet down, a mile deep. This was artesian water under pressure, so when it was released from the aquifer, it flowed all the way to the surface. It was salty but also hot, so hot that it burned plant leaves. The water had to flow up into and down from an evaporative cooling tower to mitigate the heat. This process cooled the water but also resulted in a significant evaporative loss and consequent concentration of salts.

Often, on my first drive in and around the cropland each morning, an area about fifteen square miles, there would be Bedouin camels or sheep grazing with their herders standing nearby. They simply would walk over the sand berms that served as the farm perimeter fencing. As I have noted, it was my job to feed twenty thousand head of cattle every day, and I didn't think I could do it if my inventory was being shared with the neighbors.

I reacted as might be expected for someone with this overwhelming responsibility weighing on my shoulders: I attempted to chase the intruders away. They obliged, however, only temporarily, as they simply would return a few days later. Of course. I fumed with anger, beside myself with the insult of such theft, and I was going to get to the bottom of it and make certain that right prevailed! So I began to sit and drink tea with the Bedouin guards at the farm entrance to demand they keep the intruders out. After all, that was their job. But every morning, there were camels and sheep grazing. Slowly I came to understand that the intruders were, of course, the guards' friends, their extended family, their clan. Obviously, my approach was failing.

Eventually, I figured out how to skin the cat another way by simply adjusting my production budget. I made a rough estimate that the camels and goats might consume about 10 percent of the forage I could grow. Likely not this much, but hey, I could play this game as well. So I turned in revised production figures, and they were accepted. Any additional feed I required was to be purchased off the farm. After that, rather than fuming on my morning drives around the farm, I simply waved at the herders. Eventually, it felt as if we were old friends.

Just beyond the wooden fence wall around the prefab living structure that served as our family's home were gigantic piles of manure—precious organic matter. By gigantic, I mean the piles had the footprint of a parking lot and were up to two stories high. Every day they got larger. I soon learned all the manure was from the areas where the thousands and thousands of cows loafed. Each day, these loafing areas were scraped clean with giant Volvo front-end loaders, and the manure was hauled in trucks to the growing piles and dumped. That was it, and this is the way it had been since the farm began three years earlier.

Most days, Bedouin women, clad head to toe in black robes with only their eyes and hands visible, plucked dry chunks from the pile and tossed them down into Toyota pickup trucks while their male escorts—husbands or other family—sat in the shade, cross-legged on the sand leaning against one of the truck tires, drinking tea.

My job was to feed all those cattle that produced all that manure. I had five thousand acres of pure sand with zero organic material and no natural nutrients or water-holding capacity. As noted, this required twelve feet of irrigation water per acre per year, and nitrogen fertilizer applied at such a high rate it might be considered poisonous here. Add to those inputs the balance of other fertilizer requirements. I was responsible for the farm's entire crop and feed financial budget of millions of dollars, and it was literally costing s***loads of money to make this farm work.

I know in my gut what good soil means to a farmer because I had farmed with rich soil along Lowery Creek since my youth. I thought to myself, *That pile of manure is a gold mine in the shifting sands*. And I began to imagine how I could nudge this desert sand into living soil. So shortly into my tenure I went to my Saudi bosses, as was becoming routine, to drink tea and ask for "something" essential to keep the farm running. But this time, *inshallah*, I hoped to present the notion of applying the manure piles to the crops.

Bulldozers were used to pile three years of cattle manure that had accumulated prior to my arrival to the farm.

After discussing all extended family members' health, complaining about the Bedouin's camels that were sneaking onto the farm and grazing our alfalfa at night, and a third cup of tea, I presented my case:

> Improve the sand by adding manure. In this way we will increase soil water holding capacity, which will result in reduced irrigation equipment use and water application, thereby saving money. We will also increase soil nitrogen available for the crops and reduce or eliminate nitrogen fertilizer purchase expenses. In this way, the soil structure for crop growth will improve, and we'll get higher crop yields and save more money because we won't have to purchase as much feed.

I was told the workforce would resign if they were asked to handle manure any more than the front-end loader scoop and dump method already employed, but I fully believed other folks would value this work.

I decided I needed to conduct a simple trial to see how much difference a manure application might make on crop growth and whether the difference would be readily apparent to observers. I persuaded the Volvo loader drivers to drop and spread bucketloads of their daily haul in a few strips on a field right in front of the sheik's palace on the farm. The sheik, the farm's principal owner, didn't visit the farm often, but this was a very visible location. The field was soon to be planted to oats. I reduced the nitrogen fertilizer rate dramatically where the manure had been applied, and the rest of the field was fertilized as normal.

Fast forward a month, and the oats where manure had been worked into the sand were not only taller, but they were greener. I took a few photos and shared them with my Saudi bosses, and eventually one, then several, drove their Cadillacs out to see for themselves.

Things generally don't move very rapidly in the Kingdom, but in this case, the pendulum swung quickly. Soon I had four of the world's largest manure spreaders in my equipment inventory, and sufficient employees were hired specifically to serve as manure handlers to chip away at the humongous pile that had been growing for four years. These crews worked three shifts a day, six days a week.

Nitrogen, phosphorus, and potassium fertilizer rates (the big three) were able to be reduced immediately, and in time, as organic matter built up in the sandy soil, water holding capacity increased, and the expensive irrigation water requirement declined. Crop yields increased dramatically. Plants just grow faster and bigger in soil than they do in sterile sand.

As it turned out, this trial by fire was the first of many that were to define my life's journey of finding my way toward a farming system that worked for my family and the land.

After three years, Kim and I had the experience we hoped for living overseas in a faraway culture. I had taken on a seemingly impossible assignment, and with luck, good working relationships, and very hard work, I had been able to do the job. Both of us made life-long friends from across the globe. Our Saudi hosts—from the sheiks, merchants, and government officials to rural community residents—treated my family and me respectfully during our entire tenure. (It should be noted, however, that in those three years, I only saw the unveiled faces of three Saudi women.) We felt safe, valued, and we have never looked back.

However, there was just so much about that large Saudi farm that did not feel right. It was completely dependent on intensive inputs from around the world—from the largest farm machinery to exorbitant amounts of fertilizer—to an itinerant labor force imported from wherever it could be sourced most expediently in the developing world, and management that declared its authority, not from hard-won experience, thoughtful study, or respectful listening, but solely because they held the inherited purse strings.

The farm model—a giant industrial complex plopped out of nowhere, into nowhere—was so far out of ecological and cultural context that it often seemed like a mirage in the desert. In fact, it was the only green spot on the planet for miles in any direction. It was only crude oil, which the developed world craved like an addict, that fueled such a farm pipe dream.

For both Kim and me, it was not the professional and personal life we had ever sought or dreamed of. I knew I wanted a work life where I could be my own boss, and Kim wanted much the same. We began dreaming of our "horrible hilly" little farm back in the Town of Wyoming in the Driftless Area of Wisconsin.

We came to truly comprehend and become thankful for the incredible freedoms and opportunities we had been born with as European-descendant Americans. We promised ourselves to never take these gifts for granted. It was then that I made a commitment to the responsibilities that citizenship in a democracy entails and to be a steward of our precious land and water resources for which we are so blessed.

It was an eye-opening adventure for me as a young man, and for my family. But as an independent thinking person, one who desired more than anything to be a free individual, to develop my own farm and discover my own land ethic, I had to come home.

So yes, I had just lived and worked on and helped grow the largest dairy farm in the world. Somehow, I believed our little farm *could* compete, and I believed that if we were failing, it should mean something to our greater society. And I did believe it was worth saving. Indeed, when we returned to our farm, it was no longer "horrible" to us in any way. In fact, I called it Shangri La. (See Sidebar: Brother David, the Powerful Beauty of This Land)

Brother David, the Powerful Beauty of This Land

I have always had a profound physical response to this landscape. The storms, how they can gather over the hills to the southwest somewhere; you can't see them, but the light changes, and then all of a sudden, there they are. Those big black clouds coming over the hill low enough to touch.

When you are in our valley, you're just completely surrounded by those hills. The uncountable shades of green. Every day of every season, every day of the year, the colors are different, and the shadows are different. The way the trees leaf out in the spring and then change color in the fall, each different from the next.

And winter is very profound. The silence of the woods. Looking across a frozen field of snow, it takes a tremendous amount of imagination to conceive of summer someday returning. And the sounds—birds, creatures, water flowing, wind in the leaves as they rattle and hiss ... and so different from one moment to the next.

It's all so powerful to me. Some nights, looking up at the sky. Oh my God, it can feel right on top of you. Like it has been since the beginning of the Earth and will be until the end of the Earth. On a quiet clear night, it's just the peepers and the stars.

All of the elements and the variations in wind, temperature, humidity. But mainly light. This place is just a delight to the eyes. From my eyes right down into my heart. Day after day. I have been touched really strongly by the landscape of the farm.

I live in Montana, and many people come out, and they're there for a week or a few months, and they say they "just fall in love with the land!" And I get it. But that's more like you went to a nightclub and you saw a pretty girl, and just "loved" her! But that's different from the way I learned to appreciate and love land. It's tied into a deeper joy and gratitude, which can only come, really, with suffering, of course, and with loss. The farm gave me the opportunity to feel all of that and, therefore, to feel, to understand more deeply, and to respect and love the mysteries of all land.

And now, for four decades I've written about it in my novels, in everything, practically. To me it is home. There's no place on earth that makes me feel as much like "I'm home." It's like my womb. I feel like I am back in the womb.

Every day of every season, every day of the year, the colors are different, and the shadows are different.

Fast forward to spring 1986. Home in Spring Green, we purchased a modest, foreclosed older home, worked hard for several months to refurbish it, and settled into a routine. A couple of entries from our family journal illustrate our routine at the time:

> **September 30, 1987**—I've been working on my parents' farm for much of the past year, assisting David and Rosalie, but also as a carpenter to help pay the bills, and I'm preparing for my role as agriculturist for the new Sustainable Agriculture on-farm demonstration program at the Wisconsin Department of Agriculture, Trade and Consumer Protection. I was so fortunate to get this wonderful part-time opportunity to pair with work on our farm. It has allowed me to observe and learn about almost every agricultural enterprise and approach to farming in the upper Midwest.
>
> I had a wonderful autumn day with Eric (2 1/2 yrs.) and Shannon (5 1/2 yrs.). In the morning Eric and I went to the west side of the farm to fix a fence and move the cattle into the east, or front end of the farm pasture. Eric wore his cowboy boots and said, "Many cow poopies." He also said, "Nay poopy" meaning horse poopy, and tried to mimic me when I said "chicory" and "bluegrass." The words came out, barely. At one point he got stuck boot-top deep in the middle of a small dribble of stream water and started to cry (I tried not to smile). He also tried to pick up the big sledgehammer and, in doing so, fell down on his nose and again, cried. Some helper. He follows me all around at every task, and whenever a tool or a nail or anything he's not supposed to touch is laid out within reach, he gets it into his little mitts and works with it. It is sometimes annoying, of course, but priceless. He's been doing this for over a year now. Much of his work experience started in the house remodeling last summer. Eric is a small boy with a very large head. All of a sudden, he pulled his pants down and tinkled in the pasture. He thought it was so funny, and so did I.
>
> Then Shannon and I spent the rest of the day together. I took her with me in the car to visit people on business in Madison and at the Arlington Agricultural Research Station. We visited the weed garden with nearly one hundred weeds. At every name post she would ask, "And what's this one, Daddy?" When we came to the foxtail grasses—yellow, green, giant, and foxtail barley—she said, "This one's foxtail." I just couldn't believe it. I don't know where or when she learned this, but however she did, she remembered. She collected leaves and parts of the weeds we looked at. Later in the day we went to the Dairy Expo at the Coliseum in Madison. She recalled that we had seen horses jump there several months earlier at the Midwest Horse Fair. We watched a dairy auction at the show where the auctioneer talked like he had a finger moving his lips. We had treats all day long, and Shannon loved everything. She read her books in the car while we traveled home, even by flashlight after dark.
>
> When I arrived home at night, Peter, our 11-month-old who was born with Down syndrome, showed his first sign of responding to an activity today. Kim and I clapped hands and then he did too. He laughed and smiled and did it again. It was precious indeed. I love all of my children, each one so different from the other, all so very much.

October 5—Apple pressing day.

October 9—Shannon and Daddy took the old station wagon farm-chore vehicle all over the farm today to take soil samples. We saw many, many deer on the upper hayfield. Then, later Mom took all three kids to the agricultural fair at the River Valley School District homecoming. Shannon says she saw rabbits, pigs, cats, sheep, cows, horses, ponies, and one of the older girls from our neighborhood riding in the rodeo pole-bending event. (The River Valley School District, at the time of this writing, has one of the last three remaining school agricultural fairs in Wisconsin.)

Kim and I returned to a family farm that had just thirty beef cow-calf pairs, and I began to assist brother David, who continued as caretaker on behalf of our parents' investment. As noted previously, the farm "business" was not a business. The farm income was just the sale of the calves from most of the thirty beef cows to pay for all the equipment that seemed to always break down. The grazing and cropland acreage of the farm was limited, but even more significantly, the pasture acreage was minimally productive.

In the previous chapter, I discussed the mismanagement or lack of management of our cropped fields (too much tillage, manure application at spring runoff, herbicide overuse or misuse, to name a few examples) and of the pasture grazing land throughout our growing-up years on the farm. But our pastures looked just like everyone else's I had ever seen in Wisconsin—lots of

The farmstead in the mid-1980s. My family had not yet heard of the management practice called at that time, "intensive rotational grazing," so our pastures were less productive. Brother David and I implemented a managed grazing approach a couple of years later. Photo courtesy of the Cates family.

Our young family with our herd: Kim and Dick with Eric, Peter, and Shannon, and our blue heeler, Lucy. Photo courtesy of the Cates family.

grass in the early summer flush, then almost no grass regrowth during the hotter, drier mid-summer. Thistles left untouched by the grazing animals grew tall, shading the short-grazed grass and robbing it of sunlight and rainwater. The standard approach to growing more grass was to purchase nitrogen fertilizer. This practice didn't address the thistle shading and moisture robbing problem, nor did it address the short, close, and continuous livestock grazing patterns that led to domination by the Kentucky bluegrass, the most unproductive grass that only grows well mid-May through June.

In the first three months I was with the Sustainable Agriculture Program, I met several farmers in southwest Wisconsin who had implemented something called "intensive rotational grazing." This was an approach to grassland management that mimicked the way in which wild herds have grazed savannas across the globe for millennia. The key was livestock movement on and off a particular area of grass quickly for a short duration of grazing (before the plants are grazed so short that all their leaves are removed) and then a longer period of no grazing. The clear benefits for a farmer were more grass available for grazing per acre each year—a result of more plant leaves available for photosynthesis, and improved rainwater infiltration available for plant growth (and, therefore, less rainfall runoff for soil erosion and nutrient loss), and less livestock trampling.

Who could argue against this? Wisconsin practitioners of this grazing management said they had learned about it from visits to New Zealand, where it was common practice among dairy

Some of our pastures had more thistles than grass in our early years back to the farm. This photo was taken in the drought year of 1988 when only the deep-rooted thistles remained green.

and sheep farmers. I was referred to the original "bible" on the subject, *Grass Productivity* (1959), written by a French scientist-practitioner, Andre Voisin. The promise of intensive rotational grazing, or "rational grazing," as Voisin coined it, was more productive land use for livestock growth and environmental benefits in exchange for human observation and a little additional cost for fencing materials.

As serendipity would play out, a scientist-practitioner from the University of Vermont, Dr. Bill Murphy, raised on a family farm in the Driftless Area of Wisconsin, came home that holiday season to visit family. He had just written the book *Greener Pastures on Your Side of the Fence: Better Farming with Voisin Management Intensive Grazing* (1987), and he scheduled a public presentation one evening in Spring Green to share his experience.[3]

This, as it turned out, was our aha moment. Kim and I said to each other, "This is what we need to do!" Later, we put two and two together. Southwestern Wisconsin used to be part of the historical oak savanna and tallgrass prairie, and it didn't take a rocket scientist to realize that the landscape that we were on had the biological capability—and memory, if you will—to grow grass, and lots of it. By mimicking the movement of the historic grazing herds that once occupied this landscape, we could attempt to optimize grass productivity while protecting the land. Later we came to understand this concept as an example of "biomimicry, the conscious emulation of life's genius."[4] This sure made sense to us, and we prepared to "learn-to-emulate" big time. (See Sidebar: Some Benefits of Managed Grazing—a Biomimicry of Native Herbivore Movement—for the Ecosystem, the Farmer ... and Everyone)

That winter my brother David and I planned out what would be the first implementation of a rudimentary grazing plan on the Cates Family Farm. It was very exciting and held so much

Some Benefits of Managed Grazing—a Biomimicry of Native Herbivore Movement—for the Ecosystem, the Farmer … and Everyone

Research has found, conclusively, that well-managed grazing systems, when compared with other agricultural systems, contribute favorably to the following ecosystem functions that underpin ecosystem services:[1]

Soil carbon sequestration leads to climate stabilization, reduced agronomic costs, clean water, reduced flooding, and biodiversity.

- Soil formation provides agricultural opportunities and clean water.
- Rain and snowmelt retention by interception of the plant canopy and infiltration and percolation to groundwater helps reduce flooding and purifies/cleans water.
- Nutrient cycling cleans water, reduces greenhouse gas emissions, and reduces agronomic costs.
- Phosphorus and nitrogen retention leads to clean surface and groundwaters.
- Plant photosynthesis stores energy livestock can utilize to produce meat and milk.
- Resilient habitat exists for soil biota, pest predation, pollination, bird and animal diversity, and disease control.

Managed grazing, compared to continuous grazing, provides the following agronomic benefits:

- Little or no soil loss to erosion
- Fewer weeds
- More uniform soil fertility
- More stable forage production during poor growing conditions, especially drought
- Greater yield potential and higher quality forage
- Potential for increased profitability without government subsidies

Additionally, the following are some important direct human health benefits from grassland agriculture:

- Increased levels of the so-called "good fats" omega-3 fatty acids and CLA (conjugated linoleic acid) in grass-fed meat and milk
- More vitamins E, A, and carotene in grass-fed meat and milk
- Cultural: Recreation, education, spiritual, aesthetic, and heritage (for example, mimicking tallgrass prairie and oak savanna as the original ecosystems of the Driftless Area)

promise. I could hardly wait to build my first "simple, lightweight, portable, affordable, poly wire electric subdivision pasture fence" come April.[5]

By spring, we had erected the few fences planned for this first year, but mostly we explored the limits of just how simple, lightweight, and portable this poly wire actually was. We learned that a lot had to do with just how well the cow herd was willing to play along with the new approach on any given day.

I'll never forget the pleasant spring evening I went out to unroll a new line of poly wire ahead of the grazing herd to give them a fresh paddock (partitioned area) of grazing. I was in a jolly mood with the thought that we were making some kind of history along Lowery Creek, moving the cows to fresh feed while still having time to smell the roses.

Well, I didn't have time to smell any roses, but yes, I smelled some dandelions. I made a big mistake. I didn't turn the current back on before I let the herd come rambling forward. Because they were not used to this new system *at all*, they hit the poly wire and just kept going, it seemed to the next county, with the wire strand across their breasts or under their horns.

I was fuming, of course. But there was no way I was going to let go of that poly wire and have our new intensive rotational grazing system fail! So, I held on, and the herd dragged me, feet up, on my butt through the dandelions, on and on. Never again did I forget to turn the current on any new poly wire fence before I let the cows in.

Even given hardscrabble teachable moments like this one, moving on from our historical two-pasture system was something we embraced wholeheartedly. As it turned out, this change saved the cow herd from liquidation. That summer of 1988 and through the spring of 1989 presented the worst area drought in a generation. Grazing land pastures dried up and went dormant. Of course, this meant hay prices skyrocketed to previously unimaginable levels.

I was reminded of the wise guy quip I heard the summers I worked on ranches in Montana: "If a drought happens, we'll just hang them cows by skyhooks and feed 'em on scenery."

Fortunately, the subdivision fences David and I had erected allowed us to partition the feed offered into a few days at a time. If we monitored the grass height during grazing, we were able to move the herd to the next paddock before it had been eaten or "bitten down" too low.

Holy moly, it worked! Our father was even more pleased than we were, as the financial loss would have been his. I felt as if we had somehow emerged from a vat of pig manure smelling like roses. I knew I should embrace a lot of folks in thanks. I just didn't know where to start.

(I learned sometime afterward that I had lucked out again, as all the local farm supply stores had long since sold out of skyhooks!)

> **December 6, 1988, an epiphany**—Kim and I had both been very sick for four days. I'd say this was the sickest I have been that I can recall. I thought if I had to live like this I'd just as soon die. I had a very, very sore throat, headache, swollen neck glands, fever, and stuffy nose. That evening, near to death it seemed, I drove out to the farm to get

> the feeding schedule for November. It was pinned on the wall in the barn, and I wanted to get the figures and work on them at my desk at home. Near dead, but I could still do deskwork.
>
> It was near dusk when I arrived, and I got out of my car and plodded sullenly up the path to the south barn door. I could smell the ground—it was not quite yet all frozen—and I could smell the barn, the animals below, and the hay in the mow. The wind swirls on the way up and back behind the barn, in the narrow lane between the barn and hillside, and it's possible to smell everything together all at once. I looked up at the barn corner, rising to the sky. Clouds moved past, leaving the impression that the barn itself was doing the moving. It always seemed so.
>
> The hay and earth and animal smells, the barn and sky moving. The eternal flow of life embodied in that farm, in that land, seeped its way inside of my sick body. It enveloped and healed me, and I felt good. It was like magic. That place does this to me when I least expect it. The constant is that this happens and has happened regularly for the past decades since I was a boy.

I had just spent three years living and working building the largest dairy farm in the world. How could our little farm compete? If we were failing, why should my little farm mean anything to anyone else? Why would it be worth saving?

I was so immensely appreciative of the opportunity to work with my brother David for the past couple of years since returning. It was also especially gratifying to see the joy that the farm's progress brought to our father and mother. But it was time to stake a claim. It was time to make an offer to purchase the farm and make a permanent home for my growing family.

And so, during that summer, I made the following proposal to my father:

> August 1989
>
> Dear Dad,
>
> It is appropriate now for me to write to you regarding the most significant decisions in my life before and since deciding to marry Kim. I want to keep the Spring Green farm as a working farm, develop it into an exceptional livestock grazing operation, to take care of this piece of land, to live on it. We want to be a farm family; we want to make a long-term commitment to this land which has served as a basis of our memory, and which has unequaled meaning to us.
>
> I am asking and offering to purchase from you, at assessed value, the home and buildings on the Spring Green farm, forty to one hundred acres of land, and the cow herd and machinery. I will take a mortgage to pay you in one sum the value of this property. I am prepared to secure this loan in 1990. We are prepared to begin some work on the home this spring and to move in by autumn 1990. The balance of the farm acreage could remain in your name (and be passed to the family, or sold, as you so choose). I am asking to rent the agricultural acres which remain in your and Mom's names and offering to manage

the balance of the property on your behalf and to the benefit of the family. Regarding the property of which I assume ownership, the family would retain guaranteed access and use for hunting and recreation; nothing would need to change the way the family presently uses the land and bunkhouse. (I would hope in the future to be able to employ cousins in the summers; the bunkhouse would provide lodging.) Additionally, the family could retain the first option to buy if, in the future, Kim and I need to sell the property in our name.

I'm fully aware that the decisions which this proposal requests impact you, David and Rosalie, and other family members as significantly as they do Kim and me. I am very sensitive to this. We are prepared to accept the decisions that you make. We have discussed the proposal with David and Rosalie and with John. We have needed to make this proposal, and the time is correct. To say that I want to work the family farm, to farm, is to express a very significant commitment. I want the responsibility, benefits, burden, and fulfillment that accompany commitment. In my view of the world, ownership and commitment are inseparable. I am asking for ownership of the farmstead and a portion of the farmland as a symbol of my commitment and concretely as a real value to balance the risks—financial and physical—that accompany commitment. I am a builder and not merely a user, and I need a relationship that allows this to flourish.

I want the successes and failures of farming to be my own. I believe that a farm is a signature, a reflection of the family and land that live together, and that hopefully, ideally, achieve a balance together. I believe that my reasons to want to buy a portion of a family farm are not different from many other starting farmers who have done so, for so long, before me.

The relationship which I have had with the farm specifically for the past almost two years has been very, very important and, I think, mutually beneficial for you and the family. This relationship is, however, no longer appropriate. We have thought about and discussed, endlessly, this situation and the ideas expressed in this letter.

In the present situation, farming is spliced into and around my other job and Kim's jobs. That is hard enough. But living in town requires that I travel back and forth to the farm and be away from my family almost continuously. A consequence of this exhaustive shuttle, I made a costly mistake, and farming came close to taking my life this summer.

We feel that we must now establish the terms of a long-term commitment to include residence and some ownership if I am going to continue with the work, the responsibility, the risk of farming.

My understanding of the role I want to continue to develop as an agriculturalist and as a citizen has matured through these past several years of work and involvement. I am a listener and an observer, a teacher, an advocate for a land ethic and for sustainable resource use and for farmers who also believe and practice these things. But I am also a practitioner and producer.

> My singularity, but much more importantly, my motivation, is rooted in the doing—being a practitioner. I want to be deeply involved with the pleasure, the passion, the struggle, the risk, the life of doing, of farming, and raising a family on—and taking care of—land, which has very significant meaning to us.
>
> Thanks for your patience reading through this and for your consideration. It is my hope that we can discuss these ideas before the end of August.
>
> Very much love, Dick

I had seen enough of life to know that there will always be sufficient folks who are ready and willing to tell others what and how they ought to do things. But I wanted to be one who walked the walk. I wanted the crucible of making a living on the land to teach me the way. It would take me years, however, to learn to listen.

As fate would have it, that summer, brother David, a serious developing writer, was accepted for an MFA (Master of Fine Arts) program at the University of Montana, one of the top creative writing programs in the nation and, as it happens, his undergraduate alma mater. By early autumn, Rosalie and David had completed the preparations for moving a household that had been on the farm for nine years, along with their two young daughters, Anna and Margie, back out to Montana. (See Sidebar: Augs)

Augs

Dick: Years ago, you and I named the fog that comes to our valley in August when the overnight temperature begins to cool. A mist forms over the Wisconsin River just off the valley floor, and it sits there, silently, still, in the early morning light. It's as if the ghosts of the souls of the past have slid down from the hills, and they've just settled in our valley, watching us, making certain we are caring, as they did, for this place. So quiet, so stirring.

You and I have always been amazed that no one before us, no one that we know of anyhow, had ever given this dependable late summer phenomenon a name. It's a fog in August, an aug, and no one has named it before or hardly even mentions it. It is intrinsically part of the magic of this place.

Dave: Early in the morning, as you look north toward the Wisconsin River, the aug may silently serpentine its way up the valley to our farm. There's this morning-lit green grass in the pasture, and then a solid bank of aug moving closer and closer, a real-life force.

As the sun rises farther, the aug begins to dissipate, growing thinner and thinner, and the pastures start to become visible again, and soon, like cobwebs across the valley, all that remain are strands along the creek bottom. Then it's gone. The sun will be high and hot, the sky blue, the pasture gleaming and green, and you can wonder, was it ever there? It's just a very beautiful, intensely moving experience.

Dick: And soon we begin to anticipate the arrival of autumn. The air so cool and crisp, ideal for labor and harvesting the fruits of the earth. The world is aflame in a kaleidoscope of color—the oak's russet, the yellows and oranges of birch, aspen, walnut, and elm, and the reds of sumac and hard maple—grandly decorating our place's celebration of life. It's no wonder "here" has been home to so many for so long.

Finding Our Way—Imagining and Building Our Farm and a Land Ethic

"Imagination is more important than knowledge. For knowledge is limited to all we know and understand, while imagination embraces the entire world, stimulating progress."
—Albert Einstein

"To keep every cog and wheel is the first precaution of intelligent tinkering."
—Aldo Leopold, *Conservation, Round River*

Our sentinel oak surely observed that movement had been put back into the grazing of our valley and that there were more and more cattle, more than our beautiful creek-side land could accommodate—and an ever-harried farmer to boot. The ancient oak longed to whisper to the matriarch of the farm family, "You have the power to save our land ... and him."

Early Spring 1989—Some days we all feed the cows together. Shannon (7 yrs.) or Eric (4 yrs.) are in charge of cutting or collecting the bale strings. Recently, we went out to the pasture one evening after dark to check for new calves. Together we saw a newborn baby calf in the headlights. The kids got out of the vehicle in the still night air and dared to get fairly close to the mom and baby. A very beautiful moment. They asked many questions about beef cows and dairy cows and calves, milk, and "breastees."

Recently Eric and I rode together in the truck. Shortly, I stopped and turned the engine off in order to start repairing the fence. As I jumped out, and Eric could see what the program was going to be, he said, "Oh good, some work!" and promptly began rummaging through the fencing tools with excitement. He tends to rearrange things, tools, constantly in a way that makes my work more difficult. It was frustrating this time, and so I said, "Eric, give me the pliers, now! When I need a tool, you give it to me; when I need something, you don't need it, ok?"

> He handed me the pliers, and after a bit of silence, sitting on the grass lazily pounding something with the hammer, he said, "When I need the hammer, Daddy doesn't need the hammer." (My note at the time of writing this book: Eric was clearly preparing for his role reversal of eventual boss, which he assumed just 28 years later.)

I continued to work alongside my brother Dave through the summer. He and his family were preparing to leave for Montana in early autumn in time for the start of the fall semester. It was a bittersweet time, indeed. In a most significant way, we owe our life journey to the commitment Dave and Rosalie made here for those years. We are forever thankful.

We initiated the purchase of eighty acres of the 287-acre farm from my parents on a twenty-year land contract with monthly payments at 8 percent interest—the portion with the older farm home, barn, and outbuildings, and most of the grazing acres.[1] The small herd of thirty beef cows and all of the farm machinery, tools, and supplies were included in our purchase in a separate but similar contract.

Our plan was to become an intensive rotational grazing "grass farm" exclusively.[2] This transition had been in process for nearly two years, since listening to Bill Murphy evangelize about rotational grazing's potential that blustery December evening in 1987. I sold off the old equipment I wouldn't need, one piece at a time, at the best price I could get. We said goodbye and good riddance to everything that promised to rust, rot, depreciate or otherwise cost money to keep intact. (Mom and Dad lived on a small farmette about a half hour away, and Dad had built a small feedlot and silo there when I was in college. When Dad had that silo erected, I thought to myself with a swollen pride, *Now we're really farming!* But, man, I was glad I didn't offer to purchase all that added infrastructure for such a few cows. Just more "stuff" to rust, rot, etc.)

That winter I also sold off the poorer cows, those who were not in calf and those who were having a difficult time maintaining good flesh. From a fledgling business perspective, this was essential because hay was in record short supply since the recent drought and priced similarly to gold.

Kim and I also took on a substantial remodeling project of the old farmhouse, with the original portion of the home having been constructed in the 1860s. With our three young children—then ages seven, four, and three—in tow, we spent the autumn of 1989 through the summer of 1990 bringing it to life again, creating the home where we planned to raise our family. We hired expert contractors to lead the project, but we worked alongside them a portion of every day and on weekends to save money. We were both working part time off the farm, in addition to running the fledgling farm business. We spent most of the funds we had saved from our three-year stint in Saudi Arabia on this home improvement.

A few years later when I began my work training beginning farming students—and did so for nearly twenty-five years—I preached that when building a business, it's most productive that your first equity (ownership) is in assets that will earn income (livestock). Kim and I chose to invest the funds we owned into a house (home equity) we could call home for a long time. For Kim, this was of paramount importance. However, our choice left us in a more vulnerable position as far as the farm business was concerned. We would now need to borrow money for income-producing assets (livestock, again), as well as operating expenses.

So for the first time in our lives, we were fully pushed from shore on the proverbial raft. We had a significant monthly payment due on a home, land, cattle and machinery, three children, and a farm business that wasn't really yet a business. Thankfully, we had the part-time jobs and colleagues who recognized and supported what we had committed to. They provided the needed flexibility, but the pressure was on. (See Sidebar: Perchance I Met Kim Denise Johnson ... and a Love Story Ensued)

We headed into spring 1990, beginning our first full year as owners, with just seventeen cows and almost no cash. Employed with part-time work off the farm and partial equity in our home, I had, for the very first time, the credit score to obtain a loan. Some additional fencing materials needed to be purchased, and I went back into the market to purchase "good but used cows." Livestock prices were favorable (but only for us as buyers), still a result of the recent drought and prolonged pasture recovery on most area farms. Our implementation of intensive rotational grazing—referred to as "managed grazing" from now on—two summers earlier meant our pastures were able to recover well enough to be productive again.

The following year, we added a few more cows. The next year we did it again. Within a few years, the herd grew to fifty, then seventy cows. I was pleased. Cates farm pastures were never able to support more than half this number while we were growing up here. That's

Perchance I Met Kim Denise Johnson ... and a Love Story Ensued

Our mothers concur that we met each other when Kim was a newborn twin in a crib with her brother Kevin. I was three and a half years old when my mom walked me the few blocks across the Madison neighborhood where our families both lived to see the new twins. After all, it was big local news.

Fast forward nearly two decades to September 1974. I had just recently graduated college and was working for my dad here on the farm. My primary project that fall was to complete a cement pad near the barn where the hay was stored, a convenient location to feed the cows during the winter. I can look out the window from where I am writing today and see the pad about a hundred yards away. It was while working in that exact spot that I had thought to myself, *I'm starting an exciting new phase of life, but I am so lonely.*

September's moon is the harvest moon. I recall gazing at it, so bright and alive those early fall evenings, as it waxed toward full. It would be a dream come true to share this beauty, this tranquility, with someone I loved.

So I hatched a naïve but hopeful plan. As there is every Saturday in autumn, and has been every autumn for a seeming eternity, a Badger football game somewhere, I decided to travel into Madison after the next home game with the hope to perhaps meet a nice young woman looking for a guy like me. After all, I lived and worked on a beautiful farm with cows and horses, and I can ski pretty well.

It turned out Wisconsin won that game, and the campus was celebrating. I decided to head to the Sigma Chi fraternity, where I knew that some of the guys from my high school were members, and it would be fun to see them.

I chose to don a partial costume for the celebration. I think I wore an older farm cap, suspenders, fingerless gloves, and plastic Halloween teeth. Why not?

I tell her I love her often and let her know, "I was always looking for someone exactly like you."

The place was packed, teeming with hooting and hollering college students, dancing away to the blaring music and chanting at frequent intervals, "We're number one!" What else would I expect, or could I expect?

It wasn't long after I arrived at the gathering that a young lady, whom I didn't know from Eve, swiped my monster teeth right from my mouth and made them her own. She wasn't interested in speaking with me and certainly not dancing with me. But, as one never knows what might transcend in life, I fell for her in that instant. Next thing I knew, she had left the gathering with a knot of girlfriends, off to who knows where.

I inquired of some of the guys I knew from high school, members of the fraternity, what that young lady's name was and where I might call on her in the future. After all, I had to get my teeth back. With the critical information secured, early the next afternoon, I paid a visit to Miss Kim Denise Johnson at Conover dormitory on the UW–Madison campus.

It turned out Kim loved horses and always wanted one of her own, and she had loved skiing since she was a young girl and hoped to continue to improve. Within a month or so, she learned to drive a tractor.

We dated for two years. As she recalls, I was persistent. We married under the harvest moon on September 4, 1976.

We both then studied soil science, traveled together by canoe across Canada to the Arctic Ocean, climbed and skied mountains and walked more miles together than we could count, lived and worked three years in faraway Saudi Arabia, and then made a commitment to raise our three beautiful children here on the farm, so many years ago.

I met Kim almost fifty lovely harvest moons ago. She is multi-talented with the cattle, on the tractor, and much more, including in the garden, the kitchen, the sewing room, and always with the kids. She is steady, wise, kind, and loving. I continue to learn from her every day.

I guess it was meant to be. I was destined to fall in love with the girl who snitched my plastic Halloween teeth. I tell her I love her often and let her know, "I was always looking for someone exactly like you."

Kim and Dick on their wedding day, September 4, 1976. Photo courtesy of the Cates family.

why cows on the farm had also been grazed in the woods before. Now, we were able to fence off the woods and begin maintaining them for productive timber.

January 15, 1990—Moved into the farmhouse, finally.

January 29—Sunday a (hoped for) day of rest. However: septic overflowing; groundwater coming into the southwest corner of the basement like a river; fuel gauge on furnace oil tank not working, but I know that we're almost out of fuel (will likely be tonight); water pump stopped working, no potable running water. Nope, there wasn't any rest today.

Later that winter—Shannon and Eric work cutting and loading firewood on Sunday to earn a dollar each. Eric used his dollar to buy a ninja turtle. Shannon saved her dollar.

April 7—Peter's [3 1/2 yrs.] first word is "mommom." His second word "moo." He doesn't have any other words. However, curiously, there is a little gray and white bird that seems to chirp "Peter, Peter" over and over again. It can be seen clinging, upside down, to any of the trees near our yard. After speaking with my birding friends and searching my Audubon field guide, I learned this is the tufted titmouse, and there it was, in plain English: "It's commonest call, sung year-round ... a whistled series of ... notes sounding like 'Peter, Peter' repeated over and over." Well I'll be darned. Peter can't say his name, but a little bird has his back! (At the time of writing this book, I never paid any attention or even noticed this call all the years growing up working on this farm. But from that spring on, I could hear it any day, every day.)

April 22—Eric puts worms in cans and tries to shoot pigeons with a slingshot.

April 30—Spring has really arrived. The world is alive with green, plum blossoms, noises, and smells. It's absolutely beautiful. We have come through the major work of building and moving onto this farm and into the farmhouse. The stress, long hours, and chaos nearly did us in at times, but we knew we had to push forward to get to this point. After 8 1/2 months of work, we are in, but there is still very much to do.

In the middle of April, Kim took our youngest son, Peter, to his pediatrician as he had been experiencing on-and-off fevers for several weeks, which had previously been diagnosed as a treatable viral infection. Kim pointed out some unusual red dots on Peter's skin, particularly on his back, and noted that he looked especially pale. Our physician ordered a blood test and other tests, and by the end of the day Peter was officially diagnosed with one of the common forms of childhood leukemia, acute lymphoblastic leukemia, otherwise known as ALL, a disease for which the mortality rate, particularly among Down syndrome children, was very high. Peter started high doses of chemotherapy immediately, and by June he was in remission. He was to be on a chemotherapy regimen for three more years.

So, independent of the work we had to do to get the home and farm business functioning, we knew our family life had changed forever and that attention to Peter's condition was going to be paramount.

Mother's Day May 13—"We gave Mom some smelly flowers," said Eric. "We went out to the fields to pick some for her. We love her." Shannon said, "I picked some smelly plants, or whatever they are, and made a present with them." The plant was yellow rocket, a yellow-flowered weed in the mustard family.

June 14—Shannon helped Dad rake the horse hoof prints out of the newly seeded yard (They had broken through one of the poorly constructed fences). Also, Shannon fell off one of the horses named Dandy recently. Sweet little girl hit the grassy ground. She was scared but unhurt, thank God.

July 3—Shannon fell off dandy again. I think this will be the end of her riding.

Late July—Shannon was out helping me on the farm. I was attempting to lay out a fence line and decided to use Shannon as a sight post. I asked her to stand in this particular spot for me and not to move while I was sighting over her head. When I was done needing her in that position, I forgot to say anything and continued on with my work. About fifteen minutes later Shannon came up to me wearing one shoe. She said she was tired of standing in one spot and so decided to leave her shoe there so she could find the place again. Of course, only then did I realize I'd forgotten to tell her I was finished. I laughed and cried and hugged her so tightly. I said I was sorry, over and over, profusely. Sweet dear creature.

September 25—Peter is a mountain man now. We found him up the hill behind the house, where the pasture ends and woods begin, with our dog Lucy. (This is the hill we eventually named "Peter's Hill," a result of this first ascent by a not-quite-four-year-old). Another day we found him at the end of the driveway with Lucy, apparently going for the mail. Then we found him out in the pasture west of the house. Wild Mountain Peter gets a little bit scolded (and we laughed, as well) when we find him and bring him home.

End of September—Last night we sold our cattle on the Midwest Livestock video auction. Eric was confused as to what this event was and asked, "How do you get the cows to the dance?" Shannon asked me to write that Lucy knocks on the front door with her tail every morning, wanting love and to come inside.

October 8—We began kids' daily and weekly responsibilities and allowances today. Shannon and Eric were very receptive of the idea and helped decide on the jobs they were to do and the allowance amount. Allowance we decide is to be one dollar per child per week, unless they don't do their jobs. We've tried to make the kids feel these are important ways they can share in and contribute to our family work and responsibilities. The allowance is not explained as payment per se, but a sharing and an opportunity to have something of their own to use as they choose.

October 17—Peter was out in the horse pasture with a bridle trying to catch the horse named Mike. Mike came up to check the little guy out and then left. Another horse, Dandy, stayed clear. Then Peter went up to the barn to get a handful of hay to take down to the horses. Kim went up to get some more. The two made a pile of hay near the horse fence, and Peter fed all that to Mike and Dandy. The little boy is amazing, fascinating all the time.

Eric dug 25 thistles from the yard and earned two cents per thistle. Shannon dug 175 other weeds in several days and earned one cent per plant.

We began the learning process, the learning curve of developing a sustainable farming business. A farm that could pay its bills and one where the soil, water, plants, and animals—the entire ecosystem on which it depended—are treated with respect. Our values also demanded that all people be treated respectfully, not only those whom we depended on for business but the greater community with whom we have reciprocal, mutually dependent relationships. We felt such an inclusive vision was imperative for all of us to have the opportunity to enjoy our "inalienable rights" to life, liberty, and the pursuit of happiness.

We tried many, many things for a long time and tackled everything head-on, full throttle. My brother Dave told me with a sigh and a smile that he had never seen, or heard of, another farmer who jogged, no ran, between chores. I had a vision of how a successful farm would look and feel—many cattle, all healthy in grass to their bellies; contented happy family; banker begging me to borrow more money—but I sure wasn't there yet. It just felt like I had a lifetime of catching up to do after years of graduate school and working abroad. Yet, to this day, I don't know what I would have done differently.

Soon after our initial foray into managed grazing in the drought of summer 1988, I became convinced it was what our pasture-dominated farmland needed. More grass meant more cattle meant more net income—it was simple. We began tearing out an old barbed wire fence that was in the wrong location for a managed pasture system. We repurposed the muddy feed yard that was no longer planned for use and took down the decrepit and impractically located corral board fencing constructed by my brothers and me many years before.

Dick on a front-end loader with steel junk collected from the pastures. Photo by Kim Cates.

A managed grazing system requires fences, many of which can be light and portable. On a landscape like ours, all of the irregularly shaped pastureland is surrounded by woodland—thanks, as you will recall, to our European forebears who put an end to natural fire. Since early in the twentieth century, Wisconsin landowners have had a chance to reduce their property taxes if they agreed to a long-term forestry management plan *and* livestock were fenced "out" of the woods.

Many farmers choose not to enroll for a variety of reasons and continue to graze their livestock in the woods.

However, in that I already had to fence our land to control the daily movement of the cattle, I jumped at the opportunity to significantly reduce our tax burden (as well as our parents', who

Top: The fence graveyard in the woods. Old fence lines that had fallen, or were no longer in a useful location, were torn down and hauled by wagonload here. The pile was more than fifty yards long after the years of work was completed. Bottom: For a few winters I fed our cattle on a feedlot, the way many farmers choose to do. It was icy when frozen and a muddy mess when thawed.

owned the balance of the farm) and enrolled in the Managed Forest Law (MFL) by fencing our herd out of the many wooded acres which are so unproductive as grazing land to begin with.[3]

Of course, this meant building miles of pasture perimeter fence. We kept running out and were often in need of borrowing more. In order to save money, we utilized the old barbed wire we had just torn down and rolled up from somewhere we didn't need a fence, along with the rusty steel fence posts and the creosote-treated wooden corner posts where they still had life in them. This was a huge piece of work that took literally years across what eventually became four grazing systems on three different farms. By the late 1990s, I calculated we had some twenty-two miles of fence to maintain, most of which was built with used materials or was heavily repaired old existing fencing.

From the beginning, inexpensive soft steel wire and more expensive poly wire were used for subdivision fences, as it is essential that these fences can be easily rolled up and taken down or moved for pasture mowing or for adjusting the daily paddock size as grass growth changes through the season.

I often hired high school boys to assist me with the arduous work of tearing out old barbed wire fences and building new ones. For several summers I employed hockey players from a nearby high school. They were tough as heck, and the more hard work I offered, the better they liked it. Other farmers often lament that they can't find kids who want to work hard, and I always tell them, "Find yourself some hockey players!"

Of course, rock picking was another chore. Although our pastures had been in place for a very long time, no one in our lifetime had picked the rocks. Rocks show up every year. They break off from outcroppings on the hillsides above and roll down to the pasture, or the frost pushes old buried chunks to the surface, little by little. I had begun my lifetime war on thistles, and that meant mowing close to the soil surface from time to time, so I had to get rid of the rocks. I had more than seventy acres that needed scouring. I couldn't do the job myself, but I hatched a plan.

As with most farms in Wisconsin, ours had a group of hunters that kind of came with the place. I can't say precisely when this group took over the farm. It just happened gradually over time, invisibly, but right before our eyes. So when Kim and I returned and began to manage the farm, you could say we "inherited" this first group of hunters.

Anyone who has some farmland in Wisconsin likely knows the type. They take over the place for the nine-day gun deer hunting season in late November each year. While they are here, they make mud tracks around the farm with their trucks and leave gigantic pits wherever they get stuck, often in the same spots, year after year. They toss their lunch sacks, candy wrappers, and toilet paper wherever they please, assuming no one else will be here in "their" woods until they return next year. Then at the end of every hunting season, they come up to your front door and hand over a bottle of brandy, saying something like, "Oh jeez, thanks for the hunt! We'll see you next year."

Well, we had one of these inherited groups of freeloaders, but that fall I decided they would have to spend a day picking rocks with me to earn their hunting privilege. It worked ... once. I hooked a wagon up to a tractor, and we alternated between driving or picking. When the wagon was heaped full, we tossed the stones into low spots in the fields or into the woods. We picked several loads of stones that day, the first year of the new program. The group never came back to hunt on our farm. (But that was a good start to a big job, and the next wave of hunters earned their place during the first several years by completing this rock-picking task. More in Chapter 7.)

Out of pure necessity, we turned the muddy driving lanes across the bottomland pastures into graveled lanes and the muddy stream crossings for cattle, vehicles, and mowing equipment into rocked crossings. It took cash, a little at a time, over decades, first one crossing, then two, three, and now thirty-seven and counting. Before long, the Cates farm, along with all the local road contractors, were receiving annual invitations to the local gravel company's customer appreciation steak dinner.

We inter-seeded clover, a legume that transfers (fixes) nitrogen from the atmosphere to feed the grasses, a natural symbiotic relationship. Clover also shades the ground to keep it cooler in the

Top left, clockwise: Kim mowing a thistle patch; recently mowed thistles. Bottom: Eric and Kim golfing thistles; twelve broken hand scythes on the wall of the shop from decades of cutting thistles. (When Eric and his friend, Seth Alt, were summer work partners on the farm during middle and high school, I used to have them hand-cut thistles on our 22-acre ridge field, about 1.5 acres every other day, twice a summer. They never seemed to mind it and, to this day, confirm this.)

summer and provides high-quality protein and energy forage. And we cut and removed hundreds of sapling weed trees on pasture hillsides and along the stream corridor.

As I have written, I had initiated my lifetime war on the plumeless thistle, and dear Kim was a tireless and committed partner. She was the head tractor driver. Where thistles were the thickest, this could mean three cuttings a season. I occasionally drove to spell her from the task, and eventually, Eric joined the battle.

My principal contribution was to carry a hand scythe and walk (actually, I mostly jogged wearing soccer cleats so I wouldn't slip and fall so often) the fence lines, stream banks, and steep hills—anywhere the tractor mower couldn't reach. The hot, muggy mid-summer evenings in July when the thistle heads first flowered, but before seeds formed, were the prime time. With the hand scythe, I would merrily "swing the heads" from the thistle plants for hours on end.

For many years, the trek amounted to more than twelve miles in tallgrass residue, some brush, and heavy thistle patches. I first made this jaunt in the summer of 1988, and then for the next twenty-five years straight. I certainly recall that I didn't mind the exercise. In fact, I thrived on it as I always have. In contemplating this obsession years later, I must confess that it seems, well, just plain weird. Over all those years, I came to realize that I was driven to near perfection in too many endeavors. I had a clear picture in my head as to how my farm was going to look, function, and "be successful." In truth, I came near to breaking myself, time and again, by enforcing my vision of the land, the markets, and reality.

We tried a lot of things, as the cattle business was not a cash cow (yet), and many didn't work out very well. I had a family to feed, a mortgage to pay, and a dream. I wasn't going to fail because I couldn't afford to fail. We had heard that all-natural wild woods grown ginseng was worth its weight in gold, after about a decade or so left alone to grow. So when the kids were young, we thought, why not create a secret spot somewhere in our two hundred acres of woods and plant a little patch of ginseng seedlings and seeds each year. We calculated "precisely" the number of seedlings and seeds we had to hand plant each year and would call it the "kids college fund." A brilliant idea! For five years in a row, Kim, the three kids, and I would traipse up to our secret spot in May and collectively "contribute to the college fund." We believed it would certainly begin coming to fruition at just the right time when Shannon would be heading off to school, and we would have to come up with the tuition.

We would dig up a few roots each year as we checked for progress but were always disappointed. However, I just expected that the roots would be slow to grow. Call me a slow learner, but by year six, I finally concluded that something was eating our ginseng root as fast as it was growing. By then, we didn't have the enthusiasm to build a Fort Knox-like structure for the ginseng and start over, so we decided that college funds would have to come from some other empty stocking.

Maple syrup rose to the top of our cash crop ideas. Why not add a sure-fire lucrative enterprise that didn't interfere with the time of year when cattle require pasture and fence maintenance April through October or hay feeding and snow plowing November through February but tapering

off in March? Yes, that's it! We'd collect maple sap in March and boil it down to maple syrup soon after, then have all year to sell it. What could be more perfect? So I decided we'd make a test run.

Once the sap started to flow that spring, I led Kim and the kids out to the west end of the pasture, where just a few strides over the fence into the woods I had observed a likely maple prospect. We set a tap and hung a collection bucket, just as I had read in a university extension bulletin. Once everything was set, we headed home for the evening.

Several days later, I headed west to check the mother lode, and indeed, perhaps a quart or so had collected in the bucket. Perfect! It took ten quarts of sap to make one quart of syrup, and we realized our final product haul would be meager but certainly sufficient for a trial run. I figured once everyone in the family got a taste of the sweet gold, they'd be hooked, and a successful farm business enterprise would be launched!

We transferred the sap to a pot and put it on the kitchen stove to simmer. About then we got a frantic call from a neighbor saying that we had cows out on the road—again. Damn. Kim and I, the only ones old enough to cowboy, rushed off to see what the problem was this time.

Top: Kim with our Arabian mare, Dandy (Kim's all-time favorite). Bottom: Kim and Dick with our Morgan X quarter horse gelding, Prince, and Eric on Dandy. Bottom right photo by Kim Cates.

Of course, we had forgotten to turn the stove off, and that was it for the maple syrup enterprise. I couldn't ever break the inertia to get another enthusiastic family trial run underway, so our potential maple syrup dynasty never was, and we had to toss that burnt-black pot.

Although there had always been a saddle horse or two on the farm, Kim and I began to invest in horses for herding the cattle from pasture to pasture or gathering them into one of our three corrals, as the number of cattle we were running each year seemed to warrant this approach. We also used ATVs and trucks, but we enjoyed and much preferred horse work at first. At one point, we kept five saddle horses and added one of the neighbor's ponies just for the fun of it.

Early on, as our herd expanded, Kim and I grew our cowboy skills. Our opinion at the time was that there simply wasn't a more effective way to handle large groups of cattle than by horseback on a mount bred and trained for the work. It is beautiful work to watch, as our neighbor from Chicago assured us. In fact, he said he had a Chicago photographer friend in the marketing world who had the Virginia Slims cigarette account. He thought that with Kim and I as "models," perhaps it would be possible to land the Marlboro account! We would have a generous income opportunity if that happened.

Kim and I said, "Sign us up; we'll give it a try." So our friend invited his friend up one sunny autumn day. Our job was to ride our horses around and near our cattle while the photographer shot photos. However, it didn't dawn on us until he offered us a package of Marlboros that we would have to ride with lit cigarettes in our mouths the entire time.

I thought I could handle that for a few hours. After all, if our man got the gig, we'd be rich, relative to our present condition. It just wasn't going to work for Kim. No sooner than the cigarette was lit and between her lips, she began coughing vehemently. After much coaxing and several tries later, it was clearly a no-go.

So a compromise was reached: I would have a lit cigarette in my mouth, and Kim would have an unlit cigarette in hers. So far so good, until the photographer indicated he would like us to canter side by side across Lowery Creek. He decided he liked it so much he asked us to do it over and over again ad nauseam. Kim kept losing the cigarette from her mouth, a consequence of the bouncing over and through the rough terrain. It would have been extremely humorous to observe if our photographer hadn't been taking it so seriously.

Unfortunately, our friend wasn't able to steal the account away from the firm that had been doing the famed Marlboro ads forever. Once again, an easy paycheck eluded us, and Kim and I went back to our anonymous cowboying, sans cigarettes hanging from our lips.

In time, Kim and I, Shannon and Eric, one by one, all got thrown off a horse or two and injured, and we eventually changed our minds about using horses.

We took on three herding dog puppies over the years. Lucy, a blue heeler; Missy, a border collie; and Jack, an Australian shepherd, all had pedigree papers that guaranteed just how extraordinary they "could be" with proper training and handling. We sent two of the puppies to professional trainers for short sessions. I read books and worked at training them, as well, but

to little avail. I had the most success with Missy. She understood and followed all my commands like a prize-herding dog. The only problem was I had to give each command twice. The first time always caused her to stop, sit, and look at me; the second try sent her in motion, but by then it was often too late, and the herd had generally done just what I needed a dog to stop them from doing.

Some of our doggies over the years. Top left to right: Chunk (golden doodle), Jack (Australian shepherd); Lucy (blue heeler), Jack, and Missy (border collie); Bottom left to right: Missy and Lucy; Oakley (golden doodle); Eric with Lucy as a puppy; Missy, a gift from friends Reed and Carol Ludlow, Viroqua, when our son Peter was diagnosed with Leukemia. Photos courtesy of the Cates family.

I asked my friend and breeder from whom we had received Missy as a gift when our son Peter was sick what he thought Missy's problem was. He gently replied that he didn't see any problem with Missy, but rather, he was quite impressed with her. "Well," he said, "she sure has *you* trained."

Alas, the kids won each time. One after the other, the three canines became useless as working dogs but beloved as pets, playing out their days and then growing old under the shade of the trees in the farmyard.

One spring we decided to get some laying hens and a rooster to have around the farm, for eggs, of course, but also for the fun of just having them around. We pondered about how to come up with a small flock and decided to call our friends and neighbors. It just so happened that one couple had ten hens and a rooster, all Rhode Island Reds. Their kids had all flown the coop, and they wanted their flock to do the same; they'd give them to us *immediately*, without charge. The only requirements were that we had to take all eleven birds, and there were no returns. Ten hens were way too many as we only wanted a few, but we went along with the deal because it was too good to pass up.

We decided that we would give some of the hens away to neighbors, and then we'd run ads in the newspaper to get rid of all but two or three. By the next morning, we had a bunch of eggs and two dead hens. We had forgotten about Lucy, our blue heeler. She had, in that short amount of time, turned two live, colorful chickens into rubber, featherless chickens. Then she killed a third the next day.

I had heard that if you swat a dog a few times with a chicken they have freshly killed, it will cure them of the bad behavior, and this worked for a while. We gave two hens away to neighbors as we had promised, but we canceled our newspaper ad. We were down to five hens in less than a week. By week two, we were down to two hens and then one. Then Kim found a hen alive underneath an overturned bucket, so we were back up to two hens for a couple of days, but soon down to one again after another rubber chicken was found. The lone rooster remained alive and well all this time, doing his own thing. He crowed every morning, either up in the woods or on the far side of the barn, so he never woke anyone up.

Lucy had been whacked with fresh dead chickens three times by then. We took out a new ad in the newspaper, this time requesting more hens. Kim got a call from a family near Soldiers Grove with Rhode Island Reds again. She picked up four hens, and by early July we were back up to five.

A new problem developed. For a few days we were unable to figure out where this new batch had laid their eggs. We finally found some eggs below the steel pipe cattle crossing on our driveway, along with a few in the barn where we hoped to find them.

We went away for a few days in mid-July and paid our neighbors in beef to do the chores and watch the farm. We had Lucy along with us on that trip, so she had an alibi for any foul things that may have occurred to our fowl during our trip away. Well, it turns out we should have specifically included "watching the chickens" in the catchall of "watching the farm," because our hired help did not. We returned to flower beds and recently planted ornamental shrubbery decimated by chickens doing what chickens do when the coop is left open. But the chickens-gone-wild paid for their party—not a one survived the wild *this* time.

Our plans for diversification weren't working out. We decided as a family that raising chickens was no longer a specialty of choice and that we best stick to cows. But having all of our eggs—pun intended—in one basket was dangerous, as well. During one of those early difficult years, in the spring of 1991, disaster struck.

We had a very cold, wet, muddy spring. Over the course of a week, seven older mother cows became bogged up to their bellies in a saturated mud wallow near the stream. This had never happened to us before, and it has never happened to us since. I later accepted this was my fault because the hay I was providing was not of sufficient nutrition or quantity for these big cows in the eighth month of pregnancy. I was cash poor, and I had tried to save on hay I didn't want to purchase. Consequently, I paid a much higher price.

After each pregnant cow became helplessly stuck, I had to thread through the mud and secure a wide nylon cinch around her midsection. Then, with my tractor hooked to the end of a log chain up on higher ground, I carefully dragged each cow out of its muddy tomb. Sadly, they had each become chilled to the extent that they were no longer able to stand up, even with support by lifting and holding the cinch up with a borrowed front-end loader for hours at a time. Inevitably, they would surely die a slow death in this manner, and I couldn't bear it.

I had no choice but to end their lives quickly, as humanely as possible. This meant properly placed 22-gauge rifle shots, but I was unable to perform this act of mercy myself. These were my sweet, lovely mama cows. I called a neighbor and asked if he would come over and perform the duty, one at a time, over about a week. I had never had to do anything more emotionally difficult up to that point in my life. I still feel compelled, after many decades, to thank him for his courage and act of mercy.

Having endured that drama, we attempted to save the yet unborn calves, a couple of weeks from full term, one at a time by cesarean section. Right out there on the muddy, cold streambanks, I performed the role of midwife and then veterinarian-physician, with a bare knife blade, iodine, and doses of antibiotics, seven times that week of fear and horror. Three of the seven calves were born alive. With colostrum obtained from our veterinary service and fed with a stomach tube, we kept them alive under a heat lamp, nestled in clean, dry hay in the basement of our home.

Peter feeding a calf the kids named Brown Ears who had lost his mother.

Within a week or so, the new calves were able to suck milk replacer from a calf bottle, and we trained the kids to take on this task after school and then through the summer. Shannon was old enough to feed her own. She helped Eric, and they both helped Peter. The calves lived in the yard, and each child named their calf. Lolo was Shannon's, Eddie was Eric's, and Brown Ears was Peter's. It was a dear opportunity and life experience, and the kids fell in love with their calf babies.

Sadly, as the summer weather turned ghastly hot and humid, we lost all three calves one at a time. It turned out they were compromised from their early traumatic birth and having no mama around for nurture. We all shed tears, and the kids—as well as Kim and I—learned, once again, that life can be short, and it is always precious. We had lost almost a quarter of our mother cows, as well as the income potential from the calves, in just a few short months. (See Sidebar: Shannon Cates Bloom—Things I learned from Growing up on a Farm)

When my cattle, domestic animals under my watch, died this way, it wasn't just the sadness of the animal's death that grieved me. It was the sense that I, as the caretaker of this animal, had failed. After all, I made poor decisions. I was distracted. I didn't notice things. The death of those cows made me question my worth as a cattleman, my judgment, and my ability to care. It also cost a lot of money that we didn't have. For years afterward folks who didn't know me from Adam, I learned from friends, referenced me as "the guy whose cows died in the mud that spring."

Within a few years after implementing managed grazing, not just the quantity but also the quality of the grass we were able to grow spring through fall was improving. We began to see that our cows were getting bigger and fatter, but their calves, our only source of income from a beef cow herd, weren't significantly bigger. Beef cows simply don't need high-quality feed all season like a lactating dairy cow or a growing animal. This is why most of the large beef cow herds in the United States are out in the West, in the sparse, arid grass range country. We also have a long winter here, and hay is almost always more expensive than one prefers it to be. Double darn.

Shannon Cates Bloom—
Things I Learned from Growing up on a Farm

Growing up on a farm I learned about the circle of life. With the birth of animals, humans, even the grass and trees, there is always another life that is ending. Sometimes it is too soon; sometimes it's at the hand of another. Sometimes it happens unnoticed, and sometimes it's an event that you'll never forget, but it's the way of life and nature. From a very young age, I was exposed to death and believe I appreciate life more because of it.

I gained a deep appreciation of animals and the land and what they provide to us humans. They can be a direct source of food or provide benefits that improve our soil, groundwater, or air to sustain our lives. But they can also provide joy and love. Animals are magical beings and are sometimes not given the credit they deserve. They are capable of reading our thoughts and can care for humans and love us, just as we do them.

And being in nature is also magical. Whether it's an ocean that looks like it has no ending, hills that are blanketed in lush green grass, trees that are as big as a skyscraper, or a field of old thistles—they can all elicit many feelings for a human. Whether it's due to their beauty, what they offer us, or the work to obtain them, these diverse elements of nature can provide not only a physical home but also a feeling of home.

I also learned about hard work and perseverance. On a farm there is no nine to five; it's a twenty-four seven job. The work on a farm doesn't stop for bad weather or sickness. In fact, it gets harder. I saw my parents work through grief, great storms, and cows in their flowerbeds.

They never gave up, making certain the animals were cared for, the land was in working order, and their kids had a beautiful life and roof over their heads. I think this is what I took away the most and even looked for in a life partner. It is in part due to my parents' personalities, but growing up on a farm highlighted how valuable it is to have a formidable work ethic and the ability to never give up, even when times are tough.

—Shannon and her husband, Dan, are part owners of the Cates Family Farm.

As a farm family, you have to find your particular skill set and what your niche is. Indeed, we could have chosen to add value to our beef herd by focusing on higher-value markets such as raising and selling breeding stock, embryo transfer, sire genetics, or 4-H Club calf markets. We had chosen to focus on managing our grass, getting the most out of our pastures, and stocking them with animals that would bring the most return. We had to figure out what we could offer and market within this system of grassland management because just grassland management by itself was clearly not going to be a business, as the returns from our cow herd showed.

Kim and I were faced with a dilemma. Should we sell the cow herd? Could we? After all, our beef cows were descendants of the cows that my siblings and I had cared for since we were kids, more than two decades earlier, purchased from the Stapleton family. Those early cows possibly shared some bloodline with the first cows that the Thomas Stapleton family first introduced to this grassland more than a century earlier.

When Kim and I looked at the "balance sheet" at the end of each year, it didn't matter which way we turned it or tipped it on a scale; it wasn't balanced. So in a protracted decision-making process full of much angst, in 1993 Kim and I decided we had to sell the cow herd and focus on "growing" cattle (young weaned steers or heifers purchased in groups primarily from sale barns, later to be sold as bigger animals). We gathered them up in a big set of portable corral panels in the middle of that winter and loaded them on semi-trucks for another happy home.

I was tearful at that moment, but by the next day I had a hard time recalling why I had been so devastated about ridding my family of an albatross around our collective necks that didn't pay the bills.

In preparation for the potential cow herd sale, the previous grazing season I had tried out grazing around seventy head of steers owned by another cattle farmer, who became a mentor and dear friend, as he genuinely cared that I survived.[4] I grazed them for him and was paid per pound of gain. A bonus was the paychecks came to me monthly. For the first time I was able to cash flow our operation without worrying. The steers gained weight well on our good quality grass, as a result of managed grazing. I became convinced that this "stocker" cattle business—buying a small steer, grazing it in the southern states in winter and on our pastures from spring to fall, and selling a big steer in the undifferentiated commodity market—was my future sustainable farm model. So I decided to go with commodity stocker steers. I figured if I could make a dollar on one steer, why not have one thousand steers?

By the next fall, I presented a business plan to my local community bank for the purchase of several hundred small steers. As a result of that plan—and the collateral Kim and I had on our home—I was granted a substantial bank loan and began to purchase small steers in the panhandle of Florida and place them with a partner rancher, whom we paid a contract fee to graze or feed them.

However, my partner rancher had significant death loss that winter among my cattle due to improperly handled sickness. By the time the remaining head were brought to our pastures that spring, even with significant weight gain here from summer through fall, I was barely able to pay my bank loan with interest back to break even for a year of work and substantial risk.

I was bound and determined to make this approach work. By my reasoning (not Kim's), I just needed more cattle. So I began investigating the possibility of contracting or renting additional land. As it turns out, parcels of pastureland proximate to us were occasionally available for purchase at reasonable prices due to a lack of competition with the cropland and development markets. Additionally, in that I was gaining a reputation for practicing good land stewardship, multiple sellers approached me offering sale prices below market before they listed with a realtor. I could see that the purchases could turn into a fine investment in time, even if my cattle enterprise went south. However, I simply didn't have the money.

My father, the lover of farmland that he was, was moved by the opportunity to purchase reasonably priced farmland, particularly if it could help his son grow a business. He believed that agricultural land would always be a good investment.

Within a couple of years, he sold off his smaller acreage of farmland closer to Madison to purchase two larger pastureland parcels—first 142 acres and then another 320 acres near our home farm (taking advantage of Wisconsin's 1031 like-kind land exchange incentive, which defers capital gains). He also successfully encouraged my brother Bob to assist with the larger of the purchases, which likely wouldn't have taken place otherwise. I am eternally thankful for Bob's valued assistance.

On these two farms, I had one new deep well drilled immediately and eventually another well on the second farm to provide for cattle watering systems. Using a tractor-mounted pipe plow, I buried over twenty-four thousand feet of waterline fanning out from those wells to supply livestock watering tanks at various locations around the pasture systems. In this way, I was able to set up properly managed grazing systems as I had at the home farm, with portable fencing to allow the herd to be moved to fresh grass every few days.

Within a few years, I was purchasing small steers in Alabama and Mississippi as well, for wintering there, or small steers in Wisconsin, Iowa, or Minnesota to be wintered with farmers here who had feedlots to fill. At one point, I had six hundred of these steers and a registered official identification brand—the Cates Family Farm brand "Rocking Double C"—in each of those six states.

I was borrowing *a lot* of money each year to finance this enterprise. The long and short of it was that for many years I had about eight hundred head of cattle in four herds on seven hundred acres of pasture on three farms some twenty miles apart, all under my watch.[5]

And the cattle all had to be growing as rapidly as possible all season, or the thin margins of potential

profit evaporated. So even though our pastures were seeded with clover, I had to apply significant additional purchased nitrogen fertilizer two to three times a growing season to keep the grass growing at a maximum, even in hot late summer weather. And pray for rain, I did, because grass doesn't grow without it, and the fertilizer sits there unused, or worse, is lost (volatilizes) into the atmosphere.

The long and the short of it was that I had more cattle than the land could sustainably handle year in and year out because my flawed business model demanded it. When things were going well, I could breathe. When things turned south, it was a nightmare.

The stocker cattle concept was simple on paper. Buy a small steer, sell a big steer, and pocket the income after expenses; it was a very sound plan, so it seemed. The problem was that with this approach, we were working in the commodity markets. Perhaps selling six hundred steers each fall seems like a lot, but not in the commodity markets. In this undifferentiated market where 99 percent of the cattle in the U.S. are sold, we were not even a flyspeck on the wall, and the commodity markets take no prisoners.

Kim on a horse in the early morning moving a herd of close to four hundred steers down to the corral at the end of the grazing season. We'd sell them to a feedlot owner, and they'd be loaded on semi-truck trailers and hauled to feedlots for "finishing."

Once you buy a small steer, that cost is set. Then you have expenses for interest, land, labor, supplies, and any illness or death losses for a year. I was borrowing hundreds of thousands of dollars every year to run this enterprise. If the price fell when it was time to sell in the fall (at the end of the growing season) when your grass had run out, the only two options were to take the loss or to borrow more money and hold the steer for feeding through the winter and hope with proper management that sickness and death loss are negligible, and the price comes back up. No one gives a hoot whether you survive except you, your wife, and your banker.

I used the futures market for price protection. I bought feeder cattle "put options"—purchased at a "floor" selling price to allow me, at a minimum, to cover my costs of raising the cattle—or futures contracts on the Chicago Mercantile Exchange (CME). I also forward contracted the sale price for my cattle from time to time. The problem was that all of these options come at an additional expense or a locked-in upside that cuts into the potential profit margins. Except for the hit-or-miss year where one could actually "buy low and sell high"—a year I never got to experience—the best I could do was break even after a year of hard work and an inordinate amount of stress. Some folks have learned how to manipulate this world very successfully. I didn't.

The stocker cattle business could have been immensely rewarding if I could've done it well enough. Maybe I wasn't tough enough or streetwise enough. I wasn't willing to be looking over my shoulder, so people were always taking money out of my pocket for unexpected expenses. I had cattle stolen three times in three different states. Twice the thieves were apprehended, but only once did we receive partial compensation. Our cattle would get sick in the south or sick when they were trucked here in the spring.

Using our imaginations and continuing our search for ways to add value and certainty to this fluctuating, risky market, we learned about "cutting horse" competitions. Competitors pay folks like us who own a lot of cattle to use our cattle in their competition events, where a horse and rider work in an arena to keep one steer away from a small bunch. Each bunch gets "worked" a few times, just for a couple of minutes, and then another bunch gets brought in to take their place. The competitors pay the cattle owners by the "head," and they could go through a lot of them in a two-day event!

We did the math. We calculated that any weight loss from short-term stress would be more than compensated for with the promised income. It seemed we could add a guaranteed profit to our cattle in this manner. So we spent the time learning what was required to host a cutting horse show on our farm. We built relationships with competitors and then erected a portable arena with

Our family put on cutting horse competitions at our farm for a number of years in the late 1990s as a hoped-for productive business enterprise. No such luck.

sand bedding right out on our pasture. We worked at this for a few years, but no one had prepared us for the barriers to ending up with more income than expenses.

The competitors were fickle. Either the weather was too hot and too hard on the horses, or it would rain too much, which made the sand sloppy, or it was too dry, and the sand was dusty. The cattle were too "lazy" and wouldn't try hard enough to get away, or the judge wasn't good enough. So we hired well-known, expensive judges from other states, and then they supposedly "played favorites." The upshot of all these scenarios is the competitors wouldn't show up in the numbers necessary to offset the cost of the events. We had all the work and only enough income to break even if we were lucky.

In the face of these many setbacks, nevertheless, I was still hopeful. I would muse to Kim, "If we can only get to one thousand head of stocker cattle, we could make good money."

She would say to me, in exactly these words, "No, that's not going to make any difference."

We'd made a long journey to get where we were—through graduate school, to Saudi Arabia, to building our home and raising our three children—although it often seemed we hadn't come very far, as we had so far to go. We were living hand to mouth, even with two part-time jobs off the farm. During this journey we made good decisions, and we made bad decisions. Hard work alone just wasn't enough. Often, I felt like I was a person groping for a way out of a deep, dark cavern.

And then real tragedy struck our family.

On May 11, 1994, we lost our precious son, Peter Johnson Cates, at seven and a half years old, to the childhood leukemia that had first been detected four years earlier.

After an initial nine-month protocol of chemotherapy followed by three years in remission, the insidious disease returned in March. Fifty days later, after mobilizing all of our resources and those of the University of Wisconsin Children's Hospital, after spending approximately one hundred overnights with Peter in the hospital over the past four years, we had no choice but to let him go. Peter passed peacefully in his mother's arms, surrounded by family in our farm home on a sunny day in May.

An hour before Peter's passing, two semi-loads of steers from Florida arrived at our farm. I had told the man I was working with in the south that my young son was home from fifty days in the hospital, and we were preparing for his inevitable death. Would he please, *please* respect my circumstance and send the cattle the next week? But he wouldn't budge and said he was extremely busy shipping cattle, and that was the day mine had to "go north." Period.

Eric, my brother John, my father, a friend, and I were receiving and treating, "working" the recently arrived steers in the corral as my mother watched. The cattle had to be watered and fed, and some doctored, after twenty hours on a truck. Only Kim and Shannon were in the living room of our home holding, caressing, and tending to Peter. We'd be done in the corral soon enough, but the work had to be done now. Damn it.

When I saw Shannon, not yet twelve years old, strolling down the farm lane alone on the way to the corral, I knew what it meant. My mother joined her hand in hand. I began weeping uncontrollably. I had just lost a son. I couldn't be with him because of those damned cattle and that son of a bitch down in Florida. And yet, I really had no one to blame but myself.

It was a sign, just like all the others over the past years. Still I wasn't yet prepared to listen to the land or to Kim.

Peter brought an everlasting joy to all who knew him. He brings a smile to our faces whenever we think of his strength, humility, and genuine and pure love for living. He'd taught me an immeasurable amount about what is important in life and how, in turn, to live with gratitude and to never, ever forget this: Life *is* precious.

Still, he was gone, and we were bereft. We'd lost him, even after all of that trying.

Peter's ashes are on Peter's Hill above our home, in a forested area we later began to restore back to its original ecotype, historic oak savanna. We continue the restoration work to this day with fire and saw, sowing of native seeds, sweat, and prayer. (More on this restoration in Chapter 7.)

We lost a son and survived. Our marriage grew stronger with time. The bond of care, love, and pure gratitude that our nuclear family held for each other also grew stronger and more precious. We had lived through the ultimate in sadness together, a devastating loss that seemed to have no explanation. Up until this tragedy, there but for the grace of God go I.

We eschewed guilt, blame, and the choice to live our lives in darkness. We emerged believing we had been blessed that Peter was given to us for his time on Earth, and we were richer for it.

Through the grieving process, I came to the place where I believed that nothing would ever be as difficult, tragic, or impossible as losing a child, and nothing was going to get in the way of achieving my dream of building a farm that was to thrive, one that honored Peter in his final resting spot on the hill above our home, with us, watching us, always. *This* was to be my home, my family's home, for as long as I had the strength and breath to go on.

Sometime later, I wrote this letter to my little family:

> My gift to you is a promise eternal
>
> To love and support you in all that you endeavor, in all that you hold dear
>
> To celebrate your commitments and accomplishments
>
> To be there, always, through thick and thin, the urgent and important, the struggles and the joys
>
> I love you forever

CATES FAMILY FARM

Getting It Right— A Commitment to the Land and Water

"Conservation means harmony between men and land. When land does well for its owner, and the owner does well by his land; when both end up better by reason of their partnership, we have conservation. When one or the other grows poorer, we do not."
—Aldo Leopold, *The Farmer as a Conservationist*

"The ecological principle in agriculture is to connect the genius of the place, to fit the farming to the farm."
—Wendell Berry, Interview with Jim Leach, www.neh.gov. (2012)

Our ancient sentinel oak observed how the land and the harried farmer's wise spouse worked together to show him the way. It appears that he is discovering, building lifelong connections with a community of people who care deeply about ethical stewardship of the land and who care for and support the work his family is doing toward these ends.

Life was dark. After losing our precious child, we had several immensely difficult financial years to add to the burden. The sum total of both of our modest paying, part-time off-farm jobs balanced against negative farm income had placed us squarely in the poverty zone, but Kim and I took it on together. We were beaten down but not beaten.

One day she surprised me with a love note:

> Dear Dick, I love you forever. I wish I could make the worries and stress of the farm business disappear. But since I can't, I wanted you to know that I won't disappear, and I so look forward to our years together. Love, Kim

Kim: The farm "mostly" subsidized itself, and our jobs subsidized our living here. Some males think, "You got to get bigger." For Dick, for some reason, running a thousand head of cattle, that just seemed like a good number. Then he would be a legitimate farmer, and people would respect him. To me, anyway, it's just a male thing—I don't know. Otherwise, to him it would look like just another guy who moved out here from Madison to hobby farm, I guess.

He had that dream of "I want to get bigger." But we had a lot of setbacks along the way, and, like my parents, I'm a very frugal person. They were very conservative with their money. That's the way I was raised, and it was very difficult for me to think about borrowing hundreds of thousands of dollars for a farm business that didn't really make any money—except to pay its own bills. So, it was very stressful to me, but I knew he had this dream, and he had this plan.

It wasn't my dream, but I had to let it run its course for a while. It might have worked out, but at some point, I didn't see the light at the end of the day. We had lost money some years and hadn't made much for years. When you borrow money at 8, 9, or 10 percent interest, any profit you make goes to the bank, and you're working for them. We didn't need a lot to live on, but Dick was spending a lot of time on the farm, and yet there wasn't any money going toward our family living expenses. It just went to the bank and farm bills, and some years, we also had carry-over loans to pay off.

It was starting to wear on me. If I brought up my concerns, Dick felt like I was telling him he was a failure, and then he'd get mad—lots of stress—both financial and emotional. He was starting to sell some beef to people on the side, and he was growing that little herd. He seemed to like selling the beef and making contact with customers. I suggested he just do that. Downsize the operation to our home farm and concentrate on doing something well here. Get rid of the huge numbers of cattle that just sold through commodity markets that we had no control over and get rid of the stress. It was hard for him to do that because his family had purchased additional farmland so he could grow the herd. He felt like he was a failure by giving up on it. Fortunately, you can rent farmland to other people, and it all worked out fine. It just took him a while to get there—a lot of tears and stress for both of us, but we got through it.

Then, of course, the added stress was having Peter, our youngest, diagnosed with leukemia in spring 1990. For four years, we were in and out of the hospitals—one hundred nights and many more days spent in the UW Hospital.

Dick had his part-time modest paying job at the university, and my outside job was less, so we weren't bringing in a lot of money by any means, and he was building this farm. When he's working on the farm one could say he's around, but he's not really. He's fixing fence after supper and out in the machine shop at night working on the equipment. There are lots of jobs you can't do with the kids until they get older. I helped out when I could, as there was too much to do, and we couldn't afford to pay anybody to help us.

The amount of time and effort that it took to build the farm, all the fences that had to be put in, rocks picked, thistles cut, and just trying to figure everything out was overwhelming and seemingly was never going to end. Then I remember the few times we decided to entrust the oversight of the many herds of cattle to our summer help or trained neighbors. Dick would sleep for twelve hours a night or more for the few days away! And we were borrowing more and more money for more and more cattle. It became a nightmare.

Finally, he saw the light. He listened, but it took several years. I had to keep saying to him, "It has nothing to do with you being a failure. It's just trying to do the best you can. We bought this farm. Let's do a good job on this farm." Rather than getting bigger and bigger and taking on more and more debt, if we scale the direct market beef, we'll be doing something that looks like it actually has some profit in it for us.

Well, the thing is, Dick is a real people person. He seemed to really enjoy working with these new customers in the direct market business, and he began to see that this type of business seemed like a good thing to do.

Farmer direct marketing cattle as beef was still in its infancy, and that created its own challenges. He'd go to restaurants, and they had never purchased directly from a farmer. In time, things started to change. We got involved in the early start of direct marketing to household customers, restaurants, and stores.

Dick enjoyed building the customer base. From the start, we offered our beef without added growth hormones or antibiotics (within nine months of processing). At first, we were feeding some corn in the pasture. We marketed our product as "free range" or "grain on grass," "leaner," or "natural" beef. Slowly, the idea of grass-fed, that is, "no grain" beef, began to take hold with the public. People seemed interested in this, and it seemed to be taking off. For our grass farm, the timing was perfect. For me, it was getting Dick to just refocus back on this farm—the home farm.

The long and the short of it is that Kim saved the farm and saved me from myself at the same time. In retrospect, I wasn't very different from a lot of young people. I thought the way to be successful was to work as hard as I could and to grow our operation as big and as quickly as I could.

For the second time, I fell victim to the mandate of growth and size as the paramount metrics that define success. The first time had been helping to build the largest dairy farm in the world. Yet, there was so much about this farm that I was building that was not satisfying and certainly not sustainable.

In the commercial beef business, the steers we sold had a price per pound that had nothing to do with how or where they were raised. The buyer didn't care that our grasslands were thriving, our hillsides not eroding, and our riparian stream banks kept the creek water clear and the trout populations healthy. But the world was changing, and so were we.

On a day of infamy, September 11, 2001, I was on the phone with my cattle broker preparing to sell my hundreds of commodity steers via live video auction out of Brush, Colorado, when over the radio in the other room I learned, along with all the world, that the Twin Towers had been hit.

The world changed, and so did I.

These were the last stocker steers I ever sold. Realizing how little control any of us had to change the course of what had just become the most horrific event anyone my generation had ever lived through hit me like a lightning bolt. I was building a business and living a life with just way too many pieces out of my control, and I realized I was setting myself up for my own crash. In a most humble comparison, I could see, symbolically, that my towers were also collapsing. That was it. Kim had been right all along.

I was wounded, but I survived. The commodity markets "broke" when they reopened several days later, rebounded somewhat, and then fell again later that autumn.

Winston Churchill once said, "Failure is not fatal; it is the courage to continue that counts." My edited version of that truth has long been, "Failure after failure is not fatal 'if' somehow one can muster the same enthusiasm to try again, but differently." There is no substitute for understanding, wisdom, and patience.

I still believed, as I stated earlier, that our little farm *could* compete, and I truly believed it was worth saving. I believed that if we were failing, it *should* mean something to our greater society. However, that moral judgment was not going to save us. That was up to me.

So I started again with what we had learned and what we had done right. Chasing growth in the commodity marketplace had meant facing factors over which I had little control. As we learned the hard way, these markets took no prisoners. Taking unnecessary unknowns out of our farming practices and business approach seemed to be where sustainability and eventual profitability could emerge. It had to.

Using both science and our imagination, we had developed a productive grass farm. Although we were struggling to figure out the business end, we were starting to get noticed for our soil and water conservation work. We received formal recognition at the local and state levels.[1] These votes of appreciation were very meaningful for our family.

The honors began to validate our methods. They meant that even though we had cattle along Lowery Creek, a sensitive riparian area, our practices were keeping soil and nutrients in place and protecting and restoring the creek's water quality.

However, it was a few years later that Nina Leopold Bradley, Aldo's oldest daughter and my friend, helped me to appreciate and internalize the journey we had embarked upon. Nina's husband, Charley, friend and mentor, was now suffering from severe dementia. Sadly, I had missed the opportunity to ever have him back to our farm. Nina and I often exchanged written notes since the years I served as a Leopold fellow (1981–82). Mine were about our farm progress, and hers were always of keen observations of the seasonal changes of the prairie flowers, bird song, or garden abundance. Her notes were so gracious and uplifting, typical of the warm and loving person that she was. I still can't rectify why I let so many years go by, but I finally grasped that the window of opportunity for Nina to ever visit here again was closing.

So, in the lead-up to one of the field events I was asked to conduct to share our managed grazing approach with a growing and eclectic number of interested folks, I called Nina to ask if she might be willing to try to attend. Remarkably, she was available and wanted to make the trip. She was in her late eighties, and I knew travel from her home on the Leopold Memorial Reserve outside of Baraboo, a ninety-minute drive, would be dependent on the availability of her gracious escort and driver, but thankfully for my family and me, she also made the commitment.

The day of the event was a beautiful June afternoon, and, in my mind, the cattle and the grass looked exceptionally good. My heart skipped a beat when Nina arrived at our farm in time to join the tour. All in attendance greeted her warmly. Her presence was, indeed, a gift for us all.

Following the tour, we were able to capture the day together in this photograph. In a moment that will never fade, Nina gathered Kim, Eric, and me and passed on a blessing that confirmed our lives' work here. She told us that her "father would be proud."[2]

Nina Leopold Bradley visits the Cates farm, early 2000s. Photo by one of the field day attendees.

As we continued our efforts, we began discovering that some people—those who eat beef or may want to again—did care. Some had made the choice that they didn't want all meat raised in feedlots and shipped through stockyards. Many wanted meat raised on land that was cared for and utilized the way land had been used to sustain animals and humans for thousands of years.

They also wanted to get their food from farm families they could get to know and trust. Incredibly, we also discovered they would pay my family the full retail value of the meat product simply to purchase directly from us. Wow.

I finally began to grasp the notion that if we as farmers don't stake out the value we need for the products that leave through our farm gate, then in a capitalist society, someone else gladly will.

We can wait until the political process and the powers that be decide to reward us, or we can establish our own model of trade where it happens immediately, a win-win for the farmer and the consumers who share our values.

Once I really understood how much of the profit from producing food is given away by those of us who grow it, I decided I wanted to take back a portion. I recognized that I had a choice. I could advocate and wait until policy change demanded that a bigger portion of the food dollar remain with the farmer, or I could just figure out how to take charge and reclaim some of it myself.

Although I have worked as an engaged citizen in agricultural and food policy for the past thirty years—in public elected capacities and appointed boards of directors—I clearly understood that if I wanted to save my business any time soon, I needed to take action *now*. I pledged to continue my work in policy arenas over the long haul. For now, though, it was up to my imagination and initiative to forge the way.

We realized there was an opportunity in the marketplace for producing a product that consumers wanted, a product with our name on it that could secure us a living wage. We had to grow carefully from there. I wrote out these basic principles that I believed were paramount to the success of our direct market business:

- Relatively inexpensive high-quality feed (mostly pasture and some grass hay each year)
- High-quality livestock
- Vertical integration—production, warehousing, marketing, delivery; only processing is outsourced
- Building partnerships with honest and reliable individuals who have similar goals
- Working our butts off for a long time

We understood that marketing our products and our values of healthy and delicious food, clean water, aesthetics, and love of the land and place would be best accomplished through a long-term dialogue with our customers and the public. We were engaged in "relationship marketing," a term I had not encountered until many years into this journey. As we built relationships, we built our business.

Over time, we have recognized that perseverance, patience, integrity, respect, and a sense of humor are virtues for anyone who wants to build their own direct market agricultural business, or any solid business for that matter. This is not a get-rich-quick scheme or a series of business deals. Much better, it's a solid, enjoyable approach to making a living on a farm or ranch in the livestock business.

We began to build relationships with potential customers in our area, really anyone who'd show a flicker of interest in our beef and our story—families; retail store owners, managers, floor clerks, and customers; and restaurant owners, chefs, and their customers.

Slowly our customers grew in number, and once they had tried our food, they almost always ordered again. I delivered fifty-pound boxes, often two at a time, through the back doors of stores and restaurants, sometimes up a flight of stairs on the fire escape or down the cramped stairwells of so many households to a chest freezer in the basement. Through sincere commitment and engagement, customer relationships became friendships that enriched all our lives. This brought my family and me such joy and does so to this day.[3]

Following my 9/11 epiphany, we had moved completely away from the commodity markets and into a robust direct marketing business. We were even able to dictate our price in some markets. The world had grown bright again as we discovered we could have more control of our destiny. The horrific strain and stress of working hard all year long only to be taken prisoner by the commodity markets once our products left the farm gate was behind us.

My best friend, Kim, had seen the light way ahead of me, up and around all the bends on the proverbial road of hard knocks. I could and should have learned earlier to pay attention and listen to her. (See Appendix I—Principles of a Direct Market Grass-Fed Beef Business)

At the same time, a significant complementary enterprise opportunity developed for us as we moved away from ownership of cattle targeted for commodity markets. Because we had freed up pasture acreage by reducing the size of our herd, we could take on the grazing management, or contract grazing of other farmers' cattle. In Wisconsin, these cattle are usually dairy heifers or beef steers. Contract grazing became our farm's second business enterprise, and it was truly productive.

Not having to own the cattle meant no prodigious bank loan payable at the end of the year, come hell or high water, which made us very happy. Contracts were written so the cattle owner paid a portion of the management fee each month throughout the grazing season. This is a paycheck, if you will, a dependable source of income each month to assist with farm cash flow. Over the years, we have had approximately twenty contracts with six different cattle owners. Most were very successful for the owners as well as our family.[4] With time and perseverance, we had begun to find our way to a business model of modest but sufficient scale, with a balance that worked for the land, our family, and a growing community of customers and partners. We were paying attention and finally getting it right. Then, one day the phone rang.

Yes, the lure of rapid growth and potential "loss of control" came knocking on our door once again. This time it was a close friend who had much experience in the entrepreneurial world, developing businesses from scratch and scaling them successfully.

I convinced Kim to at least listen to our friend's proposal. The plan involved developing our own slaughtering/processing facility along with a warehouse for cold storage of our beef, and docks for semi-trucks to load and initiate deliveries. It involved employees performing all the daily year-round tasks, staff keeping track of everything, and a board of directors making decisions. It also involved, and would depend on, other farmers and their cattle raised to our specifications, as our regional markets would require a continuous supply. The best part about the hook as it was pitched to us, was the lure—the promise—of big money for us. We briefly contemplated.

Would our farm make a bigger difference in the arc of history if we pursued scale? Would I feel that I had come closer to fulfilling my sense of destiny and purpose in life? Would I have felt more blessed by a god, any god?

While it is not appropriate or useful for me to moralize on the subject of scale, every farmer and farm family must answer the question of scale for themselves. I asked myself the following questions: What are we really good at? If we add livestock or focus on a single crop or two, could we still be able and committed to keeping our land healthy and regenerating over the longer term? What is our competitive strength in the marketplace, and will we lose control of this unique gift with scale? And I asked: What is it we really love to do, and why not pursue it with passion?!

It took Kim about one heartbeat to say, "No," and perhaps just two beats for me to say, "Ditto." A short time later, a rancher we knew who had taken the giant leap in scale was fired by his own board of directors. My heart bled for him, but his fate reinforced our experience and concerns that a business can change in unpredictable manners when it gets too big, and one can lose control. More money, maybe. More control and satisfaction, maybe not. Kim and I were going to hold.

Over time, we began to experience the joy of community that was building around our farming choices. Community is an important part of sustainability. Our interest in sharing our conservation practices with other farmers and the public, as well as the increasing number of

Visitors come to the farm to learn about grass-fed beef production, streambank protection, heritage brook trout, and soil and water conservation. Top left photo by Barb Barzen. Top right photo by River Valley High School.

customers in the direct market business, meant our farm began to be connected to an ever-growing community.

Over the decades, the eclectic diversity of folks who have engaged in our farm is overwhelming. We have had agriculture, biology, conservation, ecology, environmental, and ethics youth and university students and interns. We have hosted farmer groups from across Wisconsin, the U.S., and the globe, including Argentina, Australia, Azerbaijan, Brazil, Cambodia, China, Columbia, El Salvador, Ethiopia, France, Ghana, Ireland, Japan, Kazakhstan, Mexico, New Zealand, Nicaragua, and South Africa.

On the farm we have engaged conservation and grassland research scientists, foresters, oak savanna ecologists, prescribed burn crews, inner-city youth, conservation educators and writers, ag reporters and film crews, Culver's and Harley Davidson and Duluth Trading Company commercial crews, food groups and many, many beef customers.

Birders, game and mushroom hunters, fishermen and women, and fish biologists are frequent visitors.

Our barn has been the chosen venue for dances and weddings for family and friends, and we have hosted annual meetings for nonprofit organizations and graduation parties. The Airstream Club International planned a tour here recently, and a few years back a horse-drawn Conestoga wagon crossing Wisconsin stopped here when one of the horses threw a shoe near our farm. Why not?

Governors, senators, agriculture secretaries, and other political and policy representatives have walked our pastures, and we are just another farm the President of the United States of America hasn't visited, but he almost did. (For a humorous account of this non-visit, see Appendix II—A President "Almost" Stops By).

L'Etoile Restaurant, Madison, staff visit. Both photos by Kim Cates.

Dick (the farmer) grilling Cates grass-fed beef for L'Etoile chefs (culinary and cooking experts).

As I noted, all our customers are from the area, but we did have a customer in the Chicago area for a number of years, a beautiful black Labrador who won show prizes. He had a special needs diet. His owner said he was only allowed to eat—or, in our case, gnaw on—"natural" products. Our beef bones from cattle that had not been treated with antibiotics or added growth hormones qualified as far as the owner was concerned. So every couple of months, she and her Labrador would drive north together and fill large coolers with the bones we had saved for them. This went on for a decade or so, until one day the dear customer, now aged, passed on. I still miss this wonderful customer and his owner.

We particularly enjoy it when staff from the grocery stores or chefs from the restaurants who use our beef spend time on the farm. I'll never forget the day I acted as chef, cooking our ground beef burgers on the grill for the team of professional chefs from L'Etoile Restaurant in Madison, one of the fanciest white tablecloth gourmet eateries anywhere. (This is a restaurant I had almost never entered through the front door, except for Kim's and my twenty-fifth wedding anniversary.) A photo was taken of me at the grill, and every time I ever look at it, even decades later, the same question pops into my mind: *What's wrong with this picture?*

The community we were able to build early on, through what I learned was "relationship marketing," worked so well we only strayed from the approach once. We engaged a marketing agency in Madison and explained our business in the hope they would open a whole new world of clientele for us. After all, they were the professionals. They happened to be working with a client that sold appliances and came up with the idea to offer freezers from their client with a gift of Cates Family Farm beef included. If we could offer our beef at a 50 percent discount (which was well below our cost of production), the deal would proceed. Thinking of the promotional value we would receive at no extra charge, the proposal sounded okay to us, so we signed the papers.

When it came time to produce the television commercial to set up this exceptional opportunity for anyone who may be contemplating a new freezer, the client representatives, marketing folks, the film crew, and a thin, young blonde woman referred to as "the personality" converged on the farm. The agency folks thought it would be unique and catchy if the crew could film the personality saying her lines to promote the deal on horseback as she rode down our farm lane. It seemed like a good idea, but the personality had never ridden a horse. Even though it was just going to be a proverbial walk in the park, she was scared s******s. After much ado, it was decided that Kim—also a thin, young blonde woman, but one who loved riding her horse—should ride down the lane while the personality read the script off-camera. It worked!

The following week, the commercials started to run. The appliance company's name was all over the screen, and sure enough, freezer buyers would get free beef. However, there was no meaningful mention of the Cates Family Farm or a conveniently placed phone number, so the many new potential customers might contact us in the future (no internet search engines yet). Darn.

Nonetheless, it was fun to watch Kim ride down the farm lane over and over again on the TV screen, and we gave away a lot of beef at a loss. So much for mass media marketing.

As another illustration of experiencing the joy of community, I need to tell you more about the folks who hunt on our land. As I have made clear previously, when Kim and I came back to the farm with our three young kids and took over the task of not just managing what was in place, but building a business, home, and life on the farm, we had a lot of work to do.

So I will never forget a particular moment in the early autumn of 1987. I was digging post holes for a corral fence up by the barn near the farmhouse. Everywhere I looked there was more work to do—a lifetime of work, it seemed. I recall the pungent odor of septic waste wafting across the pasture, emanating from a crack in our sewage effluent pipe resulting from truck and tractor ruts punched deep in the springs-moisten mud, just another inconvenience that *needed* our attention.

Some fellows drove up the lane out of nowhere, parked their truck, and walked over to me. After cordial but brief hellos were exchanged, one of the fellows asked, "Gee, do you have any space for hunting?"

I looked at these five burly working men, who I had just learned hailed from over near Milwaukee, ten years or more younger than me, and I looked around again at all the work that lay ahead of me. I formulated an offer right then and there: "You bet, but the deal is you all work a day with me, and you get to hunt one season." As they thought it over, I counted out the workdays in my mind. They wanted to bow hunt for deer; okay, that's five workdays. They also wanted to gun hunt for deer; that's five more workdays this fall. And they wanted to turkey hunt in the spring; that's another five workdays! Within a moment, they agreed to the deal, and we shook on it. I was so excited I could have kissed them all. This group of hunters replaced the group that "came with the farm."

They came back the following weekend, and we busted butt together, picking rocks and pulling old barbed wire fences. When we reached the agreed-upon end of the workday, they all looked around at me, and one of them asked me with exuberance and a palpable expression of hope, "Well, did we get everything done? We're pooped!"

I said, "Not yet." Within a few years the group of five had added a few more and then doubled again.

Working alongside these young men in the early years, I got to be known as the cheerful coach who enthusiastically offered encouragements of "good job" or "attaboy," just like my father used to do for us kids while we were growing up. Of course, my encouraging words stuck in our hunters' craw. They still get bantered around for the fun of it to this day.

After thirty-eight-plus years, those same gentlemen are here every spring and fall. They have come back year after year and have picked rocks, planted trees, painted the barn and stained our house, re-roofed the barn and our home, tuck-pointed building foundations and chimneys, torn down old fence and built new fence, bucked up fallen trees, cut and stacked cords and cords of firewood, cleaned up the pasture after flood events, helped with cattle work, removed collapsed old outbuildings, operated backhoes, tractors and mowers, and maintained our back-up heating/

cooling systems. One year they treated overhead wood cross beams at the corral with waste oil, which dripped all over them. They claimed this was the worst job, until they had to hand-cut prickly and thorny bushes in the oak savanna.

For years when they showed up for work and asked what jobs I had lined up for them, I'd say, "Well, today we're going to move the barn ..." They'd reply, "How far?" After a while, they started to bring along their kids—boys and girls, who are now grown adults—to work and to hunt. They run mentored youth hunts here some years, preparing the next generation. Sometimes they bring their friends, even those who don't hunt. They have all developed such a love for this place, and they are all always pooped by the end of each and every workday.

They attended my father's funeral, and they keep an eye on the farm if we're gone. (Dad really connected with these hardworking folks who loved the land. And they loved him right back. He'd often tease them with challenges such as, "You've been here long enough; haven't you found anything I may have lost yet?!")

It is the land that connects us all. One of the fellows first hunted here when he was twelve years old, and he holds those days precious in his memory. He lost his father tragically soon after. I was with this gentleman, my friend, recently when he pointed out a red-tailed hawk perched on a tree branch not far in the distance, its silhouette sharp against the clear blue sky. The hawk took flight and was soon soaring high over our heads, free. My now-grown friend shed a tear. He told me, "Through the years, I see a hawk every time I arrive here at the farm. I know it's a sign. The hawk is the keeper of my father's spirit. I know he has, indeed, made it to the other side, and he is free. There is nowhere else in my life I have as close a connection to my father. He is here, and I am with him. I am so thankful."

These individuals still don't own any land themselves, but this land has allowed them to create a place that feels like home. It has allowed all of us to build a relationship, a community that is like family. As Leopold wrote, "Land yields a cultural harvest." These good folks are also stewards of this place, and they care deeply for this land. It is the richest kind of relationship I could ever have imagined, and a dollar has never been exchanged.

We have also been busy growing, through restoration work, another kind of community here—an oak savanna.

Standing under the canopy of our solitary sentinel oak near the bank of Lowery Creek, you can take in the moving cattle across the grassland. Gazing upslope, you see heavily wooded hillsides with oak forest, a result of the long cessation of natural or human-induced fire on the landscape.

Over the years, we conducted multiple timber harvests and protected all of our wooded land from grazing. Eventually, we wanted to learn more about the notion of a "sustainably managed forest" and what that entailed. So in the summer of 2002, we reached out to folks with this expertise and asked them to walk the forest with us.

We expected that we would learn more about managing the forest for timber. However, while we walked, they informed us, with much excitement, that the large old stand of bur oak above our home on top of Peter's Hill, where his ashes are safeguarded, actually harbored several remnant oak savanna indicator species on the forest floor, including Pennsylvania sedge, prairie violet, Robin's plantain, azure aster, showy tick trefoil, sideoats grama, bee balm, pussy toes, and more.[5]

Our remarkable hunters work for the harvest.

As noted earlier, oak savanna is today one of the rarest ecotypes on planet Earth. There remains, however, a small, miniscule acreage in our Driftless Area that is considered "restorable." Here on the forest floor of our farm is a fifteen-acre patch above our farmhouse where these remnant oak savanna indicator species are still present.

What did this mean? Well, it meant it might be possible to restore this oak savanna remnant if we were willing to commit a lifetime to the work and were patient enough to attempt it.

If more sunlight was allowed to pass through the forest canopy to the soil surface through the physical removal of some of the trees, by fire, physical or chemical brush control, and managed grazing, eventually these remnant species could recover, become more vigorous, and multiply.

This was the only such location on our several hundred acres of oak forest. Certainly, it had never been plowed. It includes the flanks and top of a ridge with very thin soil, where there are beautiful limestone outcroppings on the hill slopes. Apparently, domestic livestock never grazed it too hard or too long, likely owing to its rugged access and lack of proximity to a water source. For whatever fortuitous reasons, we felt we had a gem in the rough.

On the surface, this is a story motivated by a desire for habitat restoration, especially for the iconic migratory red-headed woodpecker. It is also a story about honoring *all* who came before us. Poignantly, it is about honoring Peter's and eventually other beloved family members' eternal place of rest and a celebration of the sacred place where Eric and his bride, Kiley, exchanged their marriage vows.

Ultimately, this is a tale motivated by wonder and awe.

Oak savanna is an ecosystem that is driven by disturbance, mainly fire and intermittent grazing. In the absence of disturbance, oak savanna transitions to an oak-hickory forest. Oak-hickory forests thrive as a result of the thirty-five-plus inches of annual precipitation that falls here in the southern Driftless Area. Typically, bur oak and other species of the white oak group were able to withstand the prairie fires because of their thick, cork-like bark. Native grass and forbs species are not only fire tolerant, but they are fire dependent. The European-introduced exotic flora that

is now common here cannot successfully compete in a fire regime because it is not fire tolerant. With the cessation of annual prairie fires after the European colonists moved in, the introduced exotics overcame the native "fire-dependent" species.

Kim and I are agriculturists by life experience, training, and practice. We have never thought of our skill set as also being those of landscape restorationists. In time, I have come to realize restoration is exactly what we had been doing on our grasslands all along as we set out to develop, learn from, and mature our managed grazing overlay on the landscape. After all, this grazing approach, one of movement dictated by the needs of the grass, was a biomimicry of native herbivores, or grazers, on the grasslands of the world.

I came to understand that the restoration of our grasslands was the basis of our business. If whatever we tried didn't pay off, however, we sure couldn't keep it up for long.

Restoration of our oak savanna would be different. There simply would be no "profit" in the market sense, and in setting about a lifetime of work restoring an oak savanna, none at all. Yet the excitement we felt about taking on this restoration effort was palpable.

Prescribed burning in the oak savanna restoration.

So we began this journey on a path not yet traveled. This process of bringing back an oak savanna through biomimicry became yet one more effort that engendered a rich community, one of teachers, learners, and indigenous flora and fauna. Some twenty years on—nine prescribed burns, hundreds of non-savanna trees felled, brush hand-cut and mowed, native prairie grass and forbs seeded—we are still at the work today.

And our loved ones remain. I know they are present as we share a quiet moment together on each visit.

(See Appendix III—Our Oak Savanna Restoration: A Journey of Wonder and Awe, for an overview of the work that has been accomplished and the restoration progress to date.)

Early in the past decade, our family began to join with neighbors to discuss how we might better learn from each other about various conservation practices, but also with the idea of sharing our work with other farmers and the interested public located anywhere.

One group of neighbors up and down the Lowery Creek watershed is now formally known as the Lowery Creek Watershed Initiative.[6] A second group in which we participate, broader in scope with farmers across several watersheds in our county, is the Iowa County Uplands Watershed Project.

Both coalitions are focused on raising the bar on conservation innovation and regenerative agriculture practices. Our farmer members share a mutual love for our landscape, its history, culture, and beauty. We all want to be a part of stewarding this landscape for the coming generations, the people who are currently or will soon be sitting in the managers' seats of our farms. (The work and progress of the Lowery Creek Watershed Initiative is celebrated in Chapter 10.)

Stepping back in time, I want to revisit the year 2013. In early July, I looked out across the mostly thistle-less pastures, stream banks, and fencerows and thought, *I think we've made progress.* Taking in the lush grassland, I recall my lifetime war on the plumeless thistle that I began in 1988 and stayed fully engaged in for twenty-five years, mowing and wearing out hand scythes and putting on so many miles running fences in my soccer shoes. I don't deny this was an obsession for me. I recall one evening at the start of another hand-cut thistle season, after several hours of battle and just before sundown, I must have seen my effort as a "holy one," because I sat down and wrote this poem:

> Ode to the Thistle-Slayer
>
> As I sat quietly, vanquished from the good fight to kill a thistle and allow the grass to breathe once again, I was witness to a growing presence of fog sweeping down from the hilltops to the south and sliding down the draw, coming to rest upon our South Hay pasture, just where I had been working, "singing" heads from thistles with the stout hand scythe, and was now sitting to rest.
>
> The unanticipated visitor slowed its movement northward as it spilled out of the forest onto the open grass meadow and then in an instant swelled in height and puffed wide like a proud horse and rider bearing a message from the grassland gods, to say, "We honor the fine work you have done, Son; you do us proud: Long live you mortal Thistle Slayer!"
>
> And as quickly as the mist had appeared and spoken, as if its purpose had been served, it began to melt into the grassy meadow, the fresh moisture now a gift to enriching the grass, ensuring more rich grass, always the grass first.

All these years later, I can smile with pride because (with tongue planted firmly in my cheek) my heroic battle has continued to pay off.

Also in 2013, our family was selected to receive Wisconsin's Leopold Conservation Award for our longtime stewardship work to protect Lowery Creek. The recognition is offered annually by the Sand County Foundation, a nonprofit organization with a nationwide reach whose mission is to assist and celebrate private working land conservation.[7]

Our son, Eric, who was twenty-eight at the time, and I worked on the lengthy application, supporting documents, and nominations from the Iowa County Land Conservation Committee and University of Wisconsin Extension for several months together in the evenings. He was with me from beginning to end. Eric and all of my family earned this recognition through their years of dedication to this land. It is truly the most meaningful endorsement of our work in my lifetime, and it has been all I could have ever imagined—a respected recognition that has assisted us in communicating the imperative of conservation and a land ethic more effectively.

The recognition came with a significant monetary gift. My family chose to contribute much of the monetary award in the form of ongoing support for an Iowa County middle school annual Conservation Day and to fund a scholarship to a River Valley School District graduate who would be pursuing post-secondary agricultural training. Applicants for our scholarship must write a five hundred-word personal statement addressing "Why soil and water conservation is imperative for the sustainability of our agriculture, and indeed, our culture itself." (See Sidebar: A Perennialized Landscape Builds Resilience—One of Nature's Ultimate Goals)

A Perennialized Landscape Builds Resilience—One of Nature's Ultimate Goals

Let's look at some of the impacts of climate change. What did we do on the Fourth of July a few years ago? Independence Day is a holiday, right? Not for us and other local farmers. We had chores to do related to yet another flood. Lowery Creek lets us know if it rains too much. It jumps its banks and floods our pastureland, often taking lots of our cross fences with it. I put all the flood events in my calendar. The reality is that no matter how many floods occur in any region, they are less intense and much less erosive on perennialized landscapes.

I recall only a few floods from my younger days on the farm. The old-timers tell me there was a "five hundred-year flood" back in the 1950s. I remember a flood in the mid-1980s, and we had a really big flood May 31–June 1, 2000, a result of about nine inches of rain in five days. That one took down a perimeter fence where Lowery Creek leaves our property, and two hundred head of our cattle stood in the middle of the county highway eyeing our neighbor's submerged and muddy cornfield two rods distant (thirty-three feet), just the width of the highway right-of-way. The only thing that saved the corn from an onslaught of eight hundred hooves was the curious yellow line—the bovines were afraid to cross it!

We had three major floods in 2007 and 2008. In 2017, 2018, and 2019, we had five flood events, and three were significant. Toward the end of June and first days of July 2024 we had ten-plus inches of rain and Lowery Creek flooded twice. We've also had numerous events through the years where the stream channel was full to the brim—"almost floods" I call them. They keep me up at night, even if they end up being false alarms. Cattle will walk out of fear, hunger, or simply pure curiosity to the next county when there is suddenly no fence keeping them where they belong.

We've learned a lot. We now place some of our fences higher above the stream channel with danglers hanging down to discourage cattle from walking underneath in normal stream flow. We've learned how to make our fences so that they release and pull up above the flood level, or so a portion can break away as the high rushing water catches and carries it away, leaving the balance of the fence intact.

More significantly, we've learned to never graze the grass down short, with the goal of always leaving four to six inches of residual after each grazing event. Why? Living plant material deflects and cushions raindrop impact and then captures the rainwater long enough to allow it to soak into the soil instead of running off. As a result of climate change, Lowery Creek will likely flood more often in the future, but because of our learned and adapted management, flood severity will be mitigated.

I believe that climate change will require all of us in agriculture, as well as those who manage land for other uses, to discover ways to become more resilient or to suffer the consequences if we do not.

If there is a bright spot to more frequent floods, it's when any of the few remaining trees along the stream fall over or lose branches, they get scoured out more frequently. This results in far less cleanup after each event than it did when floods were less frequent. I guess you have to look for a silver lining in everything in life.

The takeaway: Runoff water from a perennialized landscape is clear. This is exactly what the water of our portion of Lowery Creek looks like a day or so after a flood.

If climate change results in larger and more frequent flooding, as seems to be the trend, there will surely be a significant increase in the expense to the public when soil and nutrients leave agricultural landscapes and end up in private wells, the waters of our streams and rivers, and ultimately in the Gulf of Mexico.

Fortunately, there is a way to mitigate soil and nutrient losses and resultant costs: regenerative agriculture. (See Appendix VI—Frequently Asked Questions About Our Managed Grazing Approach to Regenerative Agriculture and a Land Ethic)

Top left: From our farmhouse, Lowery Creek tributary at flood stage. Bottom left: The day after (2018). Above: My brother John and Eric pile a wagon with flood debris from our pasture (2017).

My mother passed in 2013 after years of suffering from debilitating Alzheimer's disease. I had lost my father to pneumonia just two years earlier. They were the centering force and inspiration of my life. Their ash remains were added next to their grandson Peter's, here in the soil, on this land. I miss them all terribly and continue to seek their counsel. I count my blessings every waking day for all they taught us and hold them in my heart.[8]

In the autumn of that year, we spotted several red-headed woodpeckers in the oak savanna restoration area on Peter's Hill. We were with the Sand County Foundation film crew participating in their Leopold Conservation Award outreach video when one of the crew pointed toward a red flash. I stopped in my tracks, trained my eyes, and experienced a deep sensation of unadulterated joy. After a decade of restoration work on our oak savanna, hoping to be rewarded someday with red-headed woodpecker visitors, we finally glimpsed our first.

It was, indeed, a magical moment, one of grateful reward for Kim and me, and I know Father and Mother were smiling.

Our oak savanna restoration area. Oak forest has transitioned to an oak woodland, on its way back to savanna.

Red-headed woodpecker. Photo by Don Greenwood.

And More—A Commitment to the Lovely Animals with Whom We Share Our Lives

"It is important that our relationship with farm animals is reciprocal. We owe animals a decent life and a painless death."

—Dr. Temple Grandin, College of Agricultural Sciences, Colorado State University

"Each person, human or no, is bound to every other in a reciprocal relationship. Just as all beings have a duty to me, I have a duty to them. If an animal gives its life to feed me, I am in turn bound to support its life. If I receive a stream's gift of pure water, then I am responsible for returning a gift in kind. An integral part of a human's education is to know those duties and how to perform them."

—Robin Wall Kimmerer, *Braiding Sweetgrass: Indigenous Wisdom, Scientific Knowledge, and the Teachings of Plants*

This book is filled with stories of the land and her lessons, on how to listen, of seeking a land ethic. Stories of the people who have learned from those lessons and know the importance of passing what has been learned on to the next generation. This chapter is devoted to stories of the lovely animals with whom we share our lives and this place. These humble creatures have humbled us as they have shaped our sense of joy living with them.

Folks often ask us, "How can you raise the animals you are going to eat?"

My response is always: "Respectfully, with gratitude, and reciprocity." In this regard, I am Robin Wall Kimmerer's disciple.

But first, I want to acknowledge that some of you good folks reading this have your own deeply personal reasons why you do not and will not consume animals or use animal products in any manner. I completely respect your decision. There is nothing more sacred to me than personal freedom when it comes to decisions of the heart. Amen.

As members of the genus species *Homo sapiens*, we are by physiology heterotrophs. That is, we are only able to derive life from the oxidation of long-chain organic carbon molecules, such as sugars, starch, and protein.

As Kimmerer muses in her beautiful book, *Braiding Sweetgrass* (2013), "Sometimes I wish I could photosynthesize [that is, had the remarkable and unique capability of a plant, an autotroph] so that just by being ... I could be doing the work of the world while standing silently in the sun," consuming inorganic carbon as carbon dioxide and water while "turning sun into sugar, spinning straw into gold" and exhaling the breath of our life, oxygen.

But we can't. The reality of life for heterotrophs is that to live, we are required to consume—take a life, actually many lives in our own lifetime. Those non-human lives are plants or animals, and usually both.

There is another side to this coin. The lovely, domesticated farm animals we live with and manage for our livelihood would not have a life if it weren't for our family. They are, after all, domesticated.

Natasha Daly, in her article "Domesticated Animals, Explained" (2019) in *National Geographic* wrote, "Domesticated animals are animals that have been selectively bred and genetically adapted over generations to live alongside humans. They are genetically distinct from their wild ancestors or cousins."[1]

The more important questions from my point of view are: What is expected of my family and me in return? What are our responsibilities in this relationship? Is this a devil's bargain or a relationship based on respect, gratitude, and reciprocity?

Here, again, Kimmerer's voice resonates with me: "How do we consume in a way that does justice to the lives we take?" She shares her answer to this important question. "The indigenous canon of principles and practices that govern the exchange of life for life is known as the Honorable Harvest."

Among the acts of gratitude that could be included, several speak to my family and me as they relate to raising and harvesting our lovely animals: "Know the ways of the ones who take care of you, so that you may take care of them. Be accountable as the one who comes asking for life. Harvest in a way that minimizes harm (fear and pain). Use respectfully. Never waste what you have taken. Share. Give thanks for what you have been given. Give a gift, in reciprocity, for what you have been given. Sustain the ones who sustain you, and the Earth will last forever."

This canon begins with respect and gratitude and moves to reciprocity, which requires that we act.

My family does this through a devotion to kindness and caring. Good quality and adequate quantity of feed produced in a regenerative grass-based agricultural system to optimize carbon sequestration in an environment that allows animals to perform all their necessary daily activities, and a life free from stress and fear. Call this animal welfare, but also call it an Honorable Harvest. (See Appendix IV—The Methane Yoke of Burden Has Been Incorrectly—and Unfairly—Placed on Our Domestic Livestock)

Thanks to reciprocal relationships, our animals support the lives of our family, as well as so many caring individuals across southern Wisconsin.[2] As I have watched and tended to our lovely animals, day after day, year after year, for many decades, I know they have a good life here with us. I circle back to respect and gratitude.

People frequently ask us, "What kind of cattle do you raise?" From the beginning, the basis of our business has been Angus steers, a breed well known in Wisconsin—black in color, originally from Aberdeen in northeastern Scotland. For three decades, we have purchased Angus calves from the same family just a few miles from our farm.[3]

A more unusual part of our cattle herd is that we also raise Jersey steers. They are a British breed of smaller dairy cattle, usually light to medium brown in color, originally from the Island of Jersey in the British Channel Islands.[4]

Over time, we have had more than a few urban visitors to the farm who, in their own aha moment, have queried us if our black and tan cow herd produces chocolate milk. A fair question, I suppose ... if they were actually cows, not steers. Unfortunately, except perhaps when one of us is in a feisty mood, the answer always disappoints.

We raise Jerseys for many reasons. We buy these six-month-old calves from Jersey dairy farmers. They mix well with the Angus and help keep them nice and quiet in the herd. They do exceptionally well on pasture. They marble (deposit a modest amount of intramuscular fat) on a high grass-clover forage diet with no grain supplement required. They turn grass into lean meat protein more slowly than the Angus, but they do it dependably and do it well.

Jerseys have true personalities. We had not anticipated the added joy of having "cattle with character" in our herd. When we open a gate to a new pasture, they straighten their tails, kick up their heels, and hop and snort on their way to the new grass. A few will surely stop by to lick the windows of the pasture vehicle. And if we happen to leave a door or tailgate open, they are not shy about checking out the toolboxes, poly wire fence rolls, and any molasses in wintertime within reach of their long tongues.

As I have noted, our farm has lots of visitors, and the Jerseys are always a hit. I hate to say it, but it's not so much what I share with our guests; it's the Jerseys that our visitors remember long after they leave the farm.

Over time, everyone in our family concluded that it was pure joy to have these really colorful, friendly Jerseys on the farm. We raise them right alongside our Angus steers and collect humorous stories along the way.

The herd is in the neighbor's corn! None of our family will ever forget the Saturday evening one September when we all went to Spring Green for supper. We enjoyed our evening out, but when we returned after dark, our car headlights illuminated what appeared to be cattle manure on the gravel farm lane. As soon as we had driven over and through it, we became more than certain.

We hit the brakes, backed out of the lane, and headed south along our county road, following the line of cow pies. About a mile away, we saw the lights of a truck heading slowly our way. As we drew closer, we could hear the driver, a friend and neighbor dairy farmer, calling cattle out his pickup truck window, "Come girls. Come girls!" This is how many dairy farmers call their female cows. As we came upon him, he just smiled and waved and kept right on toward our farm, with a herd of *our* cattle following behind his truck, bellowing for a meal.

In the time it took our herd of cattle to walk a slow mile, we were back on our lane, and we shut the gate to the highway. Home safe, we thought with relief. But then our head count indicated about a third of the herd was still missing. Damn. A quick check of the pasture they had been on when we went to town came up empty, and they obviously weren't on the road. Where could they be? Damn, again. Likely still in the neighbor's cornfield!

Of course, that's about where our neighbor had first picked them up on the road and started his caravan to our farm. It was September, and the ears of corn were still soft, sweet, and juicy, just so delicious. Damn, again. There was nothing more to do that evening except fret.

After a terribly fitful night, we were out the door at first light. The longer the cattle were moving and grazing in the cornfield, if indeed that's where we might find them, the greater the damage. I could see a monumental insurance hassle coming my way. We raced down the road to the field, stood, and looked. No sign of them. We began calling, "Come boys. Come boys!"

Suddenly there was a mooing out in the cornfield amongst the tall plants. I guess we were interrupting breakfast and would have to wait. This is exactly what I dreaded. Time was of the essence. *Come on, Dick. Think, think. What to do!*

All of our Jerseys come from dairy farms. When they are calves just a day old, they are pulled from their mamas. The cows go back into the milking herd, and the infant calves are fed colostrum then milk from a bottle, and soon, some grain. In the three months or so before their rumen develops to the point where they can digest forage, they are fed a diet that almost always, in Wisconsin, includes corn grain. Of course, they get very fond of this high-energy candy corn! That's why the Jerseys had likely led the Angus to this cornfield. The delicious odor wafted in the wind for miles. If only we had some corn grain, we could put it in a bucket to shake, and I thought the rattle would likely get the Jerseys' attention.

We had a bucket for salt and mineral in the vehicle, and there were stone pebbles alongside the road. If we threw a couple of handfuls of stones in the plastic bucket, we had the potential for a heck of a rattle.

It worked! Big time. No sooner did we get to shaking the stones and calling the boys, and the Jerseys all had their heads up, looking through the tall corn plants. They trotted toward us, leading the clueless Angus as they do every day when we move them to a new pasture at home.

Kim and I jumped in our vehicle and led the parade, rattling and calling, while Shannon and Eric walked behind the stragglers to make certain we got them all home this time. We did, and the best news was the damage to the corn was still negligible. My good neighbor said not to fret. Just buy him a beer next time the opportunity arises.

Say, what? As I always say, "You never know." One typical summer day, I went out in the morning as always and called the cattle to move them to the next pasture. All but one steer came running as they usually do. Apparently, one steer had gotten his head caught in the crotch, or the V between two branches of a tree.

I'd like to be able to say that if you've been farming long enough, you've experienced everything. I've been farming for more than fifty years, and the only real truism is you never know what's going to happen next. This was the only time in my entire life—before or afterward—I have ever had a steer whose head was caught in the crotch of a tree. Say, what?

I didn't think this would be too complicated to deal with. It was as if he had walked straight into the V-crotch without looking before he leaped. The crotch was just a bit above neck height, as his front feet, although they could make contact with the ground, were a bit light, and it was strange to watch him work to scratch the ground, yet he was able when he tried hard and stretched out a bit. After all, he got his head in; he surely could get it back out. First, I approached him head-on and tried to spook him, hoping he'd just jump up and back, and that'd be that. I made several attempts using my best scary voice and Halloween grimaces, but no luck.

I thought of the electric cattle prod I had stored in the basement at home. I'd never had to use it since I started managed grazing, but I thought this would be an appropriate time to see if it still worked with some fresh batteries. Sure enough, it did. So I stuck him on the "round roast," and he jumped forward hard. No luck. I stuck him on the nose, and all he did was go limp, sort of collapsed for a moment, but then popped right back up as if to say, "Try me again!" I tried again and got the same response.

I was getting a little frustrated, but I was still hopeful. I thought about heading over to the next farm where my neighbor had a front-end loader I knew he'd let me borrow. I figured I could put a tow strap under the steer's belly and lift him out. I guessed that would work pretty well, but I had other things to do. The rest of the herd needed access to salt and water, and I probably was supposed to be somewhere else as well, of course. No, the front-end loader method was going to take too long.

Think, think, think! I came up with another brilliant idea that had to work and would surely take less time. I ran back to the farm shop, and I got a chainsaw. This should work. I'll get the saw close to the steer's neck and lop off one of the forks of the crotch—simple! So I schlepped the saw back across the pasture to the fateful tree. I quietly crept on up to the steer and then started the saw. I thought I would be done with the job before he knew what was up, but as soon as I started the saw, the steer got so jittery that he jumped and bucked in every direction—except out and free. It

was obvious there was *no way* I could get the ferociously spinning chain close enough to cut one of the stems without the potential of seriously injuring the steer.

Now I was *really* frustrated. I could see my morning was about to become history. I threw down the chainsaw (a really dumb thing to do with a piece of equipment worth almost as much as this precious steer) and stood back, snorting. At my wits' end, with no hope or patience left in me, I hauled off and slugged the steer in the nose.

The steer who thought he could ...

For a brief moment, his eyes made contact with mine as if to say, "You just did *what*?" Then he immediately pulled his head up and back and tipped over backward out of the crotch. He sat there for a moment, stunned, then he shook himself a couple of times as if awakening from a bad dream, stood up on all fours, and started a lazy saunter in the direction of the herd and breakfast.

Oh well, now I know how to do that job. Unfortunately, or rather fortunately, all that experience hasn't paid off because I haven't had to do it again. But you never know.

Over the years we have raised many animals on our farm who have become a part of the family and who live on eternally in our memories, from dogs and cats to chickens and calves who lost their mamas. Famous and favorite calves over the years, all named by our three kids, notably included Flopsy and Mopsy (of course), 20-20, Bully, Shannon, Woody, Wee Wee, Lo Lo, Eddy, the twins Brown Ears and Missy, I EEE!, Goat, Dopey, and Nutty Buddy. Though I don't know how most got their names and how they stuck—that wasn't my department—I know that the companionship, both real and imagined (I say this because the calves never seemed to care much), brought our kids immense joy.

When we began managed grazing, moving our herds almost every day, the notion of developing and keeping a lead animal seemed to make sense. There were almost always a few renegades who, most days, didn't want to get with the program. In time, we learned of experienced cattle people who had developed lead animals as part of their management approach. My friend and elder Gordon Hazard, DVM, out of West Point, Mississippi, was one. Dr. Hazard raised herds of more than a thousand head of steers on pasture and became well known for his huge 2,500-pound Holstein-cross lead steer "Ug."

Our steers seemed to pay attention to us some of the time, as exemplified in the photo below I titled "Dick, Holding Services." While some folks in the cattle business still depend on cracking whips and hollering to get their herds to follow their direction, I have said for a long time on the Cates farm we merely "reason" with them.

Dick "holding service" on pasture Photo by past field representative, Animal Welfare Institute.

We lacked a good lead steer until #95 (his ear tag number) came along.

From the moment goofy-looking Jersey #95 arrived at our farm, it was clear his brain was wired differently. He thought he was one of us and that his herd mates were his God-given responsibility when we asked them to move to a new pasture! He was not only an expert but also a comedian to watch. When we arrived on-site, he would stick his head in our vehicle to welcome us with his long, slobbery sand-paper tongue. When we stepped out of a farm vehicle, we had to make certain the windows were up and doors closed because #95 felt obligated to chew on the upholstery, suck on the rolls of poly wire, and rummage through the tools in the toolbox.

In the old parlance from back when steers were used as draft animals, after a few years of age, a steer became known as an ox. Well, our #95 graduated to ox status in time, but without the draft requirement. He became known as "Old #95" and spent the better part of a decade on the farm with us, always living up to his chosen role of lead steer. But all good things must come to an end. Old #95 became just a bit too confident and more rambunctious each year. As the years rolled on, we became concerned the great big brute would innocently hurt one of us or one of our visitors. Finally, the family decided over many tears that it was best that Old #95 enter bovine heaven.

This picture doesn't need much of an explanation. Yes, it's a picture of Old # 95 kissing my dear wife on our pasture while I look on. (We do have fun now when we farm.) No, I was not jealous. The particular significance of this picture is what happened when I used it in a presentation I gave in Rome, in front of the United Nations Food and Agriculture Organization to people from

Old #95 kissing Kim. Photo courtesy of the Cates family.

all over the world, on the animal welfare practices we follow on our farm. I was the last speaker of the day, and this was the closing slide of my presentation.

When I completed my talk, I received the polite mandatory applause one might expect from such an eclectic group. I know for a fact that some in the group did not speak English, and with my talk being the final presentation before the closing session, many were likely dozing or daydreaming about their next meal. When I finished my presentation, the stuffy old British fellow who was emceeing the day's events re-entered the room for the closing session from a side door and took his place at the head of the room. He never really took a look to see what was on the big screen behind him. He began reiterating the main points the experts made in their presentations, summarizing the testimony of the day.

This dear picture was on the screen above his head for about half an hour. I walked to the back of the room and stealthily took a photo while the British fellow was well into his summary.

All these folks in the audience were quite staid, attempting to pay attention to the program leader, and yet over the top of his head is this picture of Old #95 kissing Kim. Just look at that old steer; what a ham. That was his day of glory and world renown before joining his brethren in bovine heaven. We'll never forget Old #95.

Throughout my decades of teaching, my primary motivation was the opportunity to assist new farmers. Many new dairy farmers start out raising Jersey cattle because they're smaller animals than Holsteins, less expensive, and less daunting to handle if the new farmers aren't familiar with the larger breeds. Someone new to farming may feel more comfortable around the Jerseys.[5]

Jersey bulls and steers have very little market value. Individuals who fatten beef steers with corn almost never choose to feed and fatten a Jersey steer because their feed/gain ratio is too costly. Time is money when you run an operation with hired labor and high capital overhead. When a Jersey farmer is just starting out, and business cash flow is vital, the hope is for heifers to build the herd or to bring a fair income in the marketplace. A bull calf may hardly be worth the truck ride to the sale barn.

Kim and I decided that we'd ask a few beginning Jersey dairy farmers if they would consider keeping their bull calves from birth through the winter and feed them mostly hay, right along with their herd replacement heifers if they liked. If this were of interest, we would pay them a living wage, not as much as we generally paid to purchase Angus steer calves, but a sufficient amount, nonetheless. In this way, we would be adding value to their calf crop and an additional income source for their business.

Fast forward nearly three decades, and Eric and Kiley have continued this practice. We know where the calves come from and how they were raised. We get the benefit of very healthy animals purchased locally, right from the farm they are raised on. The beginning dairy farmers get a benefit from the additional income and cash flow. It's a closed loop and a win-win exchange.

Commodity agriculture tends to be a business where everybody is looking to turn the last nickel, and this is especially tough on young farmers. By paying these new farmers a living

Of Course, if Truth be Told, Another Prime Motivator for Raising Jerseys ...

... is that our young grandchildren love the Jerseys, and the Jerseys love them right back.

I just had an "interview" with my granddaughter, Sloane Helen Cates, who is now six years old, going on twelve, and I asked her to name her favorite steers through the years, and here's what she told me:

"JoJo, Frenchy, Elmo, Bingo, Kiley [yes, a steer has the same name as Sloane's mother], Pony, Bingo, Rolly, Marshmallow [a white steer; the only non-Jersey sufficiently esteemed by our granddaughter to be named], Hudde and Will because they have curly hair like my friends Hudde and Will, and Short Ears. He was very cute!"

Recently, a steer named Hunchy has come to rival Old #95 in the farm's lore. He stayed around for years, as well, before he "went to Strakas" (our local butcher), as his persona had created a special place for himself. As he aged, I don't really think he knew whether he was a *Bos taurus* or a *Homo sapiens*. He liked to hang out with us. Whenever Eric sorted cattle, Hunchy would come to stand by him, and head bump the others in the herd in whatever direction Eric was moving. Fun and funny, yes; helpful, not so much. But hey, you gotta love him, and we all did.

When I asked Sloane what kind of things Hunchy did and why she loved him, she said, "He licked the windows [of the pasture jeep/truck], and if I put the window down, he leaned in and licked my head. He was a silly!"

So there you go.

wage, we get healthy animals that can thrive and grow on our grass. Then we get to tell this story to our customers, and they genuinely appreciate it. Paying it forward whenever possible in life is one of the joys of living for us. What could be more meaningful? (See Sidebar: Of Course, if Truth be Told, Another Prime Motivator for Raising Jerseys ...)

We give thanks and honor our lovely animals with whom we share our lives and their lasting stories.

The cycle of life and death is indeed sacred.

The Cateses two-headed cow ... or perhaps, a once-in-a-lifetime photo? Photo by Julie Doll.

Homecoming—For Which We Are Grateful

"We have a home. It's not a pretty Greek Island either. But it is ... the most beautiful piece of ground on Earth. Several hundred acres of steep oak and hickory forest and narrow, deep soil hollows where the grass grows thick and fast, and the clear springs feed the brook trout creek. Snow falls and drifts, and the hills look naked white under crooked black trees and windless nights in the winter are as quiet as a coffin until spring and you can hear the hills seep water and the valley air begins to stir and hum and the calves grow and the air turns hazy in summer, you could eat it for the smells and the feel of it on your tongue, and on balmy nights fireflies and stars light the darkness and the morning fog on fall mornings burns away in the sun. The hillsides turn yellow and orange and scarlet, and ... the rolling smells of soil and stalk, fruit and wood, and the changing shapes of shadow on the hills and the hollows, the green the blue the yellow the gray the white the black, the light, the light, the light, the light."

—David Allan Cates from *Tom Connor's Gift*[1]

"What I stand for is what I stand on."

—Wendell Berry, *What I Stand On: The Collected Essays of Wendell Berry 1969–2017*

And life goes on. A descendant of our sentinel oak, similar in age to myself, stands just over a hundred yards from the old tree, representing yet another generation in the march of time. This past spring we transplanted four bur oak seedlings, a gift from a friend from an ancient tree that succumbed to the derecho winds that hit near here during the summer of 2020.[2] We planted one to represent each of our four grandchildren and the future and our hope for this land.

Homecoming is the magic of the return of spring on a grassland. It is spring again on the Cates Family Farm, albeit three years since I began the journey that has become this book.

Spring emerges slowly, silently, dependably, out of brown grass, mud, and cold, year after year, and wraps the landscape in rich hues of iridescent color. Lowery Creek accents this beauty as a shining silver ribbon running through it all. And the grass is back.

John James Ingalls, U.S. senator from Kansas 1873–1891, wrote, "Grass is the forgiveness of nature—her constant benediction. Forests decay, harvests perish, flowers vanish, but grass is immortal ... Its tenacious fibers hold the earth in place and prevent its soluble components from washing to the wasting sea."

Here on our farm, the return of the grass, companion legumes, and other forbs—well over thirty diverse species in a given pasture—means, quite literally, that we will be able to thrive yet another year.[3] The beauty of a grassland in spring moves the soul, and the grass itself fattens "grass-eaters" across the planet, as it has in our North American home since the late Oligocene epoch, twenty-five million years ago. For the grass, we are thankful every day.

The many migratory bird species return, enhancing the revitalized landscape and bringing along their varied song. And our year-round residents begin calling with renewed vigor. Our farmland is rich with diverse bird habitats. Walking from daybreak to mid-morning from re-established native prairie to wetlands, riparian area pastured grasslands, upland forest, and stopping at the ridgetop grassland, we hear the songs of almost fifty species. These mornings are rich in a diversity of woodpeckers, flycatchers, vireos, thrushes, warblers, sparrows, cardinals, bluebirds, and blackbirds. If we add the rarer occasionally glimpsed species, the morning silent night-time callers, as well as barn and yard dwellers, we typically have more than eighty avian species that call our farm home.

In the quiet that grassland farming allows, you can hear these songsters through mid-summer, and they become a part of everyday life.

Grandchildren Sloane Helen and Fischer Lyman, seven and four years old, respectively, know many of the bird sounds by name, or at least they think they do. Much of their bird song morphs into sameness, as one may expect. However, they definitely have mourning doves, ducks, cranes, and woodpeckers sorted As this book is readied for publication, Fischer's mom, Kiley, let me know that he can identify about forty different birds by sight or sound ... remarkable! A favorite activity of theirs each spring is making the rounds with Nana or Papa to our many bluebird (also a couple of kestrel and barred owl) boxes to check in on nesting, hatching, and fledging progress. Their unabashed biophilia—natural love of life or living things—is on display with infectious tears of joy.

Along our farming journey, we learned that leaving a portion of grassland ungrazed through the nesting season, from approximately May 15 to August 1 in our area, enhances nesting survival and boosts grassland bird populations.[4]

Setting aside a bird nesting refuge melds exceptionally well with good pasture management. Areas that perhaps need some TLC, such as a paddock that was grazed too hard during a torrential rainstorm or where an inter-seeding of clover was only marginally successful, become perfect locations to set aside from grazing for several months. Any additional seeding, as well as the grass-clover sward in place, has a chance to thicken and set seed. A mowing just before livestock turn-in to this area allows much of the tall plant growth to be consumed as hay and some of the lower leaves as fresh pasture.

As long as I can remember, we have had a single great blue heron fish along our section of Lowery Creek. Of course, it is a different giant every few years. As one ages, another takes its place. They are great big, beautiful birds. When they take flight, at first hidden below the stream bank line of sight and then suddenly emerging right in front of you, it is as if they are saying, "We have been here much longer than you." In fact, they have. Herons first appeared in the fossil record sixty million years ago. Contemporary species go back seven million years.

Speaking of ancient ones, sandhill cranes are making a comeback in Wisconsin, thanks in part to the fine work of the International Crane Foundation located in the next county north of our farm. A fossil of the present extant species was found in Nebraska, dating back ten million years. In the spring of 2020, we had our first mating pair of sandhill cranes take up season-long residence on our pastureland. They had lost their single colt (chick) early in the spring, so we never got to see the trio together. But in the summer of 2021, they romped our grasslands for a while with two precious colts, but alas, neither survived predation or injury much into the summer.

They like to hang out near the cattle and move across the pastures all summer with the herd. They certainly know where to find the spots where insects are numerous, and the picking is easy—wherever fresh cow pies are plentiful.

We have our own bald eagle on the farm as well. It's usually seen perched in a tall cottonwood or the old sentinel bur oak, hunting our grassland or fishing the waters of Lowery Creek. Right: great blue heron. Photos by Don Greenwood.

Left: Pasture left ungrazed May 15 to at least August 1 as a nesting bird refuge. Right: Our sandhill crane pair with two colts. Just one survived to migrate in the autumn. Photo at left by Eric Cates. Photo at right by Don Greenwood.

One of two colts lived and prospered through the springs of 2022 and 2023 until autumn, when it was able to take flight with its mom and dad and head south for the winter. Now we eagerly anticipate new crane life on the pasture every spring.

And our little gray and white upside-down tree-bark-feeding tufted titmice are still calling, "Peter, Peter," although with a bit more zest come each spring. My heart skips a beat, and involuntarily, I will stop whatever I'm doing and gaze up at Peter's Hill to the resting spot of our loved ones. Thank you, little Peter Bird, for never forgetting.

With jubilation and celebration, homecoming is also an indigenous trout revival, the recent return of the native "heritage" brook trout to the waters of Lowery Creek after a hiatus of the past century.

One manner of classifying cold-water streams is according to their success at growing trout. The historical trout stream classifications by the Wisconsin Department of Natural Resources (WI DNR) for Lowery Creek read as follows:[5]

1968: 1 mile of Class 2, and 2 miles of Class 3; Species: Brown Trout

1976: 1 mile of Class 2, and 2.5 miles of Class 3; Species: Brown Trout

1980: 3.5 miles of Class 2; Species: Brown Trout

2002: 3.5 miles of Class 2; Species: Brown Trout

2008: 7.5 miles—the full navigable length of the main channel—of Class 2; Species: Brown Trout

There *were* no brook trout in Lowery Creek throughout the first six decades of my lifetime, or at least not in sufficient numbers to even be noted. Only a Class 1 stream has habitat of high enough quality to support a "self-sustaining population of brook trout."[6]

My family manages 40 percent of this seven and a half miles and another two miles of a principal tributary (significantly more than any other owner or land manager), primarily with cattle in our managed grazing system and some acres cut as hay or set aside. Our cattle are the only livestock in any significant number. What my family does on the land matters, most significantly, to the ecosystem that is Lowery Creek.

There were no classification adjustments for Lowery Creek from 2008 until 2021, but the record is clear that only brown trout—a non-native fish that thrives in lower-quality water—were stocked until 2013; no stocking of any kind took place after that.

However, sometime in the past decade, Wisconsin DNR fishery biologists began to notice a change: Brook trout in Lowery Creek were present. In a sense, they started to "show up." Some explorative electro-fishing was conducted—a technique used routinely by fish managers to temporarily stun fish to net them for observation. The examined brook trout were all healthy, free of disease and parasites, and seemed to be increasing in number.

This piqued the scientists' curiosity, of course, and genomic testing was initiated. Surprisingly, the genetic map of these fish was unlike any of the propagated brook trout the DNR had been raising and releasing across Wisconsin over the past one hundred forty years!

Once European-style farming—plowing up and down the slopes—was well underway in the mid-nineteenth century in the Driftless Area, surface rainwater washed across the land rather than infiltrating into the ground and carried soil runoff along with it. This often brown, warmer water (much warmer than the cold groundwater that supported the creeks and streams throughout the Driftless Area for millions of years previously) resulted in an environment in which native cold-water brook trout could not survive.

The current theory is that small numbers of these wild native "heritage" fish had survived in isolated pools in the headwaters of Lowery Creek, where the water stayed cold and clear. Once the habitat improved such that it was habitable again for the brookies, they "went forth and multiplied." The tables turned for the brown trout when their food sources were no longer in supply in this now continuously cold, clear water.

The numbers of these wild fish seemed to be increasing at such a healthy rate, it was determined Lowery Creek's brook trout could be sustainably harvested for the DNR wild trout propagation program for release into streams across Wisconsin.

In autumn 2016, the team from Nevin State Fish Hatchery decided to harvest for the propagation program on the main channel that runs through our grazing land. In late October, after a few hours of electro-fishing, walking the section of the creek just below the bridge on our farm lane, they ended up collecting 125 adult female brook trout and keeping 64 for spawning through the next three weeks. They were able to retrieve and fertilize just over 420 eggs per fish, yielding approximately 27,000 embryos they were able to raise in the Nevin State Fish Hatchery that winter![7]

That single event meant that Lowery Creek then joined an elite trio, one of only three streams in the state of Wisconsin with a sufficient number of native "heritage" disease-free brook trout to allow for occasional spawn harvest for the state wild trout propagation program (the other two are Melancthon Creek and Hay River in and just north of the Driftless Area, respectively). I was ecstatic to learn this. Juvenile Lowery Creek brook trout had the potential for distribution all over the state and perhaps beyond. We were sharing the greatest natural treasure a Midwest angler could wish for. (See Sidebar: A Thank You from an Unknown Fisherman, but a New Friend)

Three years later, the Wisconsin DNR fishery team conducted another trek along approximately three hundred yards of stream channel below our lane bridge. I watched as they waded the stream with their electro-fishing tool, catch nets, and five-gallon buckets as repositories for the stunned fish. The harvest was overwhelming! Had we not all been there to see it with our own eyes, it would have been hard to believe.

They ended up collecting 107 males, 163 apparently fertile females, and another 33 younger females (six to seven inches, likely just two-year-olds) that may or may not have eggs, plus some young-of-the-year and sculpins, all in less than two hours. This harvest allowed the team to fertilize approximately 50,000 eggs, almost twice the number in 2016.[8] The team harvested again in the fall of 2022, and the harvest was excellent. Earlier that year they had assessed brook

A Thank You from an Unknown Fisherman, but a New Friend

Date: August 10, 2021, at 11:14:58 AM CDT
To: eric.r.cates@gmail.com
Subject: THANK YOU!

Hi Eric,

First, let me give you a little background for context. I have spent the last 40 years fly fishing the spring creeks of the Wisconsin driftless area. Five years ago, we built a small horse farm on the German Valley Branch south of Blue Mounds. I was catching some of the most beautiful brook trout I have ever caught in the upper stretches. I did some research to find that they were heritage fish from Lowery Creek. So I had to see Lowery for myself, as oddly I had never fished it. Last Sunday I was fishing the stretch right above Hwy Z and in just a couple of hours I caught about 30 beautiful brook trout. When I returned home, I looked up who owned the parcel and learned your family owned most of the valley upstream from Z! What a coincidence, we are long-time patrons of Brix Cider in Mount Horeb and get your beef products there!

My purpose in writing today is to thank you personally for all you have done in both creating the best beef products we have had and conserving the most special fish I have had the pleasure to catch. THANK YOU SO MUCH!

When I was up there, I noticed that there was some grazed area that allowed easier access to the stream. I would like to bring my six-year-old granddaughter along sometime, but the prairie grasses would be too much for her at this time of year. Do you allow access to the stream in the pastured areas? I completely understand if you don't, which is why I always want to ask first.

Regardless, thanks again for all you have done. It truly means a lot to us!

Warmest regards,
Paul Lackner, Blue Mounds, WI

Top: The Nevin (WI) State Fish Hatchery heritage brook trout spawn harvest crew at Lowery Creek on the Cates farm. Bottom left to right: Heritage brook trout young-of-the-year; a couple of years old; three or more years old; mottled sculpin, a brook trout food source.

trout density and came up with 3,000 per mile, more than ten times the median density of all other Class 1 streams in Wisconsin.[9]

On January 1, 2021, Lowery Creek was officially reclassified as a Class 1 trout stream by the Wisconsin DNR and celebrated by fisherfolks far and wide.[10] I want to shout from the mountaintop: "The brookies are back!" (In Chapter 10, you will learn how our community has worked together for the benefit of our entire Lowery Creek watershed, the place we all call home.)

Most significantly, homecoming is the return of our children—the next generation—home to our tears of joy. Early in 2016, Kim and I, with the help of our daughter, Shannon, and her husband, Dan, purchased the 104 acres contiguous to our farm to the north, the same land John Kraemer had offered to my father in 1968.[11] The sale price had certainly increased since then!

Dan and Shannon live away now, but they love this land. They named their first-born child Peter in honor of Shannon's little brother, whose ashes remain here on the hill in the oak savanna above the home where Shannon was raised. They demonstrated their love through the shared purchase of this additional grassland to assist her brother, Eric, and his bride, Kiley, in pursuing their dream of farming here. This pulls on my heartstrings.[12]

On May 23, 2015, Eric and Kiley Ann Prusso married on top of Peter's Hill. The following spring, the newly wedded couple came back to the farm for good.

Eric continued to return to the farm most summers through college, and over the next eight years he pursued a profession as an alpine (downhill) ski racing coach in the western states. Typically, I would spend the previous nine months each year making "Eric's list," as we came to call it, which identified all the things that needed repair and all the jobs I hadn't quite gotten around to. Upon Eric's arrival each summer, I'd hand him the list, scratched out in a sloppy shorthand only Eric or I could read, and he'd have at it. He always said that his job was to straighten the place up, fix everything I'd broken, and go away again long enough for the next list to be made.

But one day back in the summer of 2012, he had a stroke of luck, and his life began to soar. He met *the one* who would light up his life, Kiley Ann Prusso, from southern California by way of Vermont and Dodgeville.

Kiley had worked for a well-known cheese purveyor in San Francisco after college and, through that experience, decided she wanted to become a cheesemaker. She landed a cheese-making internship in northern Vermont and, within a year, was wooed to southwest Wisconsin by a well-known cheese-maker friend of Eric's who needed assistance and had identified Kiley as a burgeoning talent.[13]

Soon after Kiley arrived here, it dawned on our friend that he ought to find a local boy for this California girl if he was going to keep her around. So he brought her along to the local eatery one afternoon, where he was going to meet Eric. The rest is a story about love and forging a dream and a life of purpose together.

Our friend was certainly successful at keeping the Golden State girl in Dairyland, but she traded the cheese vat for the cowgirl life on the Cates Family Farm, arm in arm with Eric. Kim and I are the lucky ones, and we bask in their joy.

They've been here ever since. Now they run the farm. They make the decisions, and although Kim and I help when asked, they do most of the work. I joke that I work hard at just keeping out of their way, and even that's difficult. A few years ago, winter temperatures dropped to minus thirty degrees. From the comfort of our home, Kim and I observed these two tough, innovative folks feed and coddle the herd in the pasture just to the north. We looked at each other. What a miracle.

Eric: We got married here not long after we announced to my parents that we wanted to come back to the farm. Then, that fall, the gentleman who owned the place next to my parents' farm reached out and said that he wanted to sell, and he wanted to give the right of first refusal to my folks. My parents and my older sister and her husband all agreed that they wanted to purchase the hundred-or-so acres with the home. They closed on it in the summer of 2016, a few months after we moved back. We lived with Mom and Dad from May until September, and we all worked on the house together, making the changes we needed. We moved in by October, and now we rent that home and all the farmland from them.

Kiley: We love it.

Eric: Yeah, it's really grown on us.

Kiley: And our daughter, Sloane, loves it.

Eric: She's seven now, but she's been part of our life on the farm from day one.

Kiley: She's been doing farm chores since she was born. Eric was gone that first winter, his final season as a professional downhill ski racing coach, and I was out there with Sloane on my chest, moving the boys (the steers) in the middle of winter, feeding them. I fell on my back more than once with her on my chest, and I would freak out. This morning, in fact, she was a little bummed that she didn't get to go help with chores before school. Now our son, Fischer, has been accompanying Eric for the past couple of years, as well.

Eric: But one of the nice things about living here on the farm is we don't have to gather all of our stuff to go somewhere else to go do something. I can just put Sloane and Fischer in the farm vehicle with me. You can go out there quickly and get the small jobs done. They both love it.

Kiley: Sloane can identify grasses and birds. When the pandemic happened, we pulled her out of daycare for two months and filled so much of our time just exploring the farm and playing in the stream and teaching her about things. She wasn't even three years old at that point.

And the cattle love Sloane and Fischer! They love coming up to give kisses, and the kids love 'em right back. So for us, their enjoyment just makes the work that we're doing even more meaningful. This spring, Sloane kept so busy digging up hay piles looking for bugs!

Eric: I'd always been the third hand on all the farm projects growing up—our oak savanna project and some of the burns that we've been doing, and then a lot of the pasture and weed management, whether it's tractor mowing or by hand. So I've always tagged along or just been there to help. Obviously, my dad really loves the work and loves the outcome, and so my appreciation for it has grown through that. I think for me, my enjoyment is more, not so much the fact that we've established a prairie, or we've established a savanna; it's more the beauty that comes along with it. An aesthetic appreciation, I think.

As far as cattle, the stream and the water quality, and the actual pasture management, I've been so involved with it all from a young age, as well. We've embraced this statement: "A commitment to conservation." What I tell our customers is that our goal is first to take care of the land and the water. We're trying to create as healthy a habitat as possible. Then the habitat will take care of the cattle. So we're not necessarily animal caretakers; we're land caretakers, and the land is taking care of the animals. So that's where more of my appreciation for it all comes from. I look at it as a chain of care and stewardship. It's a connected process.

Kiley: We love our animals, and we find that a healthy environment keeps them healthy and comfortable for their time with us.

Eric: It's good and it's been fun. When we moved back, my parents were probably at the tail end of their interest in running things. They kind of limped the business along for a little while just to

see what I might do. They definitely downsized a lot. Since then, we've grown it pretty well, but we are still a small family farm.

What's been fun is that a lot of the folks that my dad used to work with are still active in the food business, perhaps in a new location or with different responsibilities. When I came back, they were like, "You guys are still doing that? Oh, we miss it. We want to keep working with you." So those connections were meaningful on a personal level but also on a business level to help jumpstart us. We've also found new markets and other unique opportunities as well, and it's been wonderful.

Eric and Kiley, Sloane and Fischer (autumn 2022).

With the direct market beef business in place for more than thirty years and never needing to own more than a hundred head of cattle a year (since selling our last large group of commodity steers), our family has created a viable, profitable business that has stood the test of time. (See Appendix I—Principles of a Direct Market Grass-Fed Beef Business)

I think back to all of the years I spent growing up working on this farm and others and the early years here after our return, before Kim showed me the light. Never once did I have the opportunity to influence the price I might receive for my production costs, my risk, or my labor. Nor did I ever have anyone ever thank me for anything I grew and sent out beyond the farm gate. Now, I can't imagine living like that again. Yet almost all farmers have lived like this, and most still do today. The feeling of accomplishment and sheer gratitude when a customer writes a check that will cover your costs and then says thank you for caring for the land and the animals and for growing delicious and healthy food for my family is one of sheer joy, ecstasy. One never tires or takes for granted such gifts. We are immensely and forever thankful.

Kim stopped working off the farm in 2010. I continued teaching part time until retirement in 2018 because I loved it. The opportunity to share what I had learned from the successes and the many failures building our farm business over decades, as well as the love and lore I had developed for the ecology of our place, gave me great joy. I was able to assist many of the next generation in starting farming successfully, as well as help many more students develop a knowledge of and appreciation for our Driftless landscape, as well as the savanna and grasslands of the world.

The biomimicry of managed grazing we have spent decades fitting to this land has allowed us to raise healthy grass-fed beef cattle and enhance our native brook trout stream habitat. Our regenerative, perennial pasture-based farming approach honors the welfare of our livestock and our sacred place. On our family farm we have made a lifelong commitment to conservation, community, and a sustainable and enriching livelihood.[14]

I understand now, after a long journey, what it means to have discovered a land ethic, one we choose to live by every day.

And I have eternal gratitude and burgeoning hope for our place into the future.

My son Eric posted the following Thanksgiving blessing:

> I am thankful for these three, my wife and two children, and the life we have together. What they provide is immeasurable, second to none; for my parents next door and the never-ending support, wisdom, and care they provide to us all; for our teachers and daycare providers who dote on and teach our "littles" and who provide an extension of love and life to fill their hopes and needs; for our butchers, customers, clients, restaurants, and grocers for their everlasting appreciation in what we do; and for this beautiful valley, this land, and all who came before us. We are lucky to call this place home.

There is simply nothing more exalted or deeply felt beyond the blessing of sharing our lives on this piece of the Driftless landscape, working along with and honoring its genius. To be a part of the magic and mystery of the rhythms of the seasons as they play out on our landscape, offering us gifts of life.

Fischer and Sloane's new golden doodle puppy. They named him Oakley (May 2023). Photo by Eric Cates.

Eric and Kiley, you stand in this place as farmers. Perhaps one or more of our grandchildren will as well. We hope they will know that we have all tried our best to care for these gifts.[15]

In the next and final chapter of our journey, I want to tell the story of how our community is "working together to get it right." Along with friends and neighbors, through our collective effort of the Lowery Creek Watershed Initiative, we are engaged in activities and relationships that build land health and community—reciprocity for Earth's gifts. It is an inspiring, hopeful story, and it brings me much joy.

Fischer assists Nana Kim and father Eric at recording Lowery Creek water quality. We teach 'em young.

PART III

We Can Only Save What We Love

Visitors to the Cates farm learn about stream bank protection and get to electro-fish for heritage brook trout with WI DNR Fisheries Biologist, Justin Haglund. Drone view by Randy Manning.

Photo by WI DNR.

The Lowery Creek Watershed Initiative—It Takes a Community

"The health of our waters is the principal measure of how we live on the land."

—Luna B. Leopold

"It would not be possible to affect change on a watershed level without cooperative and collaborative thinking, even in this small watershed. The benefit is in understanding our role as stewards of the land and sharing that understanding with others. This creek is important to the history of the valley and is arguably one of its oldest residents."

—Ryan Hewson, director of preservation, Frank Lloyd Wright Foundation

"I have been so enlightened by the various partners involved in this initiative. They have given me tools I never imagined that will help protect and enhance farmlands, prairies, forests, bottomlands, wetlands, fish, and aquatic animals. Exchange of information is a key to success with this group. I have newfound and wonderful friendships."

—Jean Unmuth, aquatic ecologist,
Wisconsin Department of Natural Resources, retired

"A land comprised of wilderness islands at one extreme and urban islands at the other, with vast food and fiber factories in between, does not constitute a geography of hope. With a broader understanding of land and our place within the landscape, our nation's farms can serve the multiple functions that we and all other life depend upon."

—Paul Johnson, farmer, land steward, and past chief of the
USDA Natural Resources Conservation Department

Our sentinel oak stood over the valley and saw that all was good and likely mused, "You have a story to tell. Your family and neighbors have found a way to grow your food and, at the same time, restore the health of this beautiful valley. It is time to share your story." Our oak knew what was possible if we listened. The singularly colorful, beautiful brook trout, *Salvelinus fontinalis*, indigenous to our valley, here well before the arrival of Homo sapiens and before the retreat of the last glacier, were waiting in the shadows of the headwaters and springs of Lowery Creek for a return. All the brook trout asks for is cool, clear water and a gift of the community along Lowery Creek to work as one for her return.

Revival of a wild trout stream, Lowery Creek Watershed Initiative serves as a model for a way forward. Here, in this treasured prairie and oak savanna landscape of the Driftless Area, our Lowery Creek watershed, we are learning from the natural community that surrounds us and from one another. Our goal is to listen and learn from this land's soils, waters, plants, and animals that make up this life-giving community.

Our community knows the visual beauty of Lowery Creek, as it starts high on the wooded hillside and snakes across farm and prairie and, past our sentinel oak and down, down the valley to the Wisconsin River. We cherish its presence. Over the millennia, the creek has been a source of cool, clear water for countless fauna and hundreds of generations of our First Peoples. Lowery Creek has been a constant to the present day for the descendants of European immigrants and all the neighbors who live along the banks.

Working together as neighboring farmers, we are beginning to see our fields, forests, and prairies as a community whose gifts we are privileged to steward. This land is much more than "natural resources" or simply commodities for us to individually exploit. Sustainable and regenerative agriculture and forestry alongside ecological restoration is what we are about. Building our soils, restoring our waterways, and treading more lightly on this sacred ground as we recognize that we humans, from the First Peoples to today's farmers, are all relative newcomers here and just one of the many species that call this place home.

When we quiet our minds and open our ears and eyes to this landscape, we find that it speaks to us and demonstrates how replicating natural processes and biodiversity leads to better farming practices and land stewardship, in general. Together, our family and neighbors are learning to put aside the practice of agriculture dependent on monoculture crops. We are curtailing tillage practices that send the valley's precious topsoil downstream. We have learned to keep our livestock herds at a size that the land can support sustainably and where movement of the herd, in turn, nourishes and replenishes the land.

Landowners here have learned the fundamental truth that it is actually the land that shows us the way to live well in gentle partnership—once we learn to pay attention and to listen.

Drone photo by Randy Manning.

As I stated in the Preface, one of my primary motives for writing this book has been to celebrate and give thanks to my community of neighbors for cherishing this place. In this chapter, I want to share part of the story of our Lowery Creek Watershed Initiative and how good neighbors can achieve extraordinary outcomes together.

The rebirth of Lowery Creek, exemplified by its designation as a Class 1 native heritage brook trout stream,[1] is a model of the great good, both environmentally and economically, that can come from cooperation, collaboration, and thoughtful, caring interaction with the land. In short, discovering and evolving our own land ethic.

In Iowa County, Wisconsin, there are 755 miles of perennial streams. A significant number of these stream miles—165 at the latest count—are listed as "impaired." Impairments noted (beginning with the greatest number of miles) include high phosphorus levels, excessive sediment, high ammonia levels, low dissolved oxygen, high zinc, lead, cadmium, and/or mercury levels. Additionally, PCBs (polychlorinated biphenyl) are sometimes at detectable levels in the Wisconsin River, and many acres of our backwater lakes support excessive algal growth annually.[2]

The Clean Water Act (33 U.S.C. ch. 23 §1251 et seq.) is the 1972 amended Federal Water Pollution Control Act. It sets the basic structure for regulating discharges of pollutants to the waters of the United States. Since the law's passage, the Wisconsin Department of Natural Resources has been required to track the quality of the state's waters. The fiftieth anniversary of the Clean Water Act was acknowledged in autumn 2022.

For the first decades, a consistent list of "impaired waters" had not yet been developed. By 1998, the list of impaired waters in Wisconsin had 552 entries. By 2015, the list had 1,196 entries. The list grew by 231 in 2016, with only ten sites previously listed improved to the extent they could be removed from the list. By 2020, the list had grown to more than 2,000 entries (thankfully, the number of listings has declined modestly since then).[3]

The large increase in the number of impaired waters location listings begs the question: Are our waters getting worse to this significant extent? It turns out that the original list was only a percentage of impaired locations and represented a fraction of the reality on the ground. With time, additional locations were observed. Significantly, an actual phosphorus limit was imposed in 2010, and locations over the new limit were added to the list.[4]

We now have a reliable way to actually assess the relative state of the waters of Wisconsin. This is known as the Long-Term Trends (LTT) Rivers monitoring program run by the WI DNR. It was developed to track and analyze water quality trends over time in Wisconsin's rivers. The current version of the network, initiated in 2001, now consists of forty-three sites, with a minimum of one site per major river basin, generally located near the mouth of each river, at or near a USGS streamflow gauge.

Routine monitoring at many LTT sites started in the 1970s, providing a perspective on water quality trends since the passage of the Clean Water Act.[5] The upshot of the findings from this monitoring effort is that although phosphorus and sediment levels are declining in some parts of the state, where thorough monitoring has taken place in southern Wisconsin, the picture is different: There has not been an improvement in total phosphorus loads, which translates to phosphorus concentration levels still above the state standard.[6] Significantly, nitrogen levels are increasing across almost all sites in southern Wisconsin.

Much of Lowery Creek since European farming culture came to its banks could likely have been classified as "impaired waters" due to high sedimentation, phosphorus, and/or nitrogen levels, low dissolved oxygen, and warmer water temperatures, a result of more surface runoff and less groundwater recharge in the channel. These measurements were never made, or at least are not on record.

In recent years, my family and others in our Lowery Creek community have participated in an effort called Water Action Volunteers (WAV), a statewide program for Wisconsin citizens who want to learn about and improve the quality of Wisconsin's streams and rivers. The program is coordinated through a partnership between the Wisconsin Department of Natural Resources and the University of Wisconsin–Madison Division of Extension.

In 2018, our Lowery Creek watershed group established our first WAV monitoring site on the main channel of Lowery Creek. My family established a site the following year here on the Cates farm where the creek bisects our grazed pastureland. A couple of years later we added a site on the tributary that runs through our pastures. In total, our watershed group is sampling the water quality of Lowery Creek at eight or nine sites each year as it passes through farmland, restoration areas, and wildlife habitat. The collected water quality data across the years document for the

Dick, neighbor Joe Stapleton, Kim, and Eric engage in monthly (through each growing season) Water Action Volunteer (WAV) water quality sampling of Lowery Creek as it runs through the Cates farm. Photo by Jean Unmuth.

world what we know so well—Lowery Creek is cool, clear water, dazzling in all ways that a brook trout would want to call home.[7]

The condition of the ninety-two miles of the Wisconsin River included in the Lower Wisconsin State Riverway is almost entirely dependent upon the health of the tributary streams and small rivers that feed the river.

> When watershed-wide efforts are made to restore and protect these tributary waters, the effect of those efforts becomes apparent on the Wisconsin [River]. Through the adherence to the standards of the Clean Water Act of the 1970s, much of the pollution from upstream industry and effluent from urban sewage treatment plants has been substantially reduced. Non-point pollution has been more difficult to address. With groups like the Lowery Creek Initiative and Friends of Black Earth Creek, we are seeing neighbors working together to create better models for responsible and restorative agriculture. The consequences of this collaboration are reduced runoff of soil and nutrients and cleaner, healthier water in the Lower Wisconsin River. I and many others who care about the health of our rivers and streams are very grateful for these efforts.
>
> —Don Greenwood, former chair,
> Lower Wisconsin State Riverway Board

My belief is if there is a significant problem that evades progress, we need to put a face on it and make it personal, and then take ownership. The loss of topsoil and nutrients from our lands of the Midwest creates the dead zone in the Gulf of Mexico. We know this is real, and it is primarily the result of our modern farm practices but also a consequence of soil and nutrient loss from stream banks, construction sites, and over-fertilized suburban lawns, parks, golf courses, etc. The challenge is how to get farmers, land managers, and consumers (people who eat) to take it personally to own the problem to the extent that they are motivated to do something about it.

Most of us take the position that we'll wait until there is a policy that tells us what we should or shouldn't do to mitigate any given problem or concern. Unfortunately, this plan of action is often a plan of no action. At best, change and progress happen at a geological pace. I like to say that chrome rusts faster than we mortals step up to solve some of our most obvious problems.

So over the past few years, my family and a handful of others who live and farm in the greater Lowery Creek watershed area have made it a point to get to know some of the shrimpers and fishers whose livelihoods are so affected by how we steward or don't steward our land up here. We traveled down to the Louisiana Gulf and spent several days with fishers and shrimpers.

The opportunity to meet and share work with these families who make their living from the sea—many for generations, as long or longer than families have been farming in Wisconsin—has been a singular and powerful learning experience. These folks have a love for their families and communities and a deep love of their place and way of life, just as we do.

Kim said she saw many similarities with our operation. "During the season, they work long, hard hours," she noted. "We share a passion for what we do. It's not just a job but a way of life. I loved spending time with these folks. They are real down-to-earth people who I felt comfortable being around." Meeting and working with these "farmers of the sea" has been a most moving experience for all of us involved.

I believe the only way farmers and anyone who manages land are ever going to be sufficiently motivated to make meaningful broad-scale changes in their practices—changes that significantly mitigate their nutrient contribution to the dead zone in the Gulf—is when they are able to put a face on the problem. That is when—and *only* when—we understand, in our gut, that we are negatively impacting human lives at a fundamental level, their ability to support families, communities, and a cherished way of life.

Enter the Lowery Creek Watershed Initiative, my community's cooperative, collaborative effort to celebrate, enhance, and share with the world our place in the Driftless Area of Wisconsin. Taking the long view, the Lowery Creek Watershed Initiative was born of a vision that our area could and should be forever a place where forward-thinking landowners actively manage and protect its natural and agricultural resources by employing practices suitable for its Driftless topography. We were motivated by the belief that the area's vibrant beauty and ecology are essential elements of its thriving arts, culture, community, and economy. And we deeply understand that stewarding all of what we have here will take collective thought and effort.

The Coon Creek Watershed Project of the mid-1930s was noted in Chapter 3 as the first-ever cooperative, collaborative, voluntary conservation effort on private lands in America. The work at Coon Valley and throughout the region "reflected a radical new approach to conservation," writes Curt Meine.[8] "Here, conservation focused not on protecting large expanses of public land but on the restoration of private lands and collaboration among private landowners." It was a resounding success.

We are thankful that there have been pioneers in citizen-led coalitions to improve watersheds across America. In Wisconsin and beyond, such efforts have recently emerged.[9] I am thankful for all. Each is a story on its own and deserves to be held up to the light and celebrated.

In 2014, a group of my neighbors met around a table at the Spring Green General Store to discuss how we might partner to conserve and enhance our Lowery Creek watershed. They enlisted the assistance of our respected and highly visible local land trust, the Driftless Area Land Conservancy (DALC),[10] and soon after, the University of Wisconsin–Madison's Nelson Institute for Environmental Studies Conservation Planning course to provide initial guidance. Barb Barzen, a DALC staff member, then led us through more detailed strategic planning over a year of conversations to develop a vision for the future and a plan for how to make it come to life. This is when I took the opportunity to jump in with both feet and waders on!

DALC has maintained a coordinating role in this partnership, which has grown to include representatives of the Frank Lloyd Wright Foundation, Friends of the Lower Wisconsin State Riverway, Iowa County Land Conservation Department, Savanna Institute and Canopy Farm Management, Taliesin Preservation, and our Town of Wyoming, in addition to farm families and other landowners and citizens in and beyond the Lowery Creek watershed. We call our group and our mission the Lowery Creek Watershed Initiative and have made a positive difference in the quality of our unique and fragile ecosystem while building community and friendships.

With this in mind, our Lowery Creek Watershed Initiative aims to engage landowners in protecting and enhancing the area's water quality, soil health, natural ecosystems, rich beauty, cultural resources, and rural character. Our work is based on sound science, effective communication and implementation strategies that are community driven, and rooted in a strong land ethic.

In the long-term, our watershed group wants to ensure that:

- Cultural resources are preserved and appreciated.
- Climate-smart regenerative agriculture and ecosystem management practices sequester carbon while producing healthy soil and water, biodiversity, and a variety of agricultural products.
- Working lands continue to dominate the landscape.
- The economy is thriving, driven by agriculture, tourism, recreation, and the area's rural character.
- The local community is actively engaged in realizing this vision.[11]

Private landowners within the watershed are, and have been, actively engaged in restoration work and conservation and regenerative farming. These activities contribute to the self-sustaining heritage brook trout population. As Mike Degen, natural landscapes coordinator at the Frank Lloyd Wright Foundation, and long-time watershed landowner and steward, explains, "We have unique habitat types and unique creatures that should be nurtured. To succeed with so many landowners along the creek takes an awareness campaign involving education and learning from each other. One thing we are focusing on is water quality." Mike continues, "Is our water quality improving or getting poorer? It can inform the practices that we employ in this really unique landscape. Land management and everything else that we do affects our watersheds and water quality."

Farmers are practicing no-till (planting without tillage/plowing) with cover crops in their farming operations or managed grazing on perennial forages with their livestock herds. Agroforestry and silvopasture have both been introduced here recently (early 2020s) but will be expanding in scope. Numerous landowners are restoring prairie, managing pollinator habitat, grassland, woodlots, specialty crops, and more. (See Sidebars: Our Friends and Neighbors along Lowery Creek Are Engaged in Activities That Build Land Health and Bestow Reciprocity for Earth's Gifts; and Wisconsin's Driftless Area Brook Trout Fishery Depends on Cold, Clean Water)

A few years ago, we began offering topic-focused farm gatherings called Evenings Afield. One evening a month through each year's growing season, we invite folks in the watershed—and now beyond—to spend a few hours together learning about the land practices each has engaged in. We may also discuss the history of land use and the peoples who inhabited and visited our landscape through the millennia, report the findings from our monthly water quality monitoring, and more. These gatherings are invaluable opportunities, of course, for socializing and further community development.

An ambitious project is an interactive map of land use and ecological cover across the entire 8,600-acre watershed. Examples of the mapping tool's more than twenty-five overlays include water monitoring sites and results, recreation, agriculture, soil erodibility, wetlands, cultural resources, and invasive species infestations. We are just getting started on an outreach effort to share our experiences with other potential watershed groups in the Driftless Area.

Evenings Afield attendees on the Welsh Hills at Taliesin. Photo by Patrick Michaels.

We have also initiated an innovative effort to offset the point source phosphorus from the watershed's sole sanitary district by engaging in what Wisconsin calls "adaptive management" to reduce overall phosphorus entering the waters of the state. In this case, our proposed adaptive management is water quality trading (WQT). In essence, WQT allows landowners to adapt or improve land practices and vegetative cover that result in less phosphorus loss (non-point emissions as soil erosion and precipitation runoff) into Lowery Creek and then "trade" these non-point emission improvements—or credits—against the point-source emissions from the sewage treatment plant that emits its effluent into Lowery Creek near its junction with the Wisconsin River. This seems to be a win-win for all.

My family, along with conservation crop and forage farmer Joe Stapleton, organic grain and specialty crops grower Gary Zimmer and nephew Patrick Michaels, and Taliesin Preservation, are in the process of developing a new Driftless Farm Tour that highlights Frank Lloyd Wright's philosophy related to farming. The tour may visit the Midway Farm on the estate and our farms in the stream corridor. During the tour, we would plan to describe our watershed initiative, which fully embodies Wright's philosophy for integrating nature, aesthetics, and working lands.

Another inspiring and exciting outreach and recreational asset in the watershed is a segment of the Driftless Trail. This effort will connect the three state parks in our region with a continuous fifty-plus-

Our Friends and Neighbors Along Lowery Creek Are Engaged in Activities That Build Land Health and Bestow Reciprocity for Earth's Gifts

Here are some examples of what's being done along Lowery Creek:

Biological-organic, high-value grain and forage crops

Restoring remnant prairies and oak savannas

Cover cropping and rotating no-till corn-soybean-hay crops

Perennialized managed grazing for soil health and grass-fed beef and hogs

Establishing and maintaining pollinator habitat

Streambank habitat improvement

Monitoring stream water quality and sharing those results

Controlling invasive plant species

Developing perennialized silvopasture for grazing livestock

Installing solar energy for homes and farms

Regenerative fruit production

Agroforestry

Producing vegetable crops year-around

Bioengineering stream restoration

Managing woodlands for timber

Electro-fishing for brook trout age classes and population number

Documenting notable breeding birds, frogs and toads, and other wildlife

Learning and telling the local human history, from First Peoples to recent decades

Preserving cultural resources and telling their stories

Developing ecotourism that sustains and enhances the area's character mile walking trail across private lands. The Cates family is all in, and we can hardly wait to help walkers, birders, and skiers who love this land as much as we do have the opportunity to make it a part of their joy in living.

Our family has recently entered perpetual conservation easements with the WI DNR (in exchange for a one-time payment) to allow public fishing access to many miles of our beautiful fishery along Lowery Creek. Our neighbors contiguous to the north, the Savanna Institute, have begun the process, as well. In this way, citizens without land ownership have one more opportunity to enjoy the exceptional place that is the Driftless.

Barb Barzen says, "The most exciting part of this [Lowery Creek Watershed] Initiative is the community building that has started. There have been a lot of great conversations between neighbors and landowners and hopefully some new awareness happening for people who have an interest in doing restoration but don't know how to begin." Indeed, many of us are eager to share what we have learned.

The local watershed level is where to start because neighbors have an opportunity to sit around a table together, face to face, listen, and really get to know each other. If one of us improves our part of Lowery Creek, it directly benefits people right at the table. This is a very powerful motivator.

I take stock in the notion that of all the memberships we identify ourselves by, the one that has the greatest potential for healing is place.

And I believe that an increasing number of landowners are learning this. I see it happening today, slowly building momentum. Folks are making a commitment to come together to improve the quality of our Driftless Area watersheds, and beyond. This is, indeed, a geography of hope.

I take a strong stand that every human being has a right to clean water, and we all should do our part to help each other. We cannot continue to address clean water and the future of farming as separate issues. They will rise—or fall—together.

The Lowery Creek partnership has engendered a culture of mutual and collaborative care for our place. The opportunity to learn from and be inspired by our neighbors is motivating and a source of joy. Together we challenge each other to lift the bar of stewardship higher, and we are held to the imperative of living a land ethic. Nothing could be more fulfilling.

My family and our community have taken ownership of our future, and by doing so, we get to decide what our future looks like.

Every farm is a story of the land and of a family or community working on the land and with the land. So every farm is a story of relationships between people and between people and the land. This has been our story.

Wisconsin's Driftless Area Brook Trout Fishery Depends on Cold, Clean Water

Dave Vetrano, WI DNR Fish Biologist-Fishery Supervisor, retired

The water that falls into the watershed is what feeds the streams. There are artesian wells that flow from deep underground, but most streams are fed with the precipitation that falls in the watershed. With our karst topography, we get significant groundwater recharge.

This trout fishery we now have in the Driftless Area did not exist fifty years ago. It's here now because we have more perennial vegetation on the landscape. This allows more of the precipitation we get to soak in, increasing base flow, which increases spring and stream flow, providing the colder water temperatures the trout need. Just imagine if all of our agricultural land was protected with cover crops or perennial grass pasture. We would see less flooding and fewer droughts. So that's why I'm still involved with the land use aspect.

I said for years, why would I not encourage a producer to practice managed grazing, plant a prairie, or farm with no-till and cover crops when with these practices, all the issues that I would have otherwise had with stream flow and stream quality simply vanish? It's not just for groundwater percolation. It's fewer pesticides. Less possibility for manure to run off. No sediment (soil erosion). I mean, for all the issues I have to deal with, it'd make my job a hell of a lot easier.

I am optimistic about all of the talk about regenerative agriculture that I'm hearing now, including building up the soil, increasing the organic material, increasing soil permeability, allowing more water to percolate in rather than running off, and creating healthy food at the same time.

Finally, I think people are starting to pay attention. It's called regenerative. I don't care what you call it, but I love that word. I think this is the direction that agriculture needs to go. And I think now, post-COVID, people are going to look more closely at locally sourcing their food. More people will want to make sure they know where their food comes from.

EPILOGUE

Hope—What I Dream for the Future of Earth's Gifts

"A healthy farm culture can be based only upon familiarity and can grow only among a people soundly established upon the land; it nourishes and safeguards a human intelligence of the earth that no amount of technology can satisfactorily replace."
—Wendell Berry, *The Unsettling of America: Culture & Agriculture*

"That land is a community is the basic concept of ecology; but that land is to be loved and respected is an extension of ethics. That land yields a cultural harvest is a fact long known, but often forgotten."
—Aldo Leopold, *A Sand County Almanac*

One last time in our story, we hear the voice of our old sentinel oak, if we listen: "I dream that a human culture that truly respects the gifts of the Earth is returning after a long absence. I dream that my children, and their children's children and beyond, will have the chance to grow and thrive in such a rich community. This is the greatest gift I could ask for."

The farm is so beautiful now as I write. The grass sparkles as these late summer morning fogs, or augs, wend their way up the valley from the Wisconsin River, only to slowly melt away in the dazzling sunlight. And there are moments of exhilarating evening chill in the air that rekindle my intense love of autumn and all that it has delivered in my life. Those are the days when I first met Kim, and I fell in love, for real. Those are the days we escorted all our children down the lane to greet the school bus and all the new adventures that school promised to offer. Those are the days our third child, Peter, was born.

And these are the days the cattle grow fat. And the mighty oaks boast their potential for a kaleidoscope of color, soon grandly book-ending our place's celebration of life. It's no wonder "here" has been home to so many for so long.

Life is precious.

There's a culturally ingrained agriculture curiosity in many of us here in the Driftless: If I say I am farming, the first questions anyone ever asks me are, "How many cattle do you have, and how many acres do you 'run' or own?" These questions are uniquely cultural because, in many parts of the world, no one would even think of asking them.

Sometimes I'm just as guilty of this inquiry as anyone else when I'm speaking with my farm colleagues. However, over time, I've come to realize these are not the questions that should be asked. The answers to these questions should not matter.

Because this is what really matters: What do you do on your landscape to help ensure health and sustainability for your family? What do you do to protect the natural world you are entrusted with, to regenerate and reciprocate Earth's gifts? How are you contributing to the betterment of your community? Are you caring, respecting, and loving one another?

Although these questions may feel quite personal to us, they are pertinent. If we are going to develop a land ethic—which I have asserted is "an ecological necessity"—these are the questions we should be asking each other.

I have come to understand in my bones, after a long journey, that a land ethic, boiled down to its essence, is as basic and as powerful as the necessity of taking personal responsibility for the care of the soil, water, plants, and animals—collectively, the land under our care. Ultimately, such a land ethic is the only thing that will save our species.

At heart, most recognize that none of us actually *own* the land on which we live and farm any more than we can own the air we breathe or the water that flows. We are caretakers rather than owners, and only in the here and now. We have the extraordinary opportunity to derive our life and sustenance from this land. And as two sides of the same coin, I have also come to understand in my bones that we have the responsibility, the obligation, to care for and pass on the gifts with which we have been blessed. How well we accept and dedicate ourselves to this task will be our only true legacy.

Ultimately, I have told our story because I want to invite people into the real possibility of living on a small farm and partnering with those who care about how we take care of the land and the water.

I have told the story of the land we embrace. I hope that it engenders your love, respect, and appreciation for your own place on Earth.

We had to figure it out and learn to do more than just work the land, but to work with the land, with this place, and to accept and embrace partners who believed in our journey.

I believe that similar journeys and experiences are accessible to anyone willing to dream, imagine, and be persistent. You've got to do the work and walk the walk, fall in love with the land and the peaceful way of life that hard work and learned lessons can bestow. We must allow ourselves to grow wiser with time.

Many folks wring their hands about how the present agricultural system benefits a few, costs the American taxpayer a significant sum, and continues to operate according to our capitalist model—the bigger survives, and the smaller just fades away.

I am often overwhelmed by how the people I meet and speak with care deeply about our rural places and about sustaining our small communities. Yet we continue to lose these communities, continuing down a declining path that sometimes seems inevitable.

But it isn't an inevitable path at all. We need to have policy changes, indeed. We need to stay at the table and work to change the course of a very big ship. As we all know, this is a daunting task. However, the opportunity for more immediate change is right in front of us.

If a person dreams of farming or ranching, it is possible to follow a model similar to where our family eventually found ourselves. (See Appendix V—Farm Business Principles for Success) One doesn't need hundreds of acres of land or much capital at all. More importantly, one needs to work with the natural capital that a few acres will provide and with the community of people who care about what you do, the people who will choose your delicious, healthy food and share, pass on, your collective values.

This community of people is not composed of those with more than an average income—far from it. It is a growing number of individuals who care deeply about the same things you do. We all vote with our pocketbook every day when we shop for or dine out for a meal. This adds up to an incredibly powerful set of votes that take place 365 days a year.

Each November, when our legislators come up for reelection, we have the power to send a clear message as to what kind of food system we want if we choose to use our food dollars to support local, regenerative, and value-added agriculture. Food dollars spent locally stay local, and that means economic activity for our communities right where we live.

So it is, indeed, possible to change this present reality by building relationships with people who care about what you do on the land. It is imperative that farmers and ranchers step up and take this opportunity and reach across the table with an open hand rather than a closed fist, and continue to build these essential, invaluable partnerships.

As we know, or should know by now, Mother Nature always has the last word. If we continue to learn to work with our natural systems, and we learn gratitude for Earth's gifts that are offered to us just by the good fortune that we live on this land, if we learn to work in partnership, we will survive and thrive.

As Kimmerer reminds us in *Braiding Sweetgrass: Indigenous Wisdom, Scientific Knowledge, and the Teachings of Plants*: "Responsibilities and gifts are understood as two sides of the same coin ... for the Earth to stay in balance, for the gifts to continue to flow, we must give back in equal measure for what we take."

As Leopold admonishes in *The Land Ethic, A Sand County Almanac*: "Examine each question in terms of what is ethically and aesthetically right, as well as what is economically expedient. A thing is right when it tends to preserve the integrity, stability, and beauty of the biotic community. It is wrong when it tends otherwise."

Our family has pursued a long journey toward our land ethic. We recall Leopold's observation: "Nothing so important as an ethic is ever written ... It evolves in the minds of a thinking community." So we continue on this journey by doing the work and paying attention.

I see more and more young people who understand this imperative. There continues to be an increasing number of high school and university studies that focus on ecology, regenerative agriculture, and soil health. This is most hopeful.

For three decades, I have helped some of the best and brightest young people in Wisconsin to stay in or get started in farming. They are often successful rural businesspeople and productive, contributing families in their communities. Significantly, taking the long view, they are perpetuating our core values by tending to our land. A next generation of farmers with an ethic of care and stewardship of the land is essential to a healthy, enduring culture in America. These bearers of a land ethic need our abiding support. We all need to commit to protecting and preserving our farmland and the waters of the nation. We all need to share with the next generation of farmers what we have learned along the way and why we love what we do.

Our story, putting in place a perennial farming model and partnering with people who share our story, offers an unlimited opportunity for young people who see farming as a life of purpose, a life of value, a life of dignity. A life of balance on the land can be a rich life filled with gratitude.

I am going to repeat something I wrote at the beginning of this book. The greatest existential crisis human civilization faces is the destruction of the natural conditions necessary for our own survival.

I believe that the most significant work any of us can do at this time in the history of human beings on Earth is to live in reciprocity for her gifts in a way that cares deeply for all she has bestowed.

This is respectful, honorable work. It is work we should all be engaged in—not just those of us who produce food, but all of us who leave any sort of footprint of our time here, supported by the gifts of the Earth.

I have followed my heart through life. A land ethic has guided my journey on this place. The wisdom of my dearest friend, Kim, guided our business in a life-giving direction, and with imagination, we worked together to put together the pieces of a life-sustaining puzzle.

For my family, conservation has indeed not been that feared set of constraints, but a very positive part of our lives, which has involved skill and learning to understand what the land can sustain. I have encouraged each of the young farmers I have trained to look at the plot of land they tend as their portrait and a statement of self and to try to understand how they and the land, living together as partners, can do better. That's an uplifting way to farm and to live. So many of us on the land long for this. It's a process of finding our way.

Here Kim and I are so many years later, with love in our hearts for our grown children, our grandchildren, and this magical land. We feel gratitude for our family, our community, and for the gifts of this place. We feel hope that the next generation of our family on this land and our community will thrive.

One must have faith that as seasons change, the Earth's gifts will always be there for us if we care for them. The greatest gift we can bestow is to be thankful, to show gratitude for these gifts, and to accept them with respect, a promise of care, and great humility. To the next generation of farmers, and to all, we need to—we must—leave a proud legacy. This is what I hope for.

What kind of ancestors do we want to be?[1]

A creek runs through this Driftless land, and it is cold and clear ... and the brookies are back.

—Nįįna wakącąkšaną

Acknowledgments

I am immensely grateful to so many good folks who offered their knowledge, believed in my family and me, and lent heartfelt support for the telling of the story that has become this book. Indeed, this multi-year effort to share a story of the land, its people, and our family's journey became a "journey" in and of itself.

I will thank all of those whose contributions I took note of in my journal, yet I fear I will have missed someone. To that someone, I am quite certain you will come to me in my pleasant thoughts at some moment, and please know you are also thanked from my heart, even though your name does not appear below.

Thank you to William Batten, James Bockheim, Eric Carson, Rich Henderson, Mark Kurz, Jed Meunier, Doug Richmond, and James Riser for assisting me with the geological, ecological, and phenological history of the Driftless Area.

Don Greenwood, Doug Gurak, Ryan Howell, Mary Kritz, Patty Loew citizen of Mashkiiziibii (Bad River Band of Lake Superior Ojibwe), Janice Rice Hoocąk (Ho-Chunk citizen), and Joe Stapleton, thank you for teaching me and helping me respectfully tell a story of the First Peoples here for millennia.

Thank you to Jerry Apps, John Halverson, John Hess, Mary Lloyd-Jones, Mary Knudson, Curt Meine, and Rob Nurre for helping me sift through the local European history to pull out pieces most relevant to our story.

Thank you to Katie Abbot, Mike Aquino, Ashley Beranek, Angie Doucette, Tristyn Forget, Justin Haglund, Jason Himebauch, Kimberly Kuber, John Lyons, Lloyd Meng, Michael Shupryt, Dave Vetrano, and Duke Welter for helping me understand the history of our surface water quality, and the journey of our Lowery Creek from a brown and muddy Class 3 stream to a cold and clear Class 1 native heritage brook trout jewel.

Blair Anderson, Jeb Barzen, Michael Casler, Fred Clark, Mike Engel, Tom Hill, Randy Jackson, Darcy Kind, Gigi La Budde, and Jason Sable, thank you all for advising and assisting us on our grassland and forest management and oak savanna restoration and helping us to communicate the ecological functions and services of each to tell our story.

Thank you to Jerry Apps, David Cates, Anna Cates, Kim Cates, Laura Daniels, Randy Jackson, Cheryll and Jonnah Mellenthin, Kevin McAleese, and Stan Temple for reading my story at its various stages of discovery, growth, and maturation. And to Barb Barzen, Michael Degen, Ryan Hewson, and Jean Unmuth, who read and contributed to the final chapter about our community effort, "The Lowery Creek Watershed Initiative," to honor our place, thank you.

Adeline Amble for her professional-quality photos of the projectile points and cultural pieces identified from the Stapleton-Wyoming Campsite.

Thank you to Darla and Rob at Any & All Media who were able to make "any and all" of my photos from the 1960s to present, across "any and all" media, print ready.

And to my amazing stalwart, extraordinary editor and reader, and now close friend, Don Greenwood, thank you for making me sound like an actual English speaker over these four years of your dedication from beginning to end.

A warm embrace to my siblings with whom I shared so many invaluable experiences in our earlier years here on the farm, including my sister Chris and brothers John, David, and Bob. And to our loving parents, Richard (Dick) Sr. and Margaret (Marnie), for providing us the opportunity to work and play together and grow as loving friends but also for putting up with our endless shenanigans in and around any real work we may have accomplished.

I so greatly appreciate the dedicated hunters who love this land and have worked their tails off here, and who have all become close friends with my family. And I give thanks to my many students and agricultural colleagues across Wisconsin and far beyond who have challenged my thinking and my actions, which helped me to take responsibility for my choices.

Thank you to the visitors from across the globe who have stopped by for a tour of our home and to share a story of their homeland.

And to our neighbors who have created a community of respect and care for our shared watershed.

Thank you to Odessa Piper, founder of L'Etoile Restaurant, the first chef so many years ago to believe in the manner in which we raised our beef on pasture; to all those in the restaurant and retail businesses who gave us a chance and embraced our work; and to the hundreds of households, families, who chose to become customers, then friends.

Thanks to Paul Lackner, who we have never met, for dropping by one day and fishing for the recently returned heritage brookies and then sending us a letter of love and gratitude—the kind of selfless gift that helps make the work here all worth it—for cherishing this place and sharing it with the greater world.

And I owe the world to the Kristin Mitchell at Little Creek Press for her design and layout work, but most of all for believing in me and taking a chance on my telling of the story of this sacred Driftless Land.

Again, to my loving children, Eric and Shannon, their spouses, Kiley and Dan, and my grandchildren, Sloane, Peter, Fischer, and Hannah, thank you for being at my side and living this story as it has unfolded over the years. And for your stalwart belief that the story of this land should be told.

And finally, I thank you dear Kim, once again, for being so wise and for sharing your life with me, through thick and thin, for fifty years now. I am so very fortunate.

For all I have been blessed, I give thanks and promise to pay it forward.

Photo by Leggett family.

About the Author

Richard (Dick) and his wife, Kim, co-own the Cates Family Farm LLC in Wyoming Township, Iowa County, with their son Eric and his wife, Kiley, and their daughter Shannon and her husband, Dan. Dick is a life-long farmer who grew up working on his family's beef cow-calf farm, a neighbor's dairy farm, Montana ranches, and in large-scale dairy forage and grain crop production overseas.

From left to right: Dan and Shannon (Cates) Bloom with children Hannah Denise and Peter Ray; Dick and Kim; Eric and Kiley with children Sloane Helen and Fischer Lyman. Photo courtesy of the Cates family.

Dick pursued professional studies in soil science and agronomy and earned an MS (1979) in soils from Montana State University and a PhD (1983) in soils and plant health from the University of Wisconsin–Madison College of Agricultural and Life Sciences while serving a Leopold Fellowship. Dick began taking over the family farm management in 1987 and then, along with Kim, purchased a portion of the land to build their own farming business.

For the next eight years, Dick helped (part time) lead the development and oversight of the Wisconsin Sustainable Agriculture Program, an on-farm demonstration and research effort of the Wisconsin Department of Agriculture, Trade and Consumer Protection with the purpose of reducing agriculture's dependence on non-renewable petroleum-based inputs. In 1995 Dick was given the opportunity (part time) to develop and direct the Wisconsin School for Beginning Dairy and Livestock Farmers, a program at UW–Madison to train new would-be farmers in business planning and managed grazing. Dick retired from this work in 2018, but over those twenty-three years, he also developed and taught courses within the College of Agricultural and Life Sciences there.

Dick and his family are members of the Iowa County Uplands Farmer-Led Watershed Project and the Lowery Creek Watershed Initiative, where they share information about and demonstrate conservation practices with other landowners and the public.

The Cates family has been recognized for their soil and water conservation work: 1998 Wisconsin Soil and Water Conservation Achievement Award, Soil and Water Conservation Society of America; 1999 and 2018 Water Quality Leadership Award, Iowa County Land Conservation; 2000 Distinguished Agricultural Award, Kiwanis Club of Downtown Madison; 2006 certification by the Animal Welfare Institute, the first beef farm in the United States to receive this certification; 2009 Wisconsin Grazing Community Communicator of the Year; 2012 UW–Madison Farm and Industry Short Course Alumni Service to Agriculture; 2016 Blue Mounds Area Project Bur Oak Award; 2016 Wisconsin Master Agriculturist; and 2020 Wisconsin Farm Bureau Federation Distinguished Service to WI Agriculture Award. In their words, the most cherished recognition was receiving the 2013 Sand County Foundation Wisconsin Leopold Conservation Award.

Dick authored the book *Voices from the Heart of the Land: Rural Stories That Inspire Community* (University of Wisconsin Press, 2008) and a children's book, *An Adventure on Sterna's Hill* (2019).

Dick and Kim enjoy walking on the farm and in wild country anywhere, canoeing, skiing, and dancing together. They have four grandchildren who are the love and joy of their lives.

APPENDIX I

Principles of a Direct Market Grass-Fed Beef Business

There are no public (taxpayer) subsidies—farm programs—or futures markets for direct marketed farm products similar to those available in commodity agriculture. Your essential job is to create a business that differentiates your products (hence, they are no longer commodities) to satisfy values desired in the marketplace, to add value to your community of customers and a living return to your farm and family. It has been a joy to be able to accomplish this, and now I can observe Eric and Kiley create their own relationships and personal metrics of success.

The success of your business is dependent on the following:

- Relatively inexpensive high-quality feed (well-managed pasture)
- High-quality livestock
- Vertical integration: production, warehousing, marketing, delivery; processing is outsourced
- Building partnerships with honest individuals with similar goals
- Working your butt off for a long time

These are the production choices our customers value the most:

- No use of antibiotics or growth hormones (minimum nine months prior to processing) or animal by-products fed (ever)
- Pasture raised and grass fed
- No excess fat
- Cattle can be sourced from birth
- Animal welfare/humane living and handling practices

(Delicious, high-quality beef will bring them back and spread the good word).

Market your products and your values—healthy and delicious food, clean water, aesthetics, love of the land and place—through personal conversation, a long-term dialogue with your customers and the public.

Create your own diversified, sustainable market by "adding value to value to value" to commodities with the following:

- A buyer for all cuts
- Households: delicious, healthy local food as a staple and for enjoyment
- Specialty retail: delicious, healthy local food as a consumer preference and for enjoyment
- Artisan and local restaurants: delicious, healthy local food for enjoyment, social gathering, and pure recreation
- Gift trade: delicious, healthy local food as a gift!
- Reasonable prices, not the highest

The best grass-fed beef is finished on pasture during the year when the weather is cool, and the grass is growing rapidly (spring and autumn flushes). Tender, delicious, pasture-raised beef is encouraged by these factors:

- Minimal, or no, stress on livestock throughout their life cycle
- Breeds that naturally marble on a high-forage diet
- Rapid growth prior to/at processing
- Dry aging after processing

Perseverance, patience, integrity, respect, and a sense of humor are virtues for anyone who has the goal of building their own business. We are not talking about a get-rich-quick scheme or a series of business deals. We are talking about a solid, enjoyable approach to making a living on a farm/ranch in the livestock business.

APPENDIX II
A President "Almost" Stops By

Dick: I had a voice message left on my cell phone at 12:59 p.m., Friday, June 18, 2021, from a White House policy adviser.

"A senior White House official is interested in visiting your farm, and we'd want to discuss that with you. If you could give me a call back ASAP today, that would be great because we're trying to finalize the location by the end of the day. Otherwise, I think we'll have to go with a different location."

I responded with my own message, and that was that. Like everyone, we receive a *lot* of "unsolicited" calls, and I put this one out of my mind. A few days later, Kim and I traveled north to our lake cottage and left the farm to those who are actually in charge, Eric and Kiley.

Eric: I had received multiple phone calls from a Washington, D.C., number on June 16. I was busy doing farm work. Of course, a phone number from Washington, D.C., just screamed out "spam." And then several more. I ignored them.

I got an email the next day from a woman at a different Washington contact, reiterating that they wanted to visit and had a few questions about the impact of economic concentration in rural areas, particularly on agriculture, as well as things related to the pandemic and broadband.

I returned the email and said, "I'm really busy. Be happy to chat but working on equipment the next couple of days and hauling hay." She responded, letting me know she totally understood, but if we could make it work really quickly, that would be great.

Then I received phone calls from another woman, a New York number. Again, I ignored them, assuming it was more spam. An email followed from this person in New York saying that a "senior administration official is interested in making a visit to Southwest Wisconsin very soon. If that's something of interest to you, we need to connect today."

So I returned the call as I was driving between farms hauling hay. The contact was from the White House. Although my cell phone dropped the call between hills, she seemed very excited that we had connected and happy to have her questions answered. That was about it.

In the meantime, unbeknownst to me, Dad had also connected with the first person to reach out to us. Neither of us was given any further information, nor did we ask. We are accustomed to fielding questions about our farm and our agricultural perspectives.

Early the next week, Mom came across a news article that announced President Biden would visit Southwest Wisconsin on June 29 to talk about ag issues. So my dad reached out to the folks in

Washington and New York on June 22, asking if there was anything else they needed from us now that we knew the President of the United States was going to be in our neighborhood.

The next day, Dad and I both received an email introduction of sorts from our personal White House contact, and we were told she would arrive in Wisconsin that evening.

At this point, all we knew for sure was a "senior official" wanted to visit our farm with no timeline hinted at, and President Joe Biden was coming to Wisconsin the following Tuesday.

The next day, June 24, I was in Madison, and our contact emailed, "Hey, there. So great to be connected. Mind sharing the best number to reach you? Our travel plans are a bit in flux, and we'd love to stop by this afternoon." The job title in her signature line read: Associate Director of Presidential Advance.

I called the contact while I was making beef deliveries in Madison. When we connected, she said, "We'll be there at 4:00 p.m. today, and the Secret Service will be there at 5:00 p.m."

I still had about two hours of deliveries and an hour's drive back to the farm. At each delivery stop, I had to say, "I've got to go. I got to go. The White House is coming at 4:00 p.m. I got to get home."

I arranged for our four-year-old daughter Sloane to be picked up from daycare by a friend. My wife, Kiley, met me at the farm with our one-year-old Fischer as I arrived at 3:56 p.m.! Sure enough, at 4:01 there was a small group of a half-dozen young ladies and one young guy. They all looked fresh out of college and dressed up a little, but they were excited to be there. They just said, "Just show us around. Show us the farm." So I said, "Okay, let's hop in the truck, and we'll go move the cattle to fresh pasture."

They asked about our grazing business, what we stood for from an ethical perspective, and what a "commitment to conservation" (our farm tagline) meant to us in our daily work. They adored our animals and asked about our animal welfare practices.

They were really excited, and I was thrilled to see their reactions! They all came from different places: D.C., New York, New Jersey, Michigan, and Arizona. Some were asking lots of questions and wanted to know what we enjoy and appreciate about our life here on the farm. Some were in the background writing notes. Besides our personal contact, the associate director of presidential advance, the others were mostly White House media and photography staff.

At one point on the tour, our contact said, "Oh, the president just loves this stuff. This is up his alley. This is what really makes him tick. He loves being out here and doing these kinds of things and seeing these things. This is the type of person he is."

This prompted Kiley to ask, "Well, what is the plan? What are you guys doing here?" The contact looked at us somewhat dumbfounded.

After a pause, she said, "Well, the president is coming on Tuesday, June 29. What, nobody told you?"

We said, "No, nobody told us anything. We didn't know."

Our contact said, "Oh, I'm so sorry. I thought you guys knew." It was pretty comical and somewhat mind-blowing.

We headed back to the farmstead, and the place was swarming with about forty more folks! Secret Service agents and a lot of military-type guys, wearing shorts and t-shirts, backpacks, hats, and hiking boots.

We were introduced to the newcomers, and then they huddled up and talked seriously for a while. One by one, folks would break from the group and ask questions: "Who owns the land? Where are the property boundaries? What's down there? What is in those buildings? Is there anything combustible? Are there people who walk around in the woods frequently? Does it get really wet here?"

One of the guys who deals with transportation issues asked how much vehicle weight the driveway bridge could support. When I told him we get gravel trucks across, he responded, "Oh, that should be enough."

Some Secret Service officers were dressed like Secret Service. A few worked with me on my phone line so they could monitor it for bomb threats. There was a lot of small talk with them, too. They were curious about the farm and what we do, and I was curious about them and their background. It was an enjoyable give and take. Some asked, "Do you mind if we walk around in the woods for the next couple of days and just canvass the area from different viewpoints?" I let them know that was fine.

They asked if we had a lot of group visits and tours. I let them know we've had folks from all over the world.

One asked if we had ever had any dignitaries visit. I let them know that my mom had worked for U.S. Senator (Herb) Kohl, and he'd been out to the farm. I told them we'd had a Wisconsin governor, agriculture secretary, and other elected officials here. Then I let them know that we've had Craig Culver out. Those from states that host the Culver's chain grinned in approval.

While we were mingling, I opened a package of our beef sticks and offered them to a few folks. They passed them around, and soon a volley of questions started coming: "Do you sell those beef sticks here? Can I buy some?" "Wait, we can buy beef sticks? How much?" They were a hit, and soon, folks were lining up. "There are beef sticks for sale! I'll take two." "Can I get some summer sausage, as well?" Within a few minutes, I sold hundreds of dollars of Cates Family Farm grass-fed beef! I guess this was almost as good as the president visiting.

The advance team let us know how much they loved the place, appreciated our time, and that they'd be here every day preparing for the president's visit.

That night I sent my parents a text: "Oh, by the way, President Biden and the U.S. Secretary of Agriculture, the governor of Wisconsin, and elected Wisconsin officials are coming on Tuesday. Surprise!" At this point, no one else knew about this except the planning team that had been on

our farm and the entourage of dignitaries that were to join him. We weren't allowed to tell anyone until the story was scheduled to hit the press on Monday!

As it turns out, Kiley's family was scheduled to arrive from California that night for a few days' visit. I sent them a text: "Heads up, President Biden will be coming here on Tuesday, and White House folks will be here all week. Just letting you know."

The next day, I expected a few people to be around, but nobody showed up. I wondered, *What's our role? Are we giving a tour to the president?* So I reached out to our contact and left her a voicemail and an email asking these questions.

It wasn't until the next day that I received an email back from her that said, "Oh, I'll call you later. There are still a few things we're working out." She called back that afternoon and initiated the conversation by letting me know how sorry she was that it wasn't going to work out. She had worked hard to make it happen, but it wasn't going to be possible. With impending rain in the forecast, the difficulty the rugged terrain posed to secure the farm, and uncertainty about whether they would be able to land five helicopters.

Then she let me know that the president would still be coming to Southwest Wisconsin on Tuesday but not to speak on agriculture issues. Instead, he was going to speak on his new Infrastructure Investment and Jobs Act. This meant the visit had to be shifted to a more appropriate location. So they chose the municipal garage in the city of La Crosse.

Dick: On Monday, the president's planned visit for the following day hit the press. The media informed readers of the original plan to address agricultural issues on the Cates Family Farm in rural Spring Green. So now the world knew that the president "almost" visited the Cates farm.

The Cates family was invited, instead, to the small La Crosse gathering, and Eric and I attended with reserved seats up front with our Wisconsin governor and other dignitaries. We had a chance to meet President Biden after his address to the crowd, and we ribbed him a bit for not making it to the farm, And, of course, he promised, "Next time."

Dick and Eric shaking hands with President Biden. Photo courtesy of the Cates family.

APPENDIX III

Our Oak Savanna Restoration: A Journey of Wonder and Awe

"He who owns a veteran bur oak owns more than a tree. He owns a historical library and a reserved seat in the theater of evolution. To the discerning eye, his farm is labeled with the badge and symbol of the prairie war."
—"Bur Oak (April)" in *A Sand County Almanac*

First Phase of the Restoration Process

Summer 2002: Fred Clark, Clark Forestry, Baraboo; and Gigi La Budde, restoration ecologist, Spring Green, toured our forest acres along with Kim and me. As stated in Chapter 7, "They informed us, with much excitement, that the large old stand of bur oak above our home on top of Peter's Hill, where his ashes are safeguarded, actually harbored several remnant oak savanna indicator species on the forest floor: Pennsylvania sedge (*Carex pensylvanica*), prairie violet (*Viola sororia*), Robin's plantain (*Erigeron pulchellus*), azure aster (*Symphyotrichum oolentangiense*), showy tick trefoil (*Desmodium canadense*), sideoats grama (*Bouteloua curtipendula*), bee balm (*Monarda didyma*), pussy toes (*Antennaria plantaginifolia*), and more."[1]

So this meant, "Here on the forest floor of our farm is a fifteen-acre patch above our farmhouse ... It might be possible to restore this oak savanna remnant if we were willing to commit a lifetime to the work and were patient, even audacious enough to make the attempt." We are forever thankful to Fred and Gigi for enlightening us about the diamond in the rough right under our feet. They had much to do with setting us off on a lifetime of adventure.

Autumn 2002–Winter 2003: Solicited partner assistance from the USDA NRCS, the U.S. Fish and Wildlife, and Clark Forestry to develop a plan of action.

Autumn 2003: Began mechanical removal (with a tractor brush hog!) of woody weed species; chemical treatment of some re-sprouting woody species.

Spring 2004: Created "a textbook" firebreak (burn line). Performed first prescribed burn of thirty-seven acres; patience ...

I grabbed a chain saw and rake and went at the task of "showing" Seth Alt and Eric Cates what the job was. We need to create a firebreak—a path through the woods about a half mile long—clean of brush and leave litter so the thirty-seven-acre prescribed and controlled burn would stay controlled. After about fifty yards of huffing and puffing, showboating, showing the boys, I retreated to other less strenuous activities on the farm. Several days later, they told me they were done! I traveled with them back to the site to take this picture. A short time later, when the burn boss of the fire crew came to inspect our work, he told me this was a textbook burn line. In fact, it was an over-the-top burn line, and would I mind if he took pictures of it to use in his classroom trainings! Well, the boys were tickled, of course, but they had to ponder what else they could have accomplished in those extra hours it took to build the Taj Mahal of burn lines.

Eric and friend, Seth Alt, hand rake a "textbook" firebreak for our first oak savanna burn, spring 2004.

Second Phase of the Restoration Process

August 2006: Enter Darcy Kind, conservation biologist, WI DNR, and a grant through the Landowner Incentive Program; additional understory indicator flora species observed: golden alexanders (*Zizia aurea*) and purple joe-pye weed (*Eutrochium purpureum*).

Autumn 2007: Enter Mike Engel, private lands biologist, U.S. Fish and Wildlife Service. Re-created/maintained firebreak and performed second prescribed burn on thirty-seven acres.

Late spring 2009: Enter Al Shea, director, WI DNR, who led us on an early morning birding outing and identified rare/declining species that benefit from oak savanna restoration: cerulean and hooded warblers.

Third Phase of the Restoration Process

Winter 2009–10: Engaged partners WI DNR (again) and Mike Healy, ecologist and owner of Adaptive Restoration LLC.

Early spring 2010: Re-created/maintained firebreak. Performed the third prescribed burn, focused on approximately twenty-five acres, keeping some refugia adjacent to the pasture for at-risk birds.

Summer 2010: Where burns had not removed all invasive understory, hand-pulled/dug herbaceous weeds, primarily common burdock (*Arctium minus*), and some garlic mustard (*Alliaria petiolata*); and mowed woody species, principally autumn olive (*Elaeagnus umbellata*), bush honeysuckle (*Lonicera tatarica*), fewer multiflora rose (*Rosa multiflora*), and excess native prickly ash (*Zanthoxylum Americanum*).

Additional understory indicator flora species observed: purple milkweed (*Asclepias purpurascens*), thimbleweed (*Anemone cylindrica*), white (death) camus (*Anticlea elegans*), and arrowleaf aster (*Symphyotrichum urophyllum*).

Fall 2010: Girdled, then herbicide-treated more than one hundred invasive or over-crowded tree stems.

Aldo Leopold Foundation staff and volunteer prescribed fire crew at the oak savanna restoration site.

Fourth Phase of the Restoration Process

Spring 2011: Maintained firebreak and performed the fourth prescribed burn, focused on approximately twenty acres.

Summer 2011: Enter John Harrington, professor of landscape architecture, UW–Madison, an oak savanna master. Additional understory indicator flora species observed: poke milkweed (*Asclepias exaltata*). The professor offered us (lots of) moral support.

Fifth Phase of the Restoration Process

Spring 2013: Engaged another new partner: the Aldo Leopold Foundation burn crew headed by ecologist Alanna Koshollek. Maintained firebreak and performed fifth prescribed burn on approximately twenty acres.

Late summer 2013: Additional understory indicator flora species observed: tall thimbleweed (*Anemone virginiana*), stiff bedstraw (*Galium tinctorium*), kitten tails (*Besseya bullii*), a species of special concern), lion's foot (*Leontice leontopetalum*), and pale-spiked lobelia (*Lobelia spicata*).

Autumn 2013: First several red-headed woodpeckers identified (read the story in Chapter 7), a marker of real progress toward our habitat restoration goal.

Sixth Phase of the Restoration Process

Spring (May 23) 2015: Eric and Kiley hold their wedding ceremony on the top of Peter's Hill.

Summer 2015: Additional understory indicator flora species observed: bottlebrush grass (*Elymus hystrix*), pale-leaf woodland sunflower (*Helianthus strumosus*), and leadplant (*Amorpha canescens*).

Spring 2016: Engaged the Aldo Leopold Foundation burn crew once again. Maintained firebreak and performed sixth prescribed burn on approximately twenty acres.

Seventh Phase of the Restoration Process

Spring 2018: Enter Bill Moore, ecologist and owner, Ecological Woodland Management LLC. Maintained firebreak and performed seventh prescribed burn on approximately twenty acres.

Summer 2018: Additional understory indicator flora species observed with Darcy Kind: false Solomon's seal (*Smilacina racemosa*), Illinois tick trefoil (*Desmodium illinoense*), violet wood sorrel (*Oxalis violacea*), and whorled milkweed (*Asclepias verticillata*) with monarch butterfly larvae! Mowed invasive woody brush not sufficiently set back by fire.

Autumn 2018: Girdled, then herbicide-treated approximately 125 invasive or over-crowded tree stems. Seeded native grasses sideoats grama (*Bouteloua curtipendula*), little bluestem (*Schizachyrium scoparium*), Canada wild rye (*Elymus canadensis*), big bluestem (*Andropogon gerardii*), Indiangrass (*Sorghastrum nutans*), forbs partridge pea (*Chamaecrista fasciculata*), and purple giant hyssop (*Agastache rugosa*) on just over an acre.

Some of our friends who "work-to-hunt" prepare to girdle and spot herbicide treat trunks of non-native tree species in the oak savanna restoration process.

Eighth Phase of the Restoration Process

Spring 2019: Enter Jeb Barzen, ecologist and owner, Private Lands Conservation LLC. Maintained burn line and performed eighth prescribed burn on approximately twenty acres.

Autumn 2019: Nephew Lucas Cates and bride Taryn Garland hold their wedding ceremony on top of Peter's Hill. Seeded the same native grasses as 2018 and a forb, Canada milk vetch (*Astragalus canadensis*).

Ninth Phase of the Restoration Process

Spring 2021: Engaged the wisdom and expertise, and now friendship of Jeb Barzen, once again. Maintained firebreak and performed ninth prescribed burn on approximately twenty acres. Herbicide-treated areas where invasive garlic mustard persists.

Summer 2023: Hand-cut and herbicide-treated woody invasives on about an acre where recent fire events had not sufficiently reduced their presence.

Engaged the wisdom and expertise, and now friendship of Darcy Kind, once again. Observed additional understory indicator flora species: hazelnut (*Corylus americana*), goldenrods: Canada (*Solidago canadensis*), elm-leaved (*S. ulmifolia*), and hairy (*S. hispida*), pale Indian plantain (*Arnoglossum atriplicifolium*), and asters: blue wood (*Symphyotrichum cordifolium*), calico (*S. lateriflorum*), panicled (*S. lanceolatum*), and Short's (*S. shortii*). But the most exciting observation was bur oak (*Quercus macrocarpa*) seedlings!

Darcy noted, with the exception of scattered patches of invasive understory species, the restoration site was (almost) exclusively natives. Our oak savanna restoration is slowly but surely becoming a reality.

Autumn 2023: Began the next stage of stem removal for opening the canopy for ever-increasing light to the oak savanna understory, including girdled, then herbicide-treated several hundred invasive or over-crowded tree stems, approximately five acres on the west side of the restoration area (between trails we had cut, in addition to Peter's Trail on top and the Rim Trail and Bucky's Draw Trail). That will likely be the last larger area for stem removal. (Areas previously thinned will still be revisited for fine-tuning of this multi-year process.)

Tenth Phase of the Restoration Process

Spring 2025: Maintained firebreak and performed tenth prescribed burn on approximately twenty acres.

Summer 2025: GRAZING!?

Our oak savanna odyssey continues, with the potential for many more years of joyous and hopeful work, weddings of our grandchildren and great nieces and nephews, and wonder and awe, and perhaps a final resting place for Kim and me, as well.

Top two rows left clockwise: half-black bumble bee; monarch butterfly larvae on whorled milkweed leaf; bur oak seedling; Illinois tick trefoil; Robin's plantain. Photos by Darcy Kind. Bottom: The diverse flora of the oak woodland understory.

APPENDIX IV

The Methane Yoke of Burden Has Been Incorrectly—and Unfairly—Placed on Our Domestic Livestock

First, a quick climate change tutorial:

Methane is one of several gases in Earth's atmosphere that creates what is known as the greenhouse effect. Since the beginning of time, carbon dioxide (CO_2), nitrous oxide (N_2O), methane (CH_4), and a few other gases have created a ceiling of sorts that traps heat from the sun and blankets our planet with it. It's not a bad thing. In fact, if it were not for the greenhouse effect, Earth would be too cold to sustain life.

However, in the last one hundred fifty years or so, we have produced a record amount of greenhouse gas emissions. These gases are behaving as they were meant to: trapping heat from the sun. Because there is an unprecedented amount, they're causing the planet to heat up. That's what is referred to as global warming, the phenomenon that is driving climate change.

Ruminant animals produce methane. So does the extraction and production of fossil fuels, as does organic waste as it decomposes in landfills and wetlands, including flooded rice fields the world over. As a matter of comparison, the amount of methane produced by wetlands and cattle stocked on well-managed grazed pastures in Wisconsin is about the same on a per-acre basis.[1]

Chemically speaking, methane is methane is methane. It is always a compound made up of one carbon atom bonded to four hydrogen atoms. That said, the source of methane is significant. Where it comes from makes a difference in how it affects our atmosphere, the greenhouse effect, and climate change.

There are two pathways for methane production:

Fossil methane, the gas that comes from the Earth's crust, has a one-way route directly to the atmosphere. It's a brand-new addition to the atmosphere, and once there, it hangs above us for about twelve years before being converted to carbon dioxide and water vapor through hydroxyl oxidation—a chemical reaction in the atmosphere. After it becomes carbon dioxide, it stays in the atmosphere for more time than we can count, simply because of the glut already there. This results in additional carbon in the atmosphere and new warming.

Another source of methane in the atmosphere is the planet's herbivores. Methane is produced by "enteric" fermentation occurring in their stomachs, intestines, or rumens. The roughly two hundred species of ruminants include both domestic and wild species. Ruminating mammals include all domesticated and wild bovids: antelopes, bison, African and water buffalos, cattle, deer, gazelles, giraffes, goats, and sheep.

Methane produced by wild or domestic fauna is part of the biogenic carbon cycle where plants take up carbon dioxide and turn it into plant tissue—primarily the carbohydrate cellulose—which is consumed by herbivores. Some of this is turned into methane, which is belched into the atmosphere.

Indigestible by humans, cellulose is a key feed ingredient for cattle and other herbivores. They are able to break it down, using the carbon that makes up the cellulose they consume and emitting a portion as methane. After about twelve years, this methane is also converted back into carbon dioxide and water. But this carbon is the same carbon that was in the air prior to being consumed by an animal. It is recycled carbon. As long as herbivore emissions remain constant for more than twelve years, no additional methane—or warming—is being added to the atmosphere in the biogenic carbon cycle.

So the biogenic cycle produces methane from animals, which is a flow gas made from atmospheric carbon that has been cycling through the atmosphere since life began. As part of the biogenic carbon cycle, plants absorb carbon dioxide, and through the process of photosynthesis, they harness the energy of the sun to produce oxygen and carbohydrates such as cellulose, which are a primary component of grasses across the globe.

That's very different than CO_2 from fossil methane, or any fossil CO_2, that hangs over us potentially forever because the carbon sinks, and oceans, soils, and plants that remove it are overwhelmed. Blame humans, not cattle, for that. Our love affair with the burning of fossil fuels is only slowly cooling down. Consequently, so goes the atmosphere.

Eating meat and dairy products is not a major driver of the problem, and it might well be part of the solution, according to Frank Mitloehner, professor and air quality specialist in the Department of Animal Science, and his team at the University of California, Davis who are monitoring methane production from cattle on varying diets.[2] Some get standard fare, while others are given feed that may reduce methane from enteric fermentation. Emissions from their belches and manure are then measured.

Their recent research finds that adding small doses of common plants, such as seaweeds, into the diets of cattle can reduce methane emissions by 80 percent with no impact on productivity.[3] Research elsewhere in the world is also revealing that diet adjustments in cattle can significantly reduce enteric fermentation.

Mitloehner says, "What gets me the most excited is that if we reduce methane from cattle, then we are actively pulling carbon out of the atmosphere. That's almost as if you were to store atmospheric CO_2 in the ground. Can it be done? It can be done, and it has been done."

Of course, we'll never be able to reduce the biogenic methane production from the wild herds of grass-eating mammals across the planet, but it appears we will be able to mitigate significantly domestic animal methane production.

This gets me excited, as well.

Photo by Sam Otto.

APPENDIX V

Farm Business Principles for Success[1]

There are always opportunities in agriculture for people who want to farm and who are willing to follow a few basic principles to get started and stay in business. As directors and educators with the Wisconsin School for Beginning Dairy and Livestock Farmers (WSBDF) at the University of Wisconsin–Madison, we have been able to follow the progress of many of our graduates. The advice and principles we share here are based on our observations of the experiences, both good and bad, of the hundreds of students who have enrolled in the WSBDF and on our own farming and business experiences. While these principles were developed with beginning dairy and livestock farmers in mind, most apply to all kinds of farm enterprises.

We are pleased that since the WSBDF began in 1995, more than 75 percent of its graduates are farming; half have started their own farm business or enterprise, and 60 percent are operating pasture-based farms. And most who aren't farming plan to do so. They are young and old, men and women, high school and college graduates, from farms and cities. Despite these differences, they are linked by their passion for farming. When we ask our students, "What gets you out of bed in the morning?"

They respond, "I want to farm."

Who succeeds in farming? What leads to the creation of both financial success and a satisfying life for farmers and their families? As with any business, starting and succeeding in farming requires time and sacrifice, and our fast-paced culture doesn't emphasize such patience. Successful farmers are passionate about the journey as well as the envisioned end point. They understand on a gut level that you can build your castles in the air, but that it takes work and commitment to anchor your dreams to a solid foundation.

Successful farmers are entrepreneurs. They value community, integrity, and trust in their relationships. We've learned from these agricultural "rock stars" that communication and business planning skills are paramount for success.

But we've also learned that everyone doesn't have to have all the required skills—at least as long as they have the humility to recognize their shortcomings and the wherewithal and good fortune to reach out and build strong partnerships with people who can fill the gaps. We often tell students that, if they are lucky, they will meet a potential spouse who not only shares their passion to farm, but also brings a complementary set of strengths to the relationship and business.

We've seen problems develop. For instance, young and not-so-young folks are often hampered by a parent who isn't willing to hand over the reins or by their uncertainty about leaving the farm or neighborhood to see the world.

There's an old bit of cowboy wisdom that goes, "Good judgment comes from experience, and a lotta that comes from bad judgment." We always tell people to go forth and learn. Get exposed to the many different ways of solving a problem. Make lots of mistakes (especially before you invest too much of your own money).

I tell these would-be beginning farmers, "You can put your head down in class, but don't snore. I suggest you all listen to me as I've already made all of the mistakes. And unless you can get beer out of a cow, I think I can teach you something." And they all walk out at the end of fifteen weeks with a business plan in their hand, and many take theirs to a lender and start their business. I have not had one student in over six hundred who could get beer out of a cow, so I still had a teaching job after twenty-five years.

Aside from this broad advice, what do you need to successfully start and maintain a farming business? Here are twelve principles that guide our work at the WSBDF, and that we recommend our students keep in mind throughout their farming careers:

Set goals. Figure out what you really want to accomplish in life and how your farm business can help get you there. Then write your goals down, review them, maybe change them, and write them down again. Patiently seek opportunities that move you toward your goals, not someone else's.

Identify your strengths and weaknesses. What parts of farming are you good at—and not so good at? Be honest with yourself. Develop partnerships with others who have the skills you lack. Identify your competitive advantage(s)—such as particular talents, farm location, or market opportunities—and capitalize on these strengths/advantages.

Develop a business plan and write it down. The adage is true: Most businesses don't plan to fail; they fail to plan. Avoid the common (and unsuccessful) American business plan: "I have to have it all and have it all now." Rather, put your left foot in front of your right and walk in a direction that sets you up for success, one step and one financial commitment at a time.

Surround yourself with a community of mentors and others who care about your survival and success. Even with the best preparations, getting started in farming is difficult, and you will find no shortage of negative people predicting your demise. However, many who have successfully gone before you are willing to share their experiences and the valuable lessons they have learned. Treat this community of wonderful people as a precious resource and vow that, in the future, you will give back to those who look to you for support.

Work to develop honest and fair relationships and partnerships. For both business and family relationships, seek to work with people who share goals similar to your own but offer different, complementary skills. In any partnership, make sure all parties are headed in the same direction and communicate, communicate, communicate. Always be gentle with the feelings and opinions of your loved ones. Without them by your side, little else matters.

Spend the first year(s) putting together a sound herd of livestock. Work for equity in cattle as a part of your paycheck. Put together a healthy herd that you know well, and that is bred and raised to fit your farming style.

Apply your (usually limited) financial resources to purchase income-producing assets. Read: livestock. Do not overinvest in assets that rust, rot, and depreciate. Read: machinery and buildings. If you spend your money wisely at first, you'll be able to afford the comforts that you'll want later, when you are older.

You don't need to own land to build a farm business, but you do need to control land. We all want to own a piece of the planet—our own land and home. But paying down a mortgage will reduce the potential for a positive cash flow in a new business. A large mortgage can make a new business difficult, and often impossible, to cash flow. Rather than purchase land before you've built equity, set up your business so that you can control the land you farm, preferably with a longer-term lease. The lease might include an option to purchase within an agreed-upon price range. Develop a good relationship with your landlord, whether this person is a family member, neighbor, or new acquaintance. Spend as much time developing this relationship as you spend on any other farm business activity, before you sign the lease.

Invest time in on-farm internships under the guidance of experienced mentors. Intern on several farms, and plan to spend a few months at each farm. Internships are the single most beneficial activity an aspiring farmer can engage in. If you're from a farm, you'll gain valuable insights about new ways to solve familiar problems. If you're not from a farm, you'll come to understand the stamina, routine, and problem-solving required to farm, and you'll have opportunities to ask questions while you learn all aspects of the business.

Work for other farmers. This experience can help you learn what you like and don't like, as well as help you discover your strengths and weaknesses. When you have a grasp on your goals for the future, consider a long-term apprenticeship, with greater responsibilities, on a farm that fits your aspirations. If possible, earn a portion of your pay in young stock, and raise these animals on or near the farm where you are working. You'll build equity as the livestock mature and grow in value, and you'll build a herd of healthy animals whose temperament you know well.

Go on your own only when you are both mentally and financially able. These days, only in rare circumstances can a farmer successfully start out by making a mortgage payment on purchased land, growing all their own feed, managing and/or milking a herd, and shipping a commodity-priced product. For dairy and other livestock farms, it is usually best to raise or purchase your own herd, lease land (for a minimum of three years) and, if needed, a milking facility, purchase feed, discover your best market, and keep a mentor close by. Consider partnering with an established or retiring farmer who may or may not be family. The established farmer might provide infrastructure and experience and raise feed, while the start-up farmer offers passion and labor in exchange for pay and an increasing equity share.

And, finally, some tried and tested wisdom offered by Gary and Holly Stankowski, start-up dairy farmers in Mosinee, Wisconsin, and first-year (1996) WSBDF graduates:

- Work with your brain first, then your back. Don't be afraid of some good old sweat equity, as it's still the lowest cost equity you can find.
- Listen to folks who have farmed for fifty years.
- Believe in and follow the KISS (keep it simple stupid) principle.
- Take care of your cows; take even better care of your calves.
- Find good in every bad.
- Have fun!
- Love your life. Breathe, let go, and remind yourself that this very moment is the only one you know you have for sure.

Many young people in Wisconsin and beyond, who don't live on farms, want to farm; they just need to know how to get into the industry. And with fewer young folks from farm families, a greater percentage of the next generation of farmers may not have a farm background. We need to continue to find ways to give those folks the proper training and experience to get started.

Successful farmers are entrepreneurs. They value community, integrity, and trust in their relationships. Communication and business planning skills are paramount for success.

When starting any business, it needs to cash flow. This is where most new businesses fail, not because they don't have the potential to be profitable in the longer term. So a business plan with a cash flow analysis is imperative.

Identify your competitive advantages, such as particular talents, farm location, and market opportunities. We live in a time when the next generation has a tremendous opportunity that we didn't have back when I was young. We have a caring public out there that will pay for your story and, in essence, pay you for caring for the natural resources of our shared home, planet Earth.

New markets are being developed continuously. Be innovative; value-added products are key. And having livestock that can produce more than one product is also key. For example, if you raise sheep, consider selling grass-fed lamb, the hides, fleece for hand spinning yarn and weaving, and breeding stock. Move toward organic, natural, local, humanely raised, or all of the above if the market is taking you there.

First of all, be patient. Second, be diligent. And third, be intentional in every choice or action.

If you don't know where you're going, any road will get you there.

Conventional wisdom says that you need a million dollars to start farming, and then you can only farm until it's gone; old paradigms die slowly. Albert Einstein reminds us that, when pursuing your dream, "Imagination is more important than knowledge." Seek knowledge continuously, but to build a successful farm business, one needs to imagine how to use this knowledge to create your successful future.

So the future is ours to invent. Let's make it one filled with successful farmers living their dreams.

APPENDIX VI

Frequently Asked Questions About Our Managed Grazing Approach to Regenerative Agriculture and a Land Ethic

Q: How do you define "regenerative agriculture"?

Aldo Leopold wrote in *A Sand County Almanac*, "Health is the capacity of the land for self-renewal. Conservation is our effort to understand and preserve this capacity." There are a variety of parameters that can be quantified in a laboratory to indicate soil health. This science is still being developed, but the four measurements most closely related to soil biological properties are soil organic matter, active carbon, protein, and respiration. Since soil organic matter affects all these properties, it is usually considered the most important indicator of overall soil health.

Is my soil healthy? A good seat-of-the-pants assessment would go something like this:

Does your soil

- allow water to soak in, drain, and not crust over when it dries out?
- mostly stay in place, i.e., doesn't blow or flow away?
- allow crops to recover most of the applied nutrients and provide for healthy crop growth all across a given area?

If the responses to the above questions are a resounding "yes," then you likely have a very healthy soil. Otherwise, it would score somewhere along a continuum.

Regenerative agriculture embodies principles and practices that, when conscientiously followed and applied to the land, help to preserve and, when possible, enhance soil health. The five generally accepted practices of regenerative agriculture are (a) minimal soil disturbance, (b) planting cover crops between main crops, (c) inter-seeding bare ground between the rows of the main crops, (d) establishing perennials, and (e) managed grazing systems which when properly designed and managed address both a and d, as well.

Regenerative agriculture is a conservation approach to farming that has the potential to keep soil in place by reducing soil erosion to nil and rebuilding or regenerating soil. This process, although often slow by our modern American expectations, can take place as a result of increased biological diversity and activity in the soil, improvement of soil water holding capacity, increased nutrient and carbon sequestration, and, in sum, increased resiliency in response to climate change. While the term "regenerative agriculture" is relatively new, the ecological principles on which it depends are as old as life on Earth.

Today we—and the USDA—often discuss or define soil health as the continued capacity of soil to function as a vital living ecosystem that sustains plants, animals, and humans. This definition speaks to the importance of managing soils so they are sustainable for future generations. This is hard to grasp for the collective mind of a mobile society in which most of our lives are lived far from the ground that supports us and in which—unlike native societies—we simply can't imagine where or how future generations will live. I believe that maintaining and building soil health is imperative for *Homo sapiens* and the biota with which we share planet Earth.

A managed grazing "grass farm" is a farm with permanent or "perennialized" grass cover on the landscape all year, every year. If it is managed and grazed to maximize soil health and ground cover, then plant growth, water retention, and nutrient retention will be optimized, along with livestock productivity. Managed grazing is truly one of the paramount approaches to resilient regenerative agriculture, which builds soil health and, in short, land health. This farming model has worked for my family, and it works for the land. It has been the path we have taken on our journey to live a land ethic.

Q: What are the basic principles of managed grazing?

Some of the pastures on our farm are not visible from the road. For decades after implementing our managed grazing system, every week, every month, one of the neighbors or friends would ask, at first, and later, random passersby would ask, "Oh, did you sell the cattle?"

I would have to reply over and over again, "No, no, they're in one of the pastures that you can't see from the road." It took a long time for folks to get used to this.

Biomimicry—from the Greek words for life (*bios*) and imitation (*mimesis*)—relies on nature as model, measure, and mentor. The notion is that the closer we can mimic natural systems in our activities, the better our chances for long-term sustainability. When it comes to managed grazing, it is a thoughtful, part art and part science, way of mimicking the movement of animals following grass that has been present on our planet's grasslands and savannas since at least the Miocene epoch, twenty-five million years ago.

Managed grazing goes by a smorgasbord of names, and here are a few: management-intensive grazing, intensive rotational grazing, controlled grazing, prescribed grazing, adaptive grazing, and adaptive multi-paddock grazing ... whew.

The essence of managed grazing can be broken down into three basic principles that focus on grazing duration, intensity, and livestock distribution:

Principle #1—The *duration* of each grazing event should be shorter than the time it takes a plant to re-grow after defoliation (no more than three to four days in the Driftless Area), and such that each plant is "harvested" only once. The grazing period is then followed by a much longer period of recovery, allowing the plants to build up and not consume root energy reserves and plant vigor.

Principle #2—The *intensity* of a grazing event should be such that sufficient plant leaf residual remains intact for efficient plant re-growth, root mass maintenance, and adequate ground cover.

Principle #3—Livestock grazing *distribution* should be more or less uniform with high livestock density so that each plant is "harvested," and urine and manure nutrient deposition is close to uniform.

To better understand these core principles, let's visit the North American grasslands prior to European settlement and recreate the life and movement of the American bison, the icon of the plains, whose herds measured in the millions. Bison are of the same family, *Bovidae*, as our domestic cattle breeds. *Bovidae* comprise the biological family of cloven-hoofed, ruminant vertebrates.

When bison, or any livestock for that matter, move in herds, they urinate and dung in concentrated areas. Native grazers instinctively know their feeding success—survival—depends on adhering to two of nature's basic rules: take half/leave half, and don't foul your own nest. The genetic code for *movement* is written in their DNA. They graze and move on before the grass is too short and the dung piles are too high. Ruminant excrement is high in nitrogen and other nutrients. These nutrients feed the soil's microbes that, in turn, die and nourish the grass. And the cycle of life continues.

Domestic livestock have not inherited the instinct of the bison that dictates movement as imperative. So today, animals *are moved* by a herder. Livestock *movement* is a keystone of grassland management.

Movement needs to take place for a variety of reasons that benefit the livestock and ecosystem goods (such as an optimum balance of forage quality and quantity) and ecosystem services (such as soil, water and nutrient retention, and carbon sequestration).

Movement also occurs in a natural grazing system with native grazers in response to season, changing weather conditions, fire, and the presence of predators. On the Cates grasslands, our fences take the role of the predators, if you will, keeping the cattle bunched in a group. Without natural fires, our mowing machines have replaced fire to keep the grass in a vegetative stage as long as adequate moisture is available and helps to weaken or rid any plants that the livestock avoid. (Mowing and fire are not exactly the same. Fire encourages native species, but the mower is useful for controlling introduced European plant species now dominant in Driftless Area pastures.)

So that's it in a nutshell.

Q: How do you protect the streambanks and keep the stream water clean when livestock are grazing along the entire area?

On our farm, we have been paying attention for a long time. We have not just been running cattle on grassland that has a trout stream down the middle of it and hoping for the best. We have been practicing conscious, conscientious, active ecosystem conservation management. We have been developing a skill set of observation and activities and a tool kit of practices that have been a source of joy. All this has provided us with a sense of accomplishment—doing the right thing, participating in the reciprocity of returning nature's gifts, and ultimately, hopefully, leaving the land in good health, perhaps even better than it was before our time on this landscape.

Here are the principles and practices the land has taught us:

Principle and practice #1: Well-sodded stream banks will remain that way if livestock have short-duration access to any given location. Cattle herds need to be moved frequently so that they rarely have access to a stretch of the stream for more than a day or so.

We keep them moving. Movement is an intrinsic law of the grasslands—movement in response to forage availability, flooding and drought, fire, and predators. Short-duration occupation keeps the woody brush down but doesn't break up the sod that is the "thatch" that holds the stream banks in place.

Principle and practice #2: Residual forage after any grazing event deflects raindrop impact to increase rainwater soil infiltration and provides a cool, comfortable environment for livestock to lie down and ruminate. Only the top halves of the grass and clover plants are consumed, and the bottom halves are left intact.

The herd is turned in when the sward is perhaps eight to sixteen inches high and removed when the residual grass is about four to eight inches high, depending on the season. It doesn't always work as perfectly in the pasture as it does on paper. Almost nothing ever does, of course, but that's the concept and the goal.

Principle and practice #3: Help the livestock drink from and cross the stream safely and without stream bank and water quality degradation by developing enhanced livestock stream crossings with crushed rock and gravel. This is the only intrusive engineering part of the process.

Principle and practice #4: There are places on every pasture that are more sensitive to overuse, so you've got to keep the cattle off these areas, either temporarily or permanently, depending on the situation.

Traffic or "keep out" signs won't work, so we developed an elegant solution, a remarkably simple practice we call a "livestock traffic controller." This is the placement of a single poly wire fence, with or without electric current, as needed. We use our traffic controllers to break up the single file nose-to-buttocks travel routes that cattle overuse, as well as to exclude cattle from areas they will overuse.

In summary, a cold-water trout stream's health is dependent on water that moves through the soil profile to the groundwater, not the water that runs over and off a soil surface. Groundwater is cold, clear, and continuously flowing from the myriad of springs that are the source of every trout stream in the Driftless. This is in stark contrast to surface water that is warm, sediment-laden, and intermittently flowing only after a hard rainfall. A well-managed perennial grassland in the Driftless Area keeps our precious topsoil in place while growing the most brook trout on Earth.

We have watched and observed Lowery Creek and our grasslands for more than five decades now. It has taken much of this time to begin to understand what we've been watching develop, and it is absolutely fascinating. The stream corridor is stabilizing, and the water runs clearer and cleaner every year. All the while, our family makes a joyful living from this land.

Q: How big are each of your pasture divisions, and is there water access in each one?

We used to operate three farms owned by Kim, me, and the extended Cates family, as well as some rented pasture. We had about seven hundred acres of grass-clover pasture, and we ran four herds of cattle. So our pasture size depended on which farm (they are larger where we can't get to a farm every day), the size of the herd, and where and how water is available. On our home farm, we have a natural water source from the stream. The other three pasture systems did not have natural water, so we watered them from wells and water lines (laid under fence lines so not to be trampled) out to water tanks in each pasture.

In general, our pastures at our home farm vary from one to five acres in size, and the herd may vary from just over one hundred head (late spring/early summer) to just under fifty head (end of winter) of cattle, averaging seven hundred fifty pounds or so. On our farms a distance from home, our pastures varied from five to forty acres, and herd sizes have ranged from one hundred up to four hundred head averaging seven hundred fifty pounds or so.

Dairy farmers who implement managed grazing will tend to move their cattle more frequently, every twelve hours, and pastures may be just an acre.

Q: How many animals can you put on your pastures?

In order to answer this, I need to describe to you the difference between "stocking rate" and "stocking density," as they are two different concepts. Stocking rate, or "carrying capacity," is the number of head of livestock of a certain size you determine your farm can support, provide feed for, or "carry" per year. Let's say your sixty-acre farm can support sixty head of one thousand-pound cows through the grazing season. This would be considered a reasonable stocking rate on a well-managed pasture in the Driftless Area.

Stocking density is how many animals at a given weight are in one area of the pasture at any given time. For managed grazing to work well, you want to have a stocking density of something like thirty thousand pounds on an acre at any one time. As an example, if you placed sixty cows that weigh one thousand pounds each on two acres (that is, thirty thousand pounds per acre), you have achieved the threshold where managed grazing in Wisconsin starts to be really productive in terms of hoof action, aeration of the soil, uniform plant clipping (biting and eating) and manure (fertilizer) deposition. Of course, these animals can only be on those two acres for a day. Much beyond that, they will begin to do more damage than good. So, in this system, the herd would rotate through the sixty acres in thirty days, about a month, before beginning the rotation again.

Q: What happens when the weather gets cold and grass isn't growing? Do you have to keep beef animals in barns or shelters, or feed them at a bunk on concrete?

Bales of hay are either set on the pasture with a ring feeder around them, or the bales are opened and spread or rolled out on the pasture. The cattle get the same thing all year, every day. We open a gate, and they go in and get fresh grass. Now, say it's November. We open a gate, and they go in and get a bale of hay that we harvested in June. It's just dried grass. We're just taking advantage of what Mother Nature offers to us: when the sun is warm and the solar collectors—plant leaves—are in place, we cut, dry, and conserve some grass for later.

Our cattle never have to feed on scenery alone and never need to go into a barn or stand on cement. And they are as happy as kids at a park. The only days of the year that are hard are minus thirty to forty degrees in winter, which rarely ever occurs, or thirty to forty degrees in March and April when it is muddy and rainy; those are the worst days. But in the middle of the winter, we open a gate, and they trot and jump when they see their hay all rolled out on the next pasture. They get excited. "Oh, there's our next meal, all fabulously laid out for us!"

And by feeding, resting, and ruminating on the same land all year long, they spread their manure, recycling their valuable nutrients, or fertilizer, all year long. This is the way nature "does livestock." We attempt to be nature's mimics, or it can be said that we practice "biomimicry."

Q: Managed grazing allows the land manager to "intensify" livestock production to some extent. Is this the same as concentrated livestock production?

It's appropriate for a farm to intensify to some extent, but this is different than concentrating. In other words, with managed grazing, we're able to count on much more productivity on our farm. We grow more grass. We use more grass. And we grow more animals on the same acreage than if we just put them out without any, or much, management. So we have intensified our production system, and in this way, made it more productive for our family. And yet, it's an alternative model to concentrated agriculture or a concentrated animal feeding operation (CAFO). In a concentrated livestock system, all the animals are confined. Say, from our example above, the sixty head would live on the same acre or so all year long. Feed would be grown somewhere else and hauled to the animals, and the manure produced might be hauled back out to some cropland acres, wherever these may be. Our system is an alternative to the CAFO model.

Q: How does the carbon footprint of raising cattle in a managed grazing approach compare with a conventional crop farming and concentrated feeding system?

I'm not going to respond by attempting to cite the absolute gallons of fuel required for field operations, fossil fuel equivalents (say, to produce fertilizers, insecticides, herbicides, machinery, and cement, etc.), or greenhouse gas (GHG) emissions equivalents for each production system. But I will describe the activities in both systems and ask you to make a mental comparison.

If I were raising cattle on a feedlot, I'd need to grow grain and forage crops to bring to them. I'd be operating tractors to prepare fields/soil (possibly shredding cornstalks, possibly plowing or discing and harrowing) and then planting the crops, later cutting and harvesting the crop/feed and hauling it from the field. Storage of dry hay is a matter of stacking, but drying grain or packing silage is time and energy consuming. To feed the cattle, I'd have to take the crop from where it's stored and haul it to the feed bunk. After feeding, I'd scrape up and haul the resultant manure back out to where the crops had been harvested. In our approach, none of these steps happen.

With our system, cutting and harvesting hay needs to happen to feed for four to five months of the year. Purchased grass hay is cut from (generally) longer-term forage stands, and hay from our farm is cut from the permanent pastureland, so in either circumstance, there is no need for field preparation and planting each year. Hay is always fed right on our pasture, and the animals graze for the rest of the year, so no manure is required to be scraped and hauled.

For fossil fuel equivalents, or BTUs, comparison studies are numerous. But they constantly get redone, reevaluated because where the research puts the sideboards on "the system" really matters. If we want to compare energy used in an entire agri-food system, for example, we really have to compare how and where food is produced and where it is consumed. The average distance food in the U.S. travels from field to fork is 1,500 miles.[1] Well, that's an energy expense as well. Growing, selling, and consuming local food reduces this footprint.

Can the same number of pounds of animal gain per acre be achieved in a grazing, grass-finished system like ours compared to a corn and alfalfa planted, harvested, hauled, stored, fed feedlot system? The answer is no. However, the managed grazing approach uses far less fossil fuel equivalents per animal. This, combined with some level of carbon sequestration by perennial grasslands instead of carbon loss from cropped fields, results in a lower carbon footprint for the managed grazing approach.

Additionally, and most significantly, nutrient and soil runoff and loss from a managed grazing, or perennialized, landscape to our public waterways is nil. Simply put, there would be no dead zone in the Gulf of Mexico if farming systems on sloping erodible landscapes across the Midwestern U.S. were shifted from row crops, used primarily to feed livestock and produce ethanol, to perennialized managed grazing.

Our system at home provides plant ground cover year-round and is powered primarily on sunlight.

Q: Some farms have too many head of livestock (many hundreds or thousands) to even think about directly marketing them to consumers. In this case, would it even be possible? And if so, how would you recommend getting started?

My first strong suggestion—and I'm not being flippant—is to have fewer head of livestock. What good are hundreds or thousands of head of livestock if they create eighty-plus hours a week of work and little or no income!? When looked at this way, say fifty head with the potential to set your own price—based on costs of production and desired return (to capital, risk, opportunity cost, and your time)—starts to look like a nice way to live. So that's where I'd start.

Repeating a statement I wrote in this book's Introduction, "In the years since my father purchased our farm from the Stapleton family in 1967, our family is the only one in our township—the Town of Wyoming, Iowa County, Wisconsin—that has started and maintained a livestock business over more than a half-century. Our farm livelihood has transferred to the third generation in this time."

So the fact that you can start a grass-based direct market farm business and hang in there has a lot to do with lower production costs and market demand for your products. See Appendix I—Principles of a Direct Market Grass-Fed Beef Business, for more.

APPENDIX VII

Resources to Learn the Rest of the Story

Geology and Oak Savanna Development of the Driftless Area

Bader, Brian J. "Developing a species list for oak savanna/oak woodland restoration at the University of Wisconsin–Madison Arboretum." *Ecological Restoration*: Volume 19, number 4 (2001): 242–250.

Baker, Richard G. "Late Pleistocene Vegetation in the Driftless Area," in *The Physical Geography and Geology of the Driftless Area*. Eric C. Carson, J.E. Rowling III, J.M. Daniels, and J.W. Attig, eds. The Geological Society of America. Special Paper 543 (2019).

Batten, William G., and John W. Attig. *Preliminary Geology of Iowa County, Wisconsin*. Wisconsin Geological and Natural History Survey (2010).

Changnon, Stanley A., Kenneth E. Kunkel, and Derek Winstanley. "Quantification of Climate Conditions Important to the Tallgrass Prairie," *Transactions of the Illinois State Academy of Science*. Volume 96, no. 1 (2003): 41–54.

Curtis, John T. *The Vegetation of Wisconsin: An Ordination of Plant Communities*. Wisconsin: The University of Wisconsin Press, 1959.

Dott, Robert H., and John W. Attig. *Roadside Geology of Wisconsin*. Montana: Mountain Press, 2004.

Knox, James C. "Geology of the Driftless Area," in *The Physical Geography and Geology of the Driftless Area*. Carson, Eric C., J.E. Rowling III, J.M. Daniels and J.W. Attig, eds. The Geological Society of America. Special Paper 543 (2019).

Nelson, Rob, and D. Bertalan. *Mysteries of the Driftless*, a documentary, 2013.

Wernerehl, Bob. *Historical Background of The Blue Mounds Region of Wisconsin*. The Blue Mounds Area Project, Wisconsin Environmental Education Board, and the Wisconsin Department of Natural Resources, 2001.

First Peoples

Birmingham, Robert A., and Amy Rosebrough, (2nd Ed.) *Indian Mounds of Wisconsin*. Wisconsin: The University of Wisconsin Press, 2017.

Eshleman, Jason A., Ripan S. Malhi, and David Glenn Smith. "Mitochondrial DNA Studies of Native Americans: Conceptions and Misconceptions of the Population Prehistory of the Americas," *Evolutionary Anthropology* 12 (2003): 7–18.

Kimmerer, Robin Wall. *Braiding Sweetgrass: Indigenous Wisdom, Scientific Knowledge, and the Teachings of Plants*. Minnesota: Milkweed Editions, 2013.

Loew, Patty. *Indian Nations of Wisconsin: Histories of Endurance and Renewal*. Wisconsin: Wisconsin Historical Society Press, 2013.

Loew, Patty. *Seventh Generation Earth Ethics Native Voices of Wisconsin*. Wisconsin: Wisconsin Historical Society Press, 2014.

Mann, Charles C. *1491: New Revelations of the Americas before Columbus*. New York: Knopf, 2005.

Millhouse, Phillip G. "Native American People in the Lower Sugar River Valley 12,000 years ago to the present." *Illinois Archeology*. 22 (1) (2010): 318–357, https://s3.amazonaws.com/lsrwa.org/wp-content/uploads/2018/11/Cultural-History-Lower-Sugar-River-Valley.pdf.

Schanen, Paul, and David Hunzicker. *Native American Artifacts of Wisconsin*. Lauric Press, 2013.

Theler, James L., and R. F. Boszhardt. *Twelve Millenia Archaeology of the Upper Mississippi River Valley*. Iowa: University of Iowa Press, 2003.

Theler, James L., and J. F. Pfaffenroth. "An archaeological Occurrence of Bison and Pronghorn Remains at Brogley Rockshelter" (47GT156), Grant County, Wisconsin. *The Wisconsin Archaeological Society*. Vol 91, no. 2 (July–Dec 2010): 63–78.

European Immigration

Apps, Jerry. *Wisconsin Agriculture: A History*. Wisconsin: Wisconsin Historical Society Press, 2015.

Carver, Jonathan. 1781. "Travels through the Interior Parts of North America." in *Jonathan Carver's Travels Through America, 1766–1768: An Eighteenth-Century Explorer's Account of Uncharted America*, by Norman Gelb, 74–75. New Jersey: John Wiley & Sons, 1993.

"History of the Fur Trade," Furbearer Education, https://www.furbearereducation.org/history.pdf.

Jones, Chester Lloyd. *Youngest Son*. Wisconsin: Democrat Printing Company, 1938.

"Lead Mining in Southwestern Wisconsin." Wisconsin: Wisconsin Historical Society, 2023, https://www.wisconsinhistory.org/Records/Article/CS408.

Leopold, Aldo. "Lessons from Coon Valley: The Importance of Collaboration in Watershed Management," 1935.

"Origin and Names of the 50 States of the USA." Knowledge Publisher.com, February 3, 2020. https://www.knowledgepublisher.com/article/449/origin-and-names-of-the-50-states-of-usa.html.

Rodesch, Jerrold C. "Jean Nicolet." University of Wisconsin–Green Bay, 1984.

Western Historical Company. *History of Iowa County, Wisconsin*. Illinois: Western Historical Company, April 1881, https://content.wisconsinhistory.org/digital/collection/wch/id/9687.

Soil Science and Soil Erosion

Bockheim, James G., and Alfred E. Hartemink. *The Soils of Wisconsin.* New York: Springer International Publishing, 2018.

Claassen, Roger, Maria Bowman, Jonathan McFadden, David Smith, and Steven Wallander. "Tillage Intensity and Conservation Cropping in the United States." United States Department of Agriculture, Economic Research Service, September 2018, https://www.ers.usda.gov/webdocs/publications/90201/eib-197.pdf.

Egan, Dan. *The Devil's Element: Phosphorus and a World Out of Balance.* New York: W. W. Norton & Company, Inc., 2023.

Hartemink, Alfred E., and J. G. Bockheim. "An Inverted Horizon Soilscape in Wisconsin." *Soil Horizons.* Soil Science Society of America (January 2013), doi:10.2136/sh12-07-0021.

Logan, William B. *DIRT: The Ecstatic Skin of the Earth.* New York: W.W. Norton & Company, Inc., 2007.

Quinn, Lauren, "Cover cropping up to 7.2% in U.S. Midwest, boosted by government programs." ACES News, University of Illinois Urbana- Champaign, College of Agricultural, Consumer and Environmental Sciences, December 5, 2022, https://aces.illinois.edu/news/cover-cropping-72-us-midwest-boosted-government-programs.

University of Massachusetts Amherst, "Saving our soil: How to extend US breadbasket fertility for centuries," Phys.org, May 25, 2023, https://phys.org/news/2023-05-soil-breadbasket-fertility-centuries.html.

Weil, Ray R., and Nyle C. Brady. *The Nature and Properties of Soils, The 15th Edition.* New Jersey: Pearson, 2016.

Grassland Agriculture and Managed Grazing

Benyus, Janine M. *Biomimicry: Innovation Inspired by Nature.* New York: HarperCollins Publishers, 2002, chaps. 1–2, 1–58.

Flack, Sarah. *The Art and Science of Grazing: How Grass Farmers Can Create Sustainable Systems for Healthy Animals and Farm Ecosystems.* Vermont: Chelsea Green Publishing, 2016.

Gerrish, Jim. *Management-intensive Grazing: The Grassroots of Grass Farming.* England: Green Park Press, 2004.

Murphy, Bill. *Greener Pastures on Your Side of the Fence: Better Farming with Voisin Management Intensive Grazing.* Arriba Publishing, 1987.

Undersander, Dan, *et al. Pastures for Profit: A Guide to Rotational Grazing.* Madison, WI: Cooperative Extension Publications, University of Wisconsin–Extension, Publication A3529, 2002.

Voisin, Andre. *Grass Productivity.* Island Press, 1959.

Wedin, Walter F., and Steven L. Fales, eds. *Grassland: Quietness and Strength for a New American Agriculture.* New Jersey: John Wiley & Sons, 2009.

White, James, and John Hodgson, eds. *New Zealand Pasture and Crop Science.* New York: Oxford University Press, 1999.

Grass-Fed Beef

Niman, Nicollette Hahn. *Defending Beef: The Ecological and Nutritional Case for Meat*. Vermont: Chelsea Green Publishing, 2021.

Schwartz, Judith D. *Cows Save the Planet: And Other Improbable Ways of Restoring Soil to Heal the Earth.* Vermont: Chelsea Green Publishing, 2013.

Shinn, Ridge, and Lynne Pledger. *Grass-Fed Beef for a Post-Pandemic World: How Regenerative Grazing Can Restore Soils and Stabilize the Climate*. Vermont: Chelsea Green Publishing, 2022.

Community, Conservation, Regenerative Agriculture, The Land Ethic

Bell, Michael M., Loka L. Ashwood, Isaac S. Leslie, and Laura H. Schlachter. *An Invitation to Environmental Sociology.* California: SAGE Publications, Inc, 2020.

Berry, Wendell. *The Unsettling of America: Culture & Agriculture.* Sierra Club, 1977.

Berry, Wendell. *What I Stand for Is What I Stand On.* Penguin Classics, 2021.

Berry, Wendell, and Gary Snyder. *Distant Neighbors: The Selected Letters of Wendell Berry and Gary Snyder.* Counterpoint Press, 2014.

Callicott, J. Baird. *In Defense of the Land Ethic: Essays in Environmental Philosophy*. New York: State University of New York Press, 1989.

Carson, Rachel. *Silent Spring.* Massachusetts: Houghton Mifflin, 1962.

Cronon, William. *Uncommon Ground: Rethinking the Human Place in Nature.* W.W. Norton & Co, 1996.

Doyle, Martin. *The Source: How Rivers Made America and America Remade Its Rivers.* New York: W. W. Norton & Company, Inc., 2018.

Hausdoerffer, John, Brooke Parry Hecht, Melissa K. Nelson, and Katherine Kassouf Cummings, eds. *What Kind of Ancestor Do You Want to Be?* Illinois: The University of Chicago Press in association with the Center for Humans and Nature, 2021.

Jackson, Randall D., "America's Dairy Grassland – Wisconsin milk production that regenerates people and land," *Agroecology and Sustainable Food Systems*, (2024): 1–18. https://doi.org/10.1080/21683565.2024.2344027.

Jackson, Wes. *Becoming Native to This Place.* Kentucky: University Press of Kentucky, 1993.

Jackson, Wes, Robert Jensen, ed. *From the Ground Up: Conversations with Wes Jackson.* Vermont: New Perennials Publishing, 2022.

Kimmerer, Robin Wall. *Gathering Moss: A Natural and Cultural History of Mosses.* Oregon State University Press, 2003.

Kimmerer, Robin Wall. *Braiding Sweetgrass: Indigenous Wisdom, Scientific Knowledge, and the Teachings of Plants.* Minnesota: Milkweed Editions, 2013.

Kirschenmann, Frederick L., Constance L. Falk, ed. *Cultivating an Ecological Conscience: Essays from a Farmer Philosopher.* Counterpoint Press, 2010.

Koch, Kevin. *The Driftless Land: Spirit of Place in the Upper Mississippi Valley.* Southeast Missouri State University Press, 2010.

Leopold, Aldo. *A Sand County Almanac: And Sketches Here and There.* New York: Oxford University Press, 1949.

Leopold, Aldo, J. Baird Callicott, and Eric T. Freyfogle, eds. *For the Health of the Land: Previously Unpublished Essays and Other Writings.* Washington, D.C., Island Press, 1999.

Leopold, Aldo, Luna B. Leopold, ed. *Round River: From the Journals of Aldo Leopold.* New York: Oxford University Press, 1953.

Leopold, Aldo, Susan L. Flader, and J. Baird Callicott, eds. *The River of the Mother of God and Other Essays by Aldo Leopold.* Wisconsin: University of Wisconsin Press, 1991.

Massy, Charles. *Call of the Reed Warbler: A New Agriculture, A New Earth.* Vermont: Chelsea Green Publishing, 2018.

Meine, Curt. *Aldo Leopold: His Life and Work.* Wisconsin: University of Wisconsin Press, 1988.

Meine, Curt, and Keefe Keeley, eds. *The Driftless Reader.* Wisconsin: University of Wisconsin Press, 2017.

Meine, Curt, and Richard L. Knight, eds. *The Essential Aldo Leopold: Quotations and Commentaries.* Wisconsin: University of Wisconsin Press, 1999.

Meine, Curt. "The Farmer as Conservationist: Aldo Leopold on Agriculture." *Journal of Soil and Water Conservation* 42 (3) (May 1987): 144–149.

Nabhan, Gary Paul. *Food from the Radical Center: Healing Our Land and Communities.* Washington, D.C., Island Press, 2018.

Provenza, Fred. *Nourishment: What Animals Can Teach Us About Rediscovering Our Nutritional Wisdom.* Vermont: Chelsea Green Publishing, 2018.

Temple, Stanley A. "An Ethical Predicament on America's Farmland." Sustainability (online). Thomson Reuters (2015).

Temple, Stanley A. "Striving Toward Land Health on Private Land," *The Leopold Outlook*, Summer 2008.

Van Horn, Gavin, and John Hausdoerffer, eds. *Wildness: Relations of People and Place.* Illinois: The University of Chicago Press in association with the Center for Humans and Nature, 2017.

White, Courtney. *Revolution on the Range: The Rise of the New Ranch in the American West.* Washington, D.C., Island Press, 2008.

Zimmer, Gary F. and Leilani Zimmer-Durand. *Advancing Biological Farming: Practicing Mineralized Balanced Agriculture to Improve Soils & Crops.* Acres U.S.A., 2011.

Inspiring Farm/Farm Family Stories

Apfelbaum, Steven I. *Nature's Second Chance: Restoring the Ecology of Stone Prairie Farm.* Beacon Press, 2009.

Cates, Richard L. Jr. *Voices from the Heart of the Land: Rural Stories that Inspire Community.* Wisconsin: University of Wisconsin Press, 2008.

Logan, Ben. *The Land Remembers: The Story of a Farm and Its People.* Heartland Press, 1975.

O'Brien, Dan. *Buffalo for the Broken Heart: Restoring Life to a Black Hills Ranch.* New York: Random House, 2002.

Rebanks, James. *Pastoral Song: A Farmer's Journey.* Massachusetts: Mariner Books, 2021.

Websites for organizations with which my family is actively engaged

Aldo Leopold Foundation *Mission:* To foster a land ethic through the legacy of Aldo Leopold. Inspired by his profound vision, we seek to cultivate an understanding and appreciation of our relationship with the environment on all levels, be it individuals or entire communities. *Vision:* Our vision is to weave a land ethic into the fabric of our society, to advance the understanding, stewardship, and restoration of land health, and to cultivate leadership for conservation. We aim to instill a deep respect for the environment in every individual and community through education, advocacy, and hands-on initiatives. One day, we hope to transform the way society interacts with the natural world, fostering a future where conservation leadership thrives at every level. https://www.aldoleopold.org

Black Earth Institute *Mission:* Black Earth Institute is a community of artist-fellows and scholar-advisers creating a more ethical world. *Vision:* BEI seeks to help create a more just and deeply interconnected world and promote the planet's health. To do so, artists are appointed as fellows for a term, and scholars join as advisors. BEI then encourages and supports its present and past fellows and scholars to address social justice, environmental issues, and the spiritual dimensions of the human condition in their art and work. https://blackearthinstitute.org

Cates Family Farm *Our Goals:* Family well-being; farm profitability—producing affordable, healthy food from livestock humanely raised; model grasslands management and environmental stewardship practices. *Our Promise:* A commitment to a land ethic and conservation through personal responsibility and gratitude for Earth's gifts. https://www.catesfamilyfarm.com

Driftless Area Land Conservancy and Lowery Creek Watershed Initiative The parent organization for the Lowery Creek Watershed Initiative (LCWI), is the focus of Chapter 10. See also the LCWI page on this website. *Mission:* To maintain and enhance the health, diversity, and beauty of Southwest Wisconsin's natural and agricultural landscape through permanent land protection and restoration, and improve people's lives by connecting them to the land and to each other. *Belief:* Protecting the natural world and engaging people in its vast wonder is one of the most important gifts that we can pass on to our children and the generations that follow. https://www.driftlessconservancy.org

Fishers & Farmers Partnership for the Upper Mississippi River Basin *Mission:* To support locally-led conservation projects that add value to farms while restoring aquatic habitat and native fish populations. *Vision:* Landowners work together with conservationists and scientists to address the needs of their own farms, local streams, and the fishes of the basin. Lessons learned are shared with neighbors, participating organizations, and others outside of the basin. https://fishersandfarmers.org

Grassland 2.0 *Mission:* A collaborative group of farmers, researchers, and public and private sector leaders working to develop pathways for increased farmer profitability, yield stability, and nutrient and water efficiency, while improving water quality, soil health, biodiversity, and climate resilience through grassland-based agriculture. We must create an agricultural system with a land ethic that intentionally restores and regenerates the health of the land while affording access to its wealth for farmers of all kinds, especially the dispossessed, oppressed, and marginalized. *Vision:* Profitable farms cultivating a next generation of farmers, healthy people, and thriving diverse communities; clean water, flood reduction, stable climate, and biodiversity. https://grasslandag.org

Iowa County Uplands Farmer-Led Watershed Group *Mission:* Protect, reduce soil and nutrients loss through farm runoff in this hilly part of the state; increase water infiltration into the soil and hold water on farmland where it's needed against droughts; and reduce costs of road, bridge, and culvert repairs when increasingly frequent extreme storm events bring heavy rainfall. *Vision:* On-farm demonstrations of producer-led solutions result in increased farmer participation in conservation and improvements in our watershed's soil and water quality. https://www.uplandswatershedgroup.com

Michael Fields Agricultural Institute *Mission:* help rural and urban farms and agricultural communities in Wisconsin and beyond be healthy environmentally, economically, and socially. Vision: An agriculture that prioritizes people and promotes human and ecosystem health, food sovereignty, and justice. https://www.michaelfields.org

Sand County Foundation *Mission:* Inspire and empower farmers, ranchers, and forestland managers to ethically care for the land to sustain water resources, build healthy soil, enhance wildlife habitat, and support outdoor recreation. Vision: A future where there is widespread adoption of what Aldo Leopold called a land ethic, based on personal responsibility, effective incentives, and science for the benefit of people and the environment. https://sandcountyfoundation.org

Savanna Institute Inspired by the native savanna ecosystems that once covered much of this region, our work is to conduct research, education, and outreach to support the growth of diverse, perennial agroecosystems. *Mission:* Catalyze the development and adoption of resilient, scalable agroforestry. *Vision:* A multifunctional agriculture in the Midwest US based on agroforestry systems of integrated trees, crops, and livestock that fosters ecological resilience, climate stability, economic prosperity, and vibrant communities. https://www.savannainstitute.org

Photo by Bob Brown.

Chapter Notes

Foreword

1 This is the position established for, and first held by, Aldo Leopold (1933 to 1948); Professor Temple held the position from 1976 until his retirement in 2008. It is within the present Department of Wildlife Ecology.

Preface

1 USDA National Agricultural Statistics Service, *Farms and Land in Farms 2021 Summary*. February 2022.

2 Personal Communication April 20, 2023, email, Angie Doucette, Midwest Farmland Protection manager, American Farmland Trust.

3 University of Massachusetts Amherst, "Saving our soil: How to extend US breadbasket fertility for centuries," Phys.org, May 25, 2023, https://phys.org/news/2023-05-soil-breadbasket-fertility-centuries.html.

4 National Oceanic and Atmospheric Administration, https://oceantoday.noaa.gov/deadzonegulf-2021/.

Introduction

1 Jed Meunier, research scientist, WI DNR Division of Forestry, and James Riser II, TREES lab research scientist, Department of Environmental Sciences and Society, University of Wisconsin–Platteville, both dendrochronologists or "tree-ring researchers," spent several afternoons on our farm, autumn 2020, coring oak trees with an increment borer to determine chronological age.

Chapter 1
Our Driftless Home Shaped by Water—A Creek Runs Through It

1 *Nįįna wakącąkšanąWater is Life* translation from *Hoocąk* by Janice Rice, a Ho-Chunk elder. Janice Rice is a peacemaker for the Ho-Chunk Nation's Trial Court, a clan mother for Ho-Chunk Nation Social Services, a past president of the American Indian Library Association, and a board member of the Ho-Chunk Nation Museum and Cultural Center and the Little Eagle Arts Foundation. In spring 2022, Rice received a certificate from Ho-Chunk Nation's Language Division for the First Listeners Program, a three-year language instruction program. See https://diversity.wisc.edu/news-archive/.

All other *Hoocqk* translations found in this book are from the website Ho-Chunk Dictionary Online https://dictionary.hochunk.org/.

2 The brook trout (*Salvelinus fontinalis*) is a species of freshwater fish in the char genus (*Salvelinus*) of the salmon family (*Salmonidae*). It is native to Eastern North America in the United States and Canada but has been introduced elsewhere in North America, as well as other locations in the world. Native "heritage" brook trout are those with genetics believed to have been in place historically, prior to any introduction of "domestic" genetics. Domestic genetics were first developed in Wisconsin at the Nevin State Fish Hatchery in 1876 to raise domestic fish—primarily brown, rainbow, and brook trout to stock around the state. See *Wisconsin Inland Trout Management Plan 2020-2029* (2019), WI Department of Natural Resources, Bureau of Fisheries Management for additional information. https://dnr.wisconsin.gov/sites/default/files/topic/Fishing/Trout_WITroutManagementPlan2019.pdf.

3 Robert H. Dott, and John W. Attig. *Roadside Geology of Wisconsin.* (Montana: Mountain Press, 2004).

4 The "true" Driftless Area that avoided all glaciation is officially 8,494 square miles (22,000 square kilometers), almost entirely in Wisconsin. The greater Driftless Area—the region where almost no glaciation happened—is often stated to be 24,103 square miles, with 85 percent of the area within Wisconsin). James C. Knox. "Geology of the Driftless Area," in *The Physical Geography and Geology of the Driftless Area.* Eric C. Carson, J. E. Rowling III, J.M. Daniels, and J.W. Attig, eds. The Geological Society of America. Special Paper 543 (2019).

5 "Trout Stream Classifications—Wisconsin Trout Fishing," Wisconsin DNR, 2023, https://dnr.wisconsin.gov/topic/Fishing/trout/streamclassification.html.

6 The following section on the development of the tallgrass prairie and oak savanna is adapted from Stanley A. Changnon, Kenneth E. Kunkel, and Derek Winstanley. "Quantification of Climate Conditions Important to the Tallgrass Prairie," *Transactions of the Illinois State Academy of Science*. Volume 96, no. 1 (2003): 41–54.

7 John T. Curtis, *The Vegetation of Wisconsin: An Ordination of Plant Communities.* (Wisconsin: The University of Wisconsin Press, 1959).

8 Wisconsin DNR. 2022. *Barrens and Savannas communities of Wisconsin.* Lowery Creek lies within the Dodgeville and Wyoming Oak Woodlands and Savanna Conservation Opportunity Area designated by the Wisconsin DNR as having "continentally significant conservation value."

9 Bob Wernerehl. *Historical Background of The Blue Mounds Region of Wisconsin.* The Blue Mounds Area Project, Wisconsin Environmental Education Board, and the Wisconsin Dept of Natural Resources (2001).

Sidebar
The Driftless Area Has an Epic Story to Tell

1 James C. Knox, Evjue-Bascom professor emeritus, Department of Geography, University of Wisconsin–Madison from *Mysteries of the Driftless, a documentary* (2013), produced by Rob Nelson and Dan Bertalan.

Chapter 2
Millennia of First Peoples Along Lowery Creek—Resilience and Reciprocity of Earth's Gifts

1 Robin Wall Kimmerer, an enrolled member of the Citizen Potawatomi Nation, attended the University of Wisconsin–Madison, earning her master's degree in botany there in 1979, followed by her PhD in plant ecology in 1983. Ms. Kimmerer likely passed by the mouth of Lowery Creek at the Wisconsin River innumerable times on her travels between her forest research sites a few miles farther west and the UW–Madison to the east. The Potawatomi origin/migration story is tied to that of the Ho-Chunk people, and a part of their ancestral lands are what is now Wisconsin.

2 Jason A. Eshleman, Ripan S. Malhi, and David Glenn Smith. "Mitochondrial DNA Studies of Native Americans: Conceptions and Misconceptions of the Population Prehistory of the Americas," *Evolutionary Anthropology* 12 (2003): 7–18.

3 Patty Loew. *Indian Nations of Wisconsin: Histories of Endurance and Renewal* (Wisconsin: Wisconsin Historical Society Press, 2013).

4 James L. Theler, and R. F. Boszhardt. *Twelve Millennia: Archaeology of the Upper Mississippi River Valley* (Iowa: University of Iowa Press, 2003).

5 Personal Communications, Ryan J. Howell, archaeologist, Warrens, WI, and Jean Dowiasch, senior research archaeologist, Mississippi Valley Archaeology Center, La Crosse, WI. And the resource *Native American Artifacts of Wisconsin* (Texas: Lauric Press: 2013) by Paul Schanen and David Hunzicker. The author recognizes and respects that the naming and dating protocol I have opted to use for respective points, arrowheads, and cultural items identified in this chapter may not represent/reflect names preferred by the entire archaeological community or all First Peoples of this region.

6 James L. Theler, and R. F. Boszhardt. *Twelve Millennia: Archaeology of the Upper Mississippi River Valley* (Iowa: University of Iowa Press, 2003).

7 Personal Communications, Ryan J. Howell, archaeologist, Warrens, WI, and Jean Dowiasch, senior research archaeologist, Mississippi Valley Archaeology Center, La Crosse, WI. And the resource *Native American Artifacts of Wisconsin* (Lauric Press: 2013) by Paul Schanen and David

Hunzicker. The author recognizes and respects that the naming and dating protocol I have opted to use for respective points, arrowheads, and cultural items identified in this chapter may not represent/reflect names preferred by the entire archaeological community or all First Peoples of this region.

8 William G. Batten, and John W. Attig. *Preliminary Geology of Iowa County, Wisconsin.* Wisconsin Geological and Natural History Survey (2010).

9 Stanley A. Changnon, Kenneth E. Kunkel, and Derek Winstanley. "Quantification of Climate Conditions Important to the Tallgrass Prairie," *Transactions of the Illinois State Academy of Science.* Volume 96, no. 1 (2003): 41–54.

10 Charles C. Mann. *1491: New Revelations of the Americas before Columbus.* (New York: Knopf, 2005).

11 James L. Theler, and J. F. Pfaffenroth. "An archaeological Occurrence of Bison and Pronghorn Remains at Brogley Rockshelter" (47GT156), Grant County, Wisconsin. *The Wisconsin Archaeological Society.* Vol 91, no. 2 (July–December 2010): 63–78.

12 Robert A. Birmingham, and Amy Rosebrough, (2nd ed.) *Indian Mounds of Wisconsin.* (Wisconsin: The University of Wisconsin Press, 2017).

13 People of the Meskwaki Nation—Sac and Fox Tribe of the Mississippi in Iowa, Kickapoo, and Potawatomi (as noted in Chapter 2 Endnote 1) used and cherished this land through the millennia as well.

14 James L. Theler, and R. F. Boszhardt. *Twelve Millennia: Archaeology of the Upper Mississippi River Valley* (Iowa: University of Iowa Press, 2003).

15 Robert A. Birmingham, and Amy Rosebrough, (2nd ed.) *Indian Mounds of Wisconsin.* (Wisconsin: The University of Wisconsin Press, 2017).

16 Patty Loew. *Indian Nations of Wisconsin: Histories of Endurance and Renewal* (Wisconsin: Wisconsin Historical Society Press, 2013).

17 James L. Theler, and R. F. Boszhardt. *Twelve Millennia: Archaeology of the Upper Mississippi River Valley* (Iowa: University of Iowa Press, 2003).

18 This site will remain unnamed in this book. However, it is registered through the Wisconsin Office of the State Archaeologist and has been assigned Smithsonian Institute cairn and burial site identification numbers.

19 Robin Wall Kimmerer, *Braiding Sweetgrass: Indigenous Wisdom, Scientific Knowledge, and the Teachings of Plants.* (Minnesota: Milkweed Editions, 2013).

20 J. Baird Callicott, *In Defense of the Land Ethic: Essays in Environmental Philosophy* (New York: State University of New York Press, 1989).

Sidebar
Patty Loew, Lowery Creek, and the Driftless Area is Ho-Chunk Ancestral Homeland

1 Text from *Indian Nations of Wisconsin: Histories of Endurance and Renewal.* 2013 (2nd ed.) by Patty Loew. Reprinted with permission of the Wisconsin Historical Society.

Chapter 3
European Immigration—Earth's Gifts of Beaver, Lead, and Soil, Free for the Taking: A Diaspora Without a Land Ethic

1 Stapleton family oral history is from personal communications with Joseph Patrick Stapleton. Stapleton family genealogical history research was conducted by Mary Knudson (May 6, 1960–February 7, 2023), genealogist, Iowa County, Wisconsin. Mary will be remembered and cherished for her long-time work benefitting the citizens of Iowa County and beyond. Thank you from the bottom of our hearts. The record indicates that Thomas Stapleton was born in 1817 in Ireland, but there is no written record or family lore as to where on the island he was born or the details of his life in Ireland. The Stapleton name may be, in fact, English but family lore has it that the clan had had enough of the big island (England) by the 1100s and had emigrated to the Emerald Isle to stay for the next 700 years.

2 Richard and Mary Thomas Lloyd Jones subsequently raised four more children, for a total of ten living children, and in time, the greater Lloyd Jones family bloomed in number and became a prominent family at the mouth of Lowery Creek through the second half of the 1800s. The most well-known descendant of Richard and Mary Thomas Lloyd Jones, Frank Lloyd Wright, was born in 1867 in Richland Center, Wisconsin. He was the son of their daughter Anna (their fifth child, later known as Hannah) and William Cary Wright, a preacher from Westfield, Massachusetts. Frank Lloyd Wright first came to the Town of Wyoming as a young man to work on his uncle James Lloyd Jones's farm, the present site of Aldebaran farm contiguous with Taliesin and proximate to the developing Stapleton farm.—From the Lloyd Jones family *Descendants and Ancestors of Richard and Mary Lloyd-Jones* (Unpublished); and personal communications with Mary Lloyd-Jones, Town of Wyoming, WI, first cousin twice removed with Frank Lloyd Wright.

It should be duly noted that eight Frank Lloyd Wright sites were inscribed on the UNESCO World Heritage list in July 2019.

3 Patty Loew. *Indian Nations of Wisconsin: Histories of Endurance and Renewal* (Wisconsin: Wisconsin Historical Society Press, 2013).

4 Jerrold C. Rodesch. "Jean Nicolet," University of Wisconsin–Green Bay, 1984.

5 James L. Theler, and R. F. Boszhardt. *Twelve Millennia: Archaeology of the Upper Mississippi River Valley* (Iowa: University of Iowa Press, 2003).

6 Jonathan Carver. 1781. "Travels Through the Interior Parts of North America" in *Jonathan Carver's Travels Through America, 1766–1768: An Eighteenth-Century Explorer's Account of Uncharted America*, by Norman Gelb, 74–75. (New Jersey: John Wiley & Sons, 1993).

7 "History of the Fur Trade," Furbearer Education, https://www.furbearereducation.org/history.pdf.

8 Philip G. Millhouse, "Native American People in the Lower Sugar River Valley 12,000 years ago to the present." *Illinois Archeology*, 22 (1) (2010): 318–357, https://s3.amazonaws.com/lsrwa.org/wp-content/uploads/2018/11/Cultural-History-Lower-Sugar-River-Valley.pdf.

9 "In the 1830s, many Ho-Chunk moved to the region north of the Wisconsin River ... those living on the ceded lands [from the treaties 1804–1832] were supposed to remove to a portion of eastern Iowa called the Neutral Ground. However, most simply moved north of the Wisconsin River. Even then, they often went back to their old residences in the ceded lands for short periods. The Ho-Chunk and the United States made another treaty in 1837 that ceded all their lands in Wisconsin. The treaty itself was made under suspicious conditions, and the Ho-Chunk did not appear to have been aware of all of its provisions, particularly the one that gave them only eight months to leave their ceded lands. By this time, large numbers of white settlers poured into the region"—Ho-Chunk Culture, Milwaukee Public Museum, 2022. https://www.mpm.edu/content/wirp/ICW-52.

10 "Lead Mining in Southwestern Wisconsin," Wisconsin: Wisconsin Historical Society, 2023, https://www.wisconsinhistory.org/Records/Article/CS408.

11 Ibid.

12 Western Historical Company, *History of Iowa County, Wisconsin*. (Illinois: Western Historical Company, 1881), https://content.wisconsinhistory.org/digital/collection/wch/id/9687.

13 "Origin and Names of the 50 States of the USA." Knowledge Publisher, February 3, 2020. https://www.knowledgepublisher.com/article/449/origin-and-names-of-the-50-states-of-usa.html.

14 Western Historical Company, *History of Iowa County, Wisconsin*. (Illinois: Western Historical Company, 1881), https://content.wisconsinhistory.org/digital/collection/wch/id/9687.

15 Personal communication, Richard Henderson, The Prairie Enthusiasts board member and vice-chair Empire-Sauk Chapter.

16 Jerry Apps. *Wisconsin Agriculture: A History*. (Wisconsin: Wisconsin Historical Society Press, 2015).

17 Ibid.

18 Virgil. *Georgics Book 1: Agriculture and Weather.* Line 73–83. 29 BCE. (Translated by A. S. Kline, 2001).

19 Aldo Leopold, "Lessons from Coon Valley: The Importance of Collaboration in Watershed Management." 1935.

20 United States Department of Agriculture. *Soils & Men: Yearbook of Agriculture 1938*. (U.S. Government Printing Office, 1938).

21 Alfred E. Hartemink, and J. G. Bockheim. "An Inverted Horizon Soilscape in Wisconsin." *Soil Horizons*. Soil Science Society of America (January 2013). https://citeseerx.ist.psu.edu/document?repid=rep1&type=pdf&doi=70580205fba66f9dd7221c366d7b8f9f5d9b260b.

22 Eric C. Carson, J. Elmo Rawling, III, J. Michael Daniels, and John W. Attig, eds. "Late Pleistocene Vegetation in the Driftless Area," in *The Physical Geography and Geology of the Driftless Area*. The Geological Society of America Special Paper 543 (2019).

23 The soils of the more sloping pasture acreage on our home farm are classified as Alfisol, lighter colored soils not as rich in carbon, that formed under forest dominant vegetation. These particular slope areas likely were somewhat sheltered from the full impact of the historic fire regime that kept the valleys as oak savanna and prairie.

24 Carbon 14 dating of the black buried (historical) surface soil at about a four-foot depth, along with two samples of wood found embedded in the same, were completed/reported on April 12 and April 16, 2021, respectively, by the National Ocean Science Accelerator Mass Spectrometry (NOSAMS) Facility at Woods Hole Oceanographic Institution, Woods Hole, Massachusetts. The age of both the embedded wood samples and organic matter in the contiguous soil was determined to be close to six thousand years old, confirming formation during the mid-Holocene after this landscape had transitioned to grassland/oak savanna. The author would like to thank James G. Bockheim, professor emeritus, Department of Soil Science, University of Wisconsin–Madison, and Mark Kurz, director emeritus, NOSAMS, for their expertise and gracious assistance through the C14 sampling and analysis process.

25 "The USDA's Conservation Reserve Program in Wisconsin." ArcGIS Online, February 17, 2023, https://storymaps.arcgis.com/stories/80bf722d106a408a94191bf516a92216. "Corn and soybean

acreage has increased since 1990." USDA, February 8, 2024, https://www.ers.usda.gov/data-products/chart-gallery/gallery/chart-detail/?chartId=76955

26 Roger Claassen, et al., "Tillage Intensity and Conservation Cropping in the United States." United States Department of Agriculture, Economic Research Service, September 2018, https://www.ers.usda.gov/webdocs/publications/90201/eib-197.pdf. AND: Lauren Quinn, "Cover cropping up to 7.2% in U.S. Midwest, boosted by government programs." ACES News, University of Illinois Urbana–Champaign, College of Agricultural, Consumer and Environmental Sciences, December 5, 2022, https://aces.illinois.edu/news/cover-cropping-72-us-midwest-boosted-government-programs.

27 James C. Knox. "Geology of the Driftless Area," in *The Physical Geography and Geology of the Driftless Area.* Eric C. Carson, J. E. Rowling III, J.M. Daniels, and J.W. Attig, eds. The Geological Society of America. Special Paper 543 (2019).

28 Ibid.

Chapter 4
My Family's Arrival—Making Hay

1 On my father's mother's side, the Wernerts arrived from Alsace-Lorraine to the Philadelphia area in the late 1800s and worked as bakers. My mother's family, Bavarian Lessigs on her father's side, arrived in the Pottstown, Pennsylvania, area in the mid-1700s. On her mother's side, the Swedish Kyn (later Keen) arrived in New Sweden, located near present-day Essington, Pennsylvania, in 1643. They were among the first European settlers in what later became the state of Pennsylvania. Some of the log homes these Swedish settlers erected and lived in still stand as memorials in Governor Printz Park, Essington. A family joke is that the patent they "must have" applied for the "log home concept" has never been granted, and our long, long overdue royalty payments have never come to fruition. My mom's parents, however, had moved to a nice suburban area near Philadelphia, and that's where she grew up with her two siblings.

2 USDA Land Capability Classification, https://efotg.sc.egov.usda.gov.

3 The University of Wisconsin–Madison Arboretum (1,260 acres) is a teaching and research facility of the University of Wisconsin–Madison and the site of historic research in ecological restoration. It was founded in 1932 with Aldo Leopold its first research director. Today the arboretum manages the oldest restored tallgrass prairie in the nation along with an extensive collection of restored ecosystems that are referred to as "ecological communities": woodlands, savannas, prairies, wetlands, springs, and the Lake Wingra shoreline. It was designated a National Historic Landmark in 2021 in recognition of its role as a pioneer site in the field of ecological restoration.

4 These dear friends were Tim Miner, Sandwich, New Hampshire, and Bob Fletcher (deceased) previously Bellingham, Washington, roommates of mine in college and fellow ski racing companions, among other grand adventures that took us together across the planet.

5 Richard L. Cates Jr., 1983. "Field and Laboratory Studies of Nitrous Oxide Production in Soils," PhD Dissertation. My major professors were Dr. Robin Harris, and Dr. Dennis Keeney who later served as the first director of the Leopold Center for Sustainable Agriculture, Iowa State University 1988–1999. Dr. Charles Bradley, who directed the Bradley Study Center on the Aldo Leopold Foundation (ALF) land, served as a lead professor for my field research there. I am ever thankful for their guidance and mentoring through this most productive three-year journey.

Chapter 5
A Sojourn in the Desert—Rediscovering Our Place

1 Kim and I had gotten to know and become close friends with Brian Schweitzer during our three years at Montana State University in Bozeman. Brian's family ranched up in north central Montana near Geyser, and they were the first to bring Simmental genetics to the U.S. from Canada (in 1967), eventually selling breeding stock to U.S. ranchers. It turned out that my family had crossed Simmental with our Hereford cows a few years before meeting Brian, likely with stock that had originated on the Schweitzer ranch.

Brian was—and is—a true-life character. We were both graduate students in soils with a passion for ranching. We teamed up with several other friends to win the "Wild Cow Riding" competition at the NCAA National Finals Rodeo held at Montana State. Brian eventually became the governor of Montana, serving from January 2005 to 2013, leaving a legacy of respect, a long time overdue, for the state's First Peoples as well as its grasslands and precious water resources. Brian also left a colorful legacy. As an example, he had a branding iron made with the word *veto* on the hot end. At times, confronted with a bill on his desk that was particularly offensive, he would respond in turn and singe his disapproval across the paperwork, adding his signature below to make it official. Brian and his wife, Nancy, remain close friends of ours.

2 Prior to 2003 the hajj was the largest annual human gathering on Earth; since then, the Arbaeen pilgrimage in Iraq has surpassed the hajj, with nearly 25 million gathered in the city of Karbala, Iraq each year.

3 Our friends, Bill Murphy's sister, Jeanne Murphy Patenaude, her husband Dan, Highland, and Charles Opitz, Mineral Point, were the first to implement intensive rotational grazing for dairy in Wisconsin. Reed and Carol Ludlow, Viroqua, and Dr. Larry Smith, DVM, Lodi were the first in Wisconsin to implement the practice for beef cattle.

4 Biomimicry comes from Greek *bios* (life) and *mimesis* (imitation). With, "nature as model ... measure ... [and] mentor ... The conscious emulation of life's genius. Innovation inspired by nature ... Biomimicry [is] based not on what we can extract from nature, but what we can learn from her."—Janine M. Benyus. *Biomimicry: Innovation Inspired by Nature.* (New York: HarperCollins Publishers, 2002).

5 Poly wire is generally a thin, twisted plastic wire wound with even thinner strands of stainless steel wire. It can be stored on and paid out from a reel or cord winder, is lightweight and portable, and can conduct the high voltage-low current (low impedance) electrical pulse that modern electric fence energizers produce to effectively teach livestock not to tangle.

Sidebar
Some Benefits of Managed Grazing, a Biomimicry of Native Herbivore Movement—For the Ecosystem, the Farmer ... and Everyone

1 Thanks to the long-term research addressing these relationships conducted by Gregg R. Sanford, Randall D. Jackson, Eric G. Booth, Janet L. Hedtcke, and Valentin Picasso at the University of Wisconsin–Madison Arlington Research Station as part of the Wisconsin Integrated Cropping Systems Trial (WICST). This trial was initiated in 1989 by the late Professor Josh Posner. For his foresight and professional commitment, we are all deeply indebted.

Chapter 6
Finding Our Way—Imagining and Building Our Farm and a Land Ethic

1 The purchase of a portion of the farm on land contract by Kim and me meant we did not have to seek a bank loan for a mortgage. However, it also meant that the deed/title to the land remained with our parents until our obligation was completed—paid in its entirety—after twenty years. Fortunately, we completed our obligation and never missed a monthly payment.

2 An intensive rotational grazing—or managed grazing—"grass farm" is a farm in permanent or "perennialized grass cover" on the landscape all year, every year, and grazed according to a management plan to optimize plant growth, ground cover, and livestock productivity. Managed grazing is one of the five core approaches/practices in what is now called "regenerative agriculture"; that term did not exist in the 1990s, whereas the ecological principles on which it depends are as old as life on Earth. The other approaches/practices of regenerative agriculture are accepted as (1) minimal soil disturbance, (2) planting cover crops between main crops, (3) inter-seeding bare ground between the rows of the main crops, and (4) establishing perennials as soil-health promoters.

3 Initiated in 1985, the Managed Forest Law (MFL) is a landowner incentive program that encourages sustainable forestry on private woodland. In exchange for following sound forest management and fencing the contracted acres from livestock, the landowner pays reduced property taxes. MFL replaced the Woodland Tax Law (1954) and the Forest Crop Law (1927). Tax savings are significant. Eventually I had enrolled just under two hundred acres on our Town of Wyoming farm.

4 Dr. Larry Smith, DVM, Lodi, Wisconsin, a fine human being by any and all standards.

5 Tragically, this excellent farmer and dear friend, Paul Bickford, passed away in the late summer of 2022 in a farm accident.

Chapter 7
Getting It Right—A Commitment to the Land and Water

1 Between 1996 and 2001, we were honored twice by our local Iowa County Land Conservation Board and received statewide recognitions from the Soil and Water Conservation Society of America and the USDA Natural Resource Conservation Service.

2 My dear friends Charles C. Bradley (b. 1911) and Nina Leopold Bradley (b. 1917) passed away May 18, 2002 (https://en.wikipedia.org/wiki/Charles_C._Bradley) and May 25, 2011 (https://en.wikipedia.org/wiki/Nina_Leopold_Bradley), respectively.

3 Contract grazing works well as a complementary enterprise but not as well as the primary enterprise that should be consistent year to year because people change their minds, or they go out of business. We experienced numerous years where the number of cattle promised was not upheld, the cattle owner suddenly couldn't pay their bills owed to us, or they were no longer in business.

4 Brian J. Bader, "Developing a species list for oak savanna/oak woodland restoration at the University of Wisconsin–Madison Arboretum." *Ecological Restoration* Volume 19, no. 4 (December 2001): 242–250, https://doi.org/10.3368/er.19.4.242.

5 Our 8,600-acre, hydraulic unit code (HUC) 12 watershed—the smallest watershed formally identified and mapped—is defined as the land area from which all precipitation, springs, tributaries, or streams that flow from higher ground end up in Lowery Creek before entering the Wisconsin River.

6 Aldo Leopold spent much of his working life and his writing focusing on the imperative of a land ethic—ethically motivated conservation—by private landowners, on private working lands. In *A Sand County Almanac* (1949), published at the end of his life, Leopold called for an ethical relationship between people and the land they own and manage, which he called "an

evolutionary possibility and an ecological necessity." See Sand County Foundation's website to learn more about their mission and their work. https://sandcountyfoundation.org/.

7 To date, the ashes of our son, Peter; my father and mother; Kim's father and mother, Kenneth and Marilyn Johnson; and her maternal grandmother, Helen Lasher, are safeguarded at this sacred spot.

Chapter 8
And More—A Commitment to the Lovely Animals with Whom We Share Our Lives

1 Natasha Daly is a writer and editor at *National Geographic*, where her investigative reporting focuses on animals' welfare, conservation, and exploitation. She has a special interest in the intersection of animals and culture: how social media and societal trends shape our perceptions and treatment of animals.

2 A most significant partner in this cycle of life is our meat processor, Straka Meats, Plain, WI, a family operated business, just a twenty-minute truck haul from the farm. Through thick and thin over the past three decades—now both businesses deep into the second generation of our relationship—and now booked out several years in advance with local farmers' livestock, they have always been there for and with us with the most careful humane handling of our animals.

3 The Gaffney family operates a registered Angus farm, Gaffney Family Cattle, and they do a first-class job with their cow herd and raising the calves. The calves we purchase from the Gaffneys at about six months old are primarily bull calves made into steers, not the ones targeted for the show ring, the big-boned tall, "framey" kind that win the ribbons in the county fairs. Instead, we look for shorter, more compact calves that "flesh" easily on grass and grow to be moderate-sized but well-muscled steers.

4 Both Jerseys and Angus but also Hereford, Devon, Galloway, and Shorthorn, to name a few, developed in a colder region of the world similar to Wisconsin, and they were bred and raised on pasture grass and clover. Consequently, they developed the capability to deposit some intramuscular fat (marbling) and body fat cover to allow them to withstand colder winters, as well as produce tender meat on pasture. All my life I had heard dairy folks in Wisconsin, most of whom raise Holsteins—black and white cows, originally from the Netherlands that everyone knows, give white milk—say they would often seek out a Jersey herd as a source for their beef. Early in our journey in the direct market beef business, one of our veterinarians who had worked with a wide range of breeds over his career, decided to raise grass-fed Jersey steers. After several years he convinced me to try his product. The meat had an extraordinary flavor, a bit like well-fed deer or elk, and was a rich red in color. We loved it, and still do. Over time many of our customers came to prefer and ask for the Jersey beef.

5 Jerseys have a higher fat and protein content in their milk than Holsteins, and so their milk is worth more on a weight basis in the marketplace. Without having to be effective at producing an exceptional milk yield, dairy farmers with Jerseys have options to sell their milk for cheese or "cheese yield" as it is termed in the dairy marketplace.

Chapter 9
Homecoming—For Which We Are Grateful

1 David Allan Cates's fifth novel, *Tom Connor's Gift* (2014), and the final in his Homecoming Trilogy after *Hunger in America* (1992) and *Ben Armstrong's Strange Trip Home* (2012).

2 Mark Hirsch. *That Tree: An iPhone Photo Journal Documenting a Year in the Life of a Lonely Bur Oak*. (Illinois: Press Syndication Group, 2013). That tree succumbed during the fatal derecho windstorm that took place on August 10–11, 2020.

3 Personal communication, site visits in the summer of 2023 with Professor Michael Casler, research (grass) geneticist, USDA Dairy Forage Research Center and University of Wisconsin–Madison. Fifteen cool-season grass, ten legumes, multiple other forb species (some desirable, such as dandelion and plantain, and some not so, such as multiple thistle species), as well as several sedges and rushes (in frequently wet areas) were identified on the grazing acreage. On our contiguous acreage where grazing is not conducted—established mesic prairies, restored sedge meadows, oak woodlands, and restoration-in-process oak savanna—there are several times as many additional species not included in this count.

4 Dr. Stan Temple, professor emeritus, forest and wildlife ecology, environmental studies College of Agricultural and Life Sciences and Nelson Institute of Environmental Studies, as well as the author of the Foreword that appears in this book, developed the concept of resting some grazing paddocks during the nesting season each year to make managed rotational grazing more bird friendly. And it works.

5 Personal communication, November 14, 2019, email from Tristyn Forget, WI DNR Fisheries program specialist. Lowery Creek, earlier known as Van Blarcum-Jones Creek, first appears in the 1968 listing of trout stream classification (by the WI DNR) as such. The creek was not included in the first Wisconsin DNR stream classifications list in 1957.

6 Wisconsin DNR Trout stream classifications—Wisconsin trout fishing, https://dnr.wisconsin.gov/topic/Fishing/trout/streamclassification.html. The full definition of a Class 1 Trout Stream is, "A stream or portion thereof with a self-sustaining population of brook trout. Such a stream contains brook trout spawning habitat and naturally produced fry, fingerling, and yearlings in sufficient numbers to utilize the brook trout habitat; or contains trout with two or more age groups, above the age of one year, and natural reproduction and survival of wild fish in

sufficient numbers to utilize the available brook trout habitat and to sustain the fishery without stocking."

7 Personal communications with Jason Himebauch, WI DNR Fisheries Technician, Nevin State Fish Hatchery, and Justin Haglund, WI DNR Senior Fisheries Biologist, Dodgeville, WI.

8 Ibid.

9 Ibid.

10 The entire navigable stream length of the main channel, 7.52 miles, as well as 4.81 miles of the two principal tributaries that were classified for the first time: A total of 12.33 miles of "Class 1 brook trout water."

11 We purchased the land with a permanent conservation easement put in place by the seller, Ted Ross, Rockford, Illinois. The conservation easement, held by the Driftless Area Land Conservancy, Dodgeville, Wisconsin, allows us to use managed grazing and/or haying on a portion of the grassland acres, but not all of them. It is restrictive as to what fertilizer and pesticide amendments may be utilized and specifically does not allow any plowing or commercial development. All of these opportunities and restrictions stay with the land (if our family was ever to sell) and are in place for perpetuity.

Approximately a year prior to our purchase, Mr. Ross had also completed a project stabilizing the stream banks and improving the brook trout habitat of the portion of Lowery Creek that flowed through this property. The project was conducted in partnership with the USDA Natural Resources Conservation Service for their engineering specifications and (possibly) cost sharing, and with a heavy equipment firm to conduct the work.

12 Dan's grandparents and his uncle were all dairy farmers near Loyal. From the age of eight, Dan helped with chores and, later, all of the farm work. When he was only fifteen, his uncle suffered from silo gas poisoning early in the summer; his wife worked full time off the farm, and their son was only eight years old. So, Dan was enlisted to help his grandmother milk the fifty cows and run the farm for the summer.

Through this trial, Dan learned about commitment, tenacity, faith, and empathy, and he grew to live in honor of these values.

Shannon told us shortly after meeting Dan at UW–Madison, "I met a new friend studying mechanical engineering who grew up on a farm. He is quiet and considerate, a hard worker, handsome, and he likes to make pancakes."

The consummate engineer, Dan chose a titanium alloy wedding ring for their wedding on May 13, 2006. Dan informed everyone, "The ring weighs 0.1216 ounces, has a density of 0.163

pounds/cubic inch, an ultimate tensile strength of nearly 132,000 psi, and can bear a load of 996.875 pounds, ignoring losses from geometry, of course."

He now oversees a design team of mechanical engineers at Apple Inc. charged with developing a product they simply call "something." He can't tell us what it is.

If I had the chance to choose a town's name from where my daughter's husband would hail from, one that matched a most hoped-for character trait, I'd select Loyal every time.

13 Kiley worked as a "cheesemonger," a seller and promoter of cheese at Cowgirl Creamery in San Francisco, as a cheese-making apprentice at Jasper Hill, Greensboro Bend, Vermont, and a cheesemaker at Uplands Cheese-Grass Dairy, Dodgeville. Our famous cheesemaker friend is Andy Hatch and his wife, Caitlin, co-owners along with Scott and Liana Mericka of Uplands Cheese-Grass Dairy. Since Eric and Kiley arrived back here in 2016, Kiley has earned her registered nurse (RN) licensure and in the process of furthering her nursing education. Eric and Kiley have been busy raising two children, Sloane Helen and Fischer Lyman.

14 We have heated our home with wood since moving here in 1989, and my brother's family heated with wood before us, and the Stapleton's before them. But in 2015, and again in 2022 we installed solar voltaic systems to a total of 17.3 kW electricity which is sufficient to power the home and farm most days. What a feeling of freedom.

15 These final two paragraphs are a respectful paraphrase from the closing pages of James Rebanks's poignant memoir, *Pastoral Song: A Farmer's Journey* (Massachusetts: Mariner Books, 2021). I have never met Mr. Rebanks, but I feel a close kinship with him through his expression of the deep passionate love he holds for his family caring for their land together.

Chapter 10
The Lowery Creek Watershed Initiative—It Takes a Community

1 Personal communication with Justin Haglund, Wisconsin DNR senior fisheries biologist, Dodgeville, Wisconsin. The process for upgrading a stream classification is lengthy and rigorous. The process requires approval of reclassification by the immediate supervisor and district supervisor, followed by consultation with other DNR staff involved in water regulation, water resource specialists, water management specialists, and drinking water/groundwater staff. Public notice must be published in the local newspaper and/or other media followed by a wait of thirty days to determine if a public hearing is requested. Notices are to local government clerks and state legislators for the districts where the stream is located. Notices are also sent to chairs of Conservation Congress and legislative committees. Once all of these conditions are met, the reclassification packet with all pertinent information is sent to the DNR central office for processing. Finally, official classification is changed as of January 1, odd years only.

2 Personal communication, Katie Abbott, Iowa County conservationist in a April 15, 2021, email. These data are from GIS mapping layers downloaded from the WI DNR, and mapping software for measured miles within Iowa County: high phosphorus levels (130 miles), excessive sediment (48 miles); high ammonia levels (15 miles), low dissolved oxygen (15 miles), high zinc, lead, cadmium, and/or mercury levels (6 miles).

3 Wisconsin DNR, "Water Condition Lists," https://dnr.wisconsin.gov/topic/SurfaceWater/ConditionLists.html.

4 In 2010, the WI DNR (codified in NR 102.06(6)) established a state standard of 0.075 and 0.100 mg/L for the upper limit of P (phosphorus) in Wisconsin streams and rivers, respectively. Lakes and reservoir upper limits are even lower.

5 Wisconsin DNR. "Long-Term River Water Quality Trends in Wisconsin," https://wisconsindnr.shinyapps.io/riverwq/.

6 Personal communication via May 17, 2023, email with Eric Booth, PhD., associate scientist—Hydroecology, Department of Agronomy and Department of Civil & Environmental Engineering, Nelson Institute for Environmental Studies, University of Wisconsin–Madison.

7 Water quality parameters measured monthly, across the 2022 sampling season, on the main channel of Lowery Creek at the Cates Family Farm Water Action Volunteers (WAV) site (normal ranges reported):

Water Temperature 14–16 °C. Brook trout require water at or below 19–20 °C/66.2–68 °F to flourish. A "cold-water stream" is defined as less than 22 °C/71.6 °F year-round.

Dissolved Oxygen 10.5–13 mg/L. The best brook trout habitat is greater than 7 mg/L.

Transparency 95–120 cm. This is the visibility through a standing column of water; the reading translates to an extremely low turbidity of <10 NTUs (Nephelometric Turbidity Units).

Biotic Index 2.7. Some invertebrates that only live in the highest quality water were observed.

The following two parameters are median values across 2020–2022, and 2020–2021, respectively. Sampling and data summary were done by Kimberly Kuber, Water Resources Management specialist, WI DNR:

Phosphorus </= 0.04 mg/L. In Wisconsin 0.075 mg/L is considered the lower limit for impairment.

Nitrate Nitrogen <0.8 mg/L. 10 mg/L is considered the lower limit for potable water.

8 Curt Meine, Aldo Leopold's biographer, in his essay, "The Edge of Anomaly" in *Wildness: Relations of People and Place*. Gavin Van Horn and John Hausdoerffer, eds. (Illinois: The University of Chicago Press, 2017).

9 See Producer-Led Watershed Protection projects supported by the Wisconsin Department of Agriculture, Trade and Consumer Protection (DATCP). "Projects focus on nonpoint source pollution abatement activities ... with the goal to improve Wisconsin's soil and water quality by supporting and advancing producer-led solutions that increase on-the-ground practices and farmer participation in local watershed efforts." https://datcp.wi.gov/Pages/Programs_Services/ProducerLedProjects.aspx.

See also Sand County Foundation Municipal-Agricultural Watershed Partnerships, Performance-Based Conservation, and Leopold Conservation Award Program among others at https://sandcountyfoundation.org.

See also the Quivira Coalition, Santa Fe, NM, https://quiviracoalition.org, and Malpai Borderlands Group, Douglas, AZ, http://www.malpaiborderlandsgroup.org, for well-known, successful partnerships in the Western U.S.

10 The Driftless Area Land Conservancy's purpose is to "maintain and enhance the health, diversity and beauty of Southwest Wisconsin's natural and agricultural landscape through permanent land protection and restoration and improve people's lives by connecting them to the land and to each other." To learn more, See the DALC website and the Lowery Creek Watershed Initiative page, https://www.driftlessconservancy.org/lowery-creek-watershed.

11 Ibid.

Epilogue: Hope—What I Dream for the Future of Earth's Gifts

1 I have been inspired and personally compelled to answer this essential existential question, posed by Michael Dahl, White Earth Anishinaabe, ever since I was first introduced to the challenge in *Wildness: Relations of People and Place* (2017; Gavin Van Horn and John Hausdoerffer, eds.) and again more recently by the poignant work, *What Kind of Ancestor Do You Want to Be?* (2021; eds. John Hausdoerffer, Brooke Parry Hecht, Melissa K. Nelson, and Katherine Kassouf Cummings). Both works were published by The University of Chicago Press in association with the Center for Humans and Nature.

Appendix III
Our Oak Savanna Restoration: A Journey of Wonder and Awe

1 Brian J. Bader, "Developing a species list for oak savanna/oak woodland restoration at the University of Wisconsin–Madison Arboretum." Ecological Restoration Volume 19, no. 4 (December 2001): 242–250, https://doi.org/10.3368/er.19.4.242. I made use of this reference in this appendix to cross check plant common names used in the field with formal Latin name identification.

Appendix IV
The Methane Yoke of Burden Has Been Incorrectly—and Unfairly—Placed on Our Domestic Livestock

1 Personal communication, Professor Randall Jackson, grassland ecologist, University of Wisconsin–Madison.

2 "Methane has been the Achilles heel for cattle emissions, but it may be part of a climate solution." November 4, 2020. Clarity and Leadership for Environmental Awareness and Research (CLEAR), University of California, Davis.

3 Breanna M. Roque, et al. March 17, 2021. "Red Seaweed (*Asparagopsis taxiformis*) supplementation reduces enteric methane by over 80 percent in beef steers." PloS ONE 16(3): e0247820.

Appendix V
Farm Business Principles for Success

1 Richard L. Cates Jr., director emeritus WSBDF, with (at the time of the original draft, 2013) Jennifer Taylor, associate director WSBDF, and Thomas Cadwallader, professor UWEX Lincoln and Marathon Counties.

Appendix VI
Frequently Asked Questions About Our Managed Grazing Approach to Regenerative Agriculture and a Land Ethic

1 Becky Henne, "How far did your food travel to get to you?," Michigan State University Extension, September 20, 2012, https://www.canr.msu.edu/news/how_far_did_your_food_travel_to_get_to_you.

Photo by Eric Cates.

Printed in the United States
by Baker & Taylor Publisher Services